Wordly Wise

Kenneth Hodkinson

BOOK 9
Revised

Educators Publishing Service, Inc. Cambridge, Mass. 02138

Cover Design/Hugh Price

July 1998 Printing

ISBN 0-8388-0439-X

Printed in U.S.A.

Contents

Word List

(Numbers in parentheses refer to the Word List in which the word appears.)

ABASE (3)
aberration (1)
abeyance (20)
abjure (28)
abrade (16)
abrogate (12)
accretion (8)
acerbity (26)
acumen (5)
adduce (25)
adipose (17)
adjure (15)
ado (21)
aeon (11)
affidavit (18)
afflatus (20)
allergy (3)
alluvial (19)
altercation (2)
amatory (10)
amenities (1)
anathema (3)
anchorite (27)
ancillary (11)
anemia (23)
animadversion (21)
anneal (14)
annular (12)
aphorism (26)
aplomb (7)
apocryphal (6)
apogee (7)
apostate (22)
apothegm (23)
apotheosis (10)
appellation (25)
appendage (16)
apposite (27)
apprise (4)
archipelago (20)
argot (11)
arpeggio (17)

arrant (12)
ascribe (29)
atelier (19)
atoll (2)
atone (5)
atrophy (26)
attenuate (10)
avail (30)
avuncular (18)

BADINAGE (28)
batten (21)
bawdy (11)
beget (16)
behemoth (12)
behoove (17)
belabor (25)
bellicose (24)
benediction (18)
benighted (1)
bicameral (29)
bier (8)
bilateral (9)
bilingual (30)
bludgeon (6)
bolus (7)
boss (4)
brackish (27)
brindled (3)
brio (28)
bucolic (5)
bullion (22)
burgeon (26)

CABAL (25)
cacophony (6)
calcify (16)
cambric (10)
canard (8)
canon (17)
caparison (9)
carnal (13)

cartel (2)
casuistry (20)
caulk (29)
cavil (27)
cerebration (1)
cerements (18)
checkered (4)
chiaroscuro (14)
chimerical (11)
choreography (30)
ciliated (23)
cite (3)
citrus (12)
clarion (10)
coagulate (16)
codicil (5)
cognomen (2)
cohere (17)
collation (19)
colloquy (18)
comatose (7)
concatenation (15)
concurrent (28)
contentious (24)
contumacious (13)
coquette (26)
corporeal (25)
coup (16)
covert (11)
crescendo (14)
cumulative (21)
cupidity (12)
curia (10)

DAIS (29)
dastard (8)
dative (1)
debacle (3)
debilitated (22)
decimate (27)
declivity (2)
decoction (26)

defalcate (1)
deleterious (3)
demure (30)
deposition (6)
depraved (28)
deprecate (25)
descry (15)
despoil (11)
desuetude (17)
detritus (2)
deviltry (4)
devolve (27)
dialectic (13)
diapason (1)
dictum (9)
dissension (5)
dissipate (7)
diurnal (23)
diva (3)
divine (6)
donor (26)
dory (14)
dotage (25)
dragoon (12)
dulcet (20)

EBULLIENT (24)
eclectic (10)
eclogue (2)
effulgent (27)
effusive (19)
egregious (4)
egress (5)
ejaculation (26)
élan (6)
elide (11)
elixir (21)
elucidate (29)
emend (25)
emetic (4)
emollient (12)
emolument (5)

enamored (27)
encomium (10)
encroach (11)
endemic (8)
endow (26)
enervate (18)
engender (1)
enjoin (6)
ensconced (30)
entente (4)
equanimity (12)
equity (5)
equivocate (25)
escutcheon (27)
espouse (10)
estranged (3)
eulogy (6)
exacting (11)
execrable (4)
exegesis (5)
expatriate (16)
expedient (9)
expeditious (2)
extemporize (28)
extirpate (20)
extrinsic (26)
extrude (6)

FACTIOUS (15)
factitious (17)
fauna (4)
fealty (25)
fecund (7)
fell (1)
feral (8)
fetid (19)
fetish (5)
fiat (21)
flagellate (22)
foible (27)
forensic (9)
frenetic (12)

v

freshet (18)
fulminate (20)
fulsome (13)

GAFF (3)
gainsay (12)
garrote (14)
gastronomy (10)
genocide (16)
genuflect (11)
germane (2)
gestation (23)
gigolo (6)
grapnel (24)
gratis (12)
gyrate (26)

HEGEMONY (29)
heinous (25)
hiatus (22)
hybrid (1)

ICONOCLASTIC (7)
idealize (11)
idyllic (3)
igneous (19)
imbibe (15)
immanent (4)
immolate (8)
immunize (21)
imperious (12)
impugn (17)
impute (13)
inchoate (18)
incipient (9)
incubate (16)
incubus (7)
incursion (5)
indemnity (20)
indent (17)
indeterminate (30)
indigenous (2)
indigent (23)
ineffable (28)
infidel (19)
infinitesimal (24)

ingenuous (22)
ingrate (8)
ingratiate (14)
inhibit (6)
inimical (21)
inordinate (27)
insensate (4)
insular (23)
interdict (29)
intestate (24)
intransigent (10)
inveigh (1)
invidious (22)
inviolable (30)
isthmus (15)
iterate (28)
itinerant (5)

JADED (13)
jingoism (29)
jocose (6)
jocular (20)
jocund (26)
junto (14)

KINETIC (15)
kleptomaniac (23)

LACHRYMOSE (4)
lacuna (18)
lambent (3)
lampoon (19)
largo (9)
lascivious (21)
laud (13)
legate (20)
leonine (19)
levy (14)
liaison (16)
libation (5)
libretto (24)
licentious (30)
limn (21)
litigation (15)
longevity (7)
lorgnette (17)

lucent (8)
lucubrate (11)
luminary (9)

MACHETE (6)
machinations (20)
macroscopic (27)
maelstrom (2)
malleable (19)
mandible (1)
maniac (28)
mawkish (29)
mensuration (12)
mercurial (25)
mikado (21)
mince (7)
minutiae (10)
miscarry (22)
mode (30)
moiety (3)
moot (11)
mountebank (13)
mulct (8)
mundane (20)

NADIR (14)
natal (12)
natation (15)
neologism (23)
neophyte (4)
nepotism (13)
nexus (18)
nihilism (14)
nodule (2)
notary (9)
numismatist (19)
nuptial (5)

OBDURATE (7)
obeisance (28)
obelisk (10)
obloquy (16)
obstreperous (17)
obverse (26)
occult (25)
ocher (11)

oleaginous (12)
olfactory (8)
oligarchy (27)
opalescent (24)
optometrist (9)
orifice (1)
orison (22)
orotund (15)
orthodox (18)
ossify (21)
ostracize (20)
ouster (19)
overrule (29)

PALPABLE (6)
paradigm (4)
parity (2)
parricide (23)
passé (21)
patina (7)
patrimony (5)
peccadillo (6)
pectoral (26)
peculate (25)
pellucid (10)
pendant (20)
pendent (24)
penumbra (4)
peon (19)
perfunctory (11)
peripatetic (22)
periphery (13)
permeable (23)
permeate (14)
perspicacious (8)
perspicuous (15)
philander (16)
piscatorial (30)
plenary (24)
plenitude (17)
pleonasm (28)
pommel (22)
porcine (13)
preamble (21)
precedent (5)
precept (23)

predilection (10)
prelate (14)
prevaricate (9)
pristine (15)
progeny (6)
prolix (18)
propitiate (24)
prorogue (22)
prosody (27)
provender (13)
puerile (23)
pusillanimous (7)

QUARANTINE (16)
querulous (11)
quiescent (29)
quondam (4)

RANT (24)
rarefied (17)
ratify (20)
rational (1)
reactionary (3)
recalcitrant (18)
recipient (19)
reciprocal (30)
recondite (28)
recreant (21)
rectitude (26)
redeem (29)
redundant (14)
refectory (12)
regime (15)
reincarnation (9)
remiss (8)
repertoire (2)
resonant (25)
resuscitate (16)
retrograde (13)
revelation (27)
rhapsodize (22)
risible (7)
rococo (8)
roseate (20)
rustic (19)

Introduction

This book has four main purposes: (1) to familiarize you with a large number of words (about 500) that you are likely to encounter in your reading or in various achievement tests designed to measure the extent of your vocabulary, (2) to give you a knowledge of how words are formed and how they are used, (3) to increase your ability to perform well at various kinds of vocabulary tests (entrance to college and to many occupations depends to a large extent on a person's demonstrated ability in this area), and (4) to accomplish the above in a way that you will find interesting, even enjoyable.

Each of the thirty lessons in this book has three exercises. Exercise A is designed to give you a firm grasp of the meaning or meanings of the words on the Word List. Exercise B is designed to make you familiar with how these words may and may not be used in sentences. These two exercises are the same throughout the book; Exercise C varies from lesson to lesson. Be sure to read carefully the instruction for each one.

Following each lesson is a Wordly Wise section which discusses the origin and formation of words, distinguishes between words commonly confused, provides a guide to pronunciation where needed, and generally deals with any points that may need clarification.

At the end of every third lesson there is a review of all the words in those lessons plus some review words. This is in the form of a crossword puzzle in which the clues are definitions of the words that have been studied. In order to get the most enjoyment out of these puzzles, come adequately prepared with a sure knowledge of the words covered.

Before beginning the first lesson, study the terms defined below. Refer back to this page if you encounter any of these terms and are unsure of their meanings.

Etymology is the science that studies the origins and histories of words; it is also the name given to the history of a word which shows where it came from and how it changed into its present form and meaning.

A *root* is a word or part of a word that is used as a base for making other words. The word *move* is the root of such words as *remove* and *movement*.

A *prefix* is a syllable or group of syllables joined to the beginning of a word to change its meaning. Some common prefixes are *un-*, *non-*, *anti-*, and *in-*. In the word *remove*, *re-* is a prefix.

A *suffix* is a syllable or group of syllables added to the end of a word to change its meaning. Some common suffixes are *-able*, *-ary*, *-ful*, *-tion*. In the word *movement*, *-ment* is a suffix.

A *synonym* is a word having the same or nearly the same meaning as another word in the same language. The English *cheese* has the same meaning as the French *fromage*, but they are not synonyms. *Little* and *small* are synonyms; so are *valiant* and *brave*.

An *antonym* is a word that is opposite in meaning to another word. *Strong* and *weak* are antonyms; so are *up* and *down*.

A *homonym* is a word that is pronounced the same as another word but has a different meaning and usually a different spelling. *Hoarse* and *horse* are homonyms; so are *bow* and *bough*.

An *analogy* is a similarity in some respect between two things; it is also a comparing of something with something else. Word relationship tests make use of analogy in the following way. A pair of words is given and the relationship between them must be established. The third word must then be matched with one of a number of choices (usually four or five) to express the same kind of relationship. Here is an example:

ant is to *insect* as *robin* is to which of the following:
(1) fly (2) nest (3) bird (4) sing (5) wing

The relationship between the first pair, *ant* and *insect*, is one of class; ants belong to the class of living things called insects. By selecting choice (3), we express the same kind of relationship since robins belong to the class of living things called birds. The form in which analogy questions are usually put together with the correct answer is shown here:

ant:insect :: robin:
(1) fly (2) nest (3) bird (4) sing (5) wing

Note that balance must be maintained between each pair of words. If we go from *ant* to *insect* on one side, we cannot go from *bird* to *robin* on the other since the relationship between the two pairs would not then be identical. The parts of speech of each of the two pairs must also match; *noun:verb* must be followed by *noun:verb*, *noun:adjective* by *noun:adjective,* and so on.

In addition to the example given, there are many other possible relationships between words. Here are some of the more common ones:

(1) synonyms (sad:gloomy)
(2) antonyms (true:false)
(3) homonyms (rough:ruff)
(4) part:whole (page:book)
(5) worker:tool (painter:brush)
(6) worker:article produced (poet:poem)
(7) function (knife:cut)
(8) symbol (dove: peace)
(9) description (circle:round)
(10) size (twig:branch)
(11) lack (invalid:health)
(12) cause (germ:disease)
(13) sex (bull:cow)
(14) parent:child (mother:daughter)
(15) noun:adjective (warmth:warm)
(16) type:characteristic (cow:herbivorous)

A *metaphor* is a figure of speech in which a term or phrase is applied to something to which it is not literally applicable in order to show a likeness. The exclamation "What a pig!" would refer to a greedy person if meant metaphorically; it would refer to the animal raised for its pork and bacon if meant literally. Metaphor extends the meanings of words; *pig* has acquired its secondary meaning, "a greedy or filthy person," in this way.

To *denote* is to provide with a factual, exact definition. The word *mother* denotes a female parent. To *connote* is to suggest some feeling or idea in addition to the actual meaning. The word *mother*, to most people, connotes love, care, warmth, and tenderness.

Chapter One

Word List 1

ABERRATION	DIAPASON	ORIFICE
AMENITIES	ENGENDER	RATIONAL
BENIGHTED	FELL	SIDEREAL
CEREBRATION	HYBRID	TORRID
DATIVE	INVEIGH	VENAL
DEFALCATE	MANDIBLE	

Look up the words above in your dictionary. Note that many of them have more than one meaning. When you feel that you know *all* the meanings of *all* the words, go on to the exercises below.

EXERCISE 1A

From the four choices following each phrase or sentence, you are to circle the letter preceding the one that is closest in meaning to the italicized word. Where the same word appears more than once, you should note that it is being used in different senses.

1. a mental *aberration*
   (a) stimulus (b) defect (c) exercise (d) reservation

2. the *amenities* of the city
   (a) worst features (b) rise and fall (c) public buildings (d) attractive features and comforts

3. the *amenities* of diplomacy
   (a) little white lies (b) social advantages (c) socially correct acts (d) political consequences

4. a *benighted* people
   (a) ignorant (b) noble (c) wandering (d) gentle

5. intense *cerebration*
   (a) joy (b) despair (c) thought (d) pain

6. the *dative* case
   (a) showing possession (b) of the direct object (c) of the subject (d) of the indirect object

7. to *defalcate*
   (a) resign (b) waver (c) embezzle (d) authorize

8. the *diapason* of the voice
   (a) highest note (b) entire range (c) particular quality (d) lowest note

9. the morning *diapason* of the birds
   (a) activity (b) flight (c) flocking together (d) burst of harmonious song

10. to *engender* strife
    (a) revel in (b) fear (c) prevent (d) produce

11. their own *fell* purpose
    (a) cruel (b) private (c) authorized (d) mysterious

12. an assassin's *fell* plot
    (a) secret (b) deadly (c) treasonous (d) elaborate

13. a strange *hybrid*
    (a) species of animal now extinct (b) object out of its proper historical time (c) object believed to be of non-terrestrial origin (d) offspring of parents of different species

14. to *inveigh* against someone
    (a) strike out (b) vote (c) speak out vehemently (d) stand firm

15. a human *mandible*
    (a) grinding tooth (b) collar bone (c) jawbone (d) kneecap

16. a large *orifice*
    (a) underground chamber (b) charitable offering (c) abnormal growth (d) mouthlike opening

17. a *rational* animal
    (a) trained (b) supernatural (c) imaginary (d) reasoning

18. a *rational* choice
    (a) unlimited (b) unwise (c) difficult (d) sensible

19. *sidereal* astronomy

(a) of the moon (b) of the planets (c) of the stars (d) of the sun

20. the *torrid* zone

(a) mild (b) hot (c) forbidden (d) freezing

21. *venal* officials

(a) unpaid (b) honorable (c) corrupt (d) honorary

Check your answers against the correct ones given below. The answers are not in order; this is to prevent your eye from catching sight of the correct answers before you have had a chance to do the exercise on your own.

11a. 21c. 4a. 19c. 5c. 14c. 2d. 16d. 8b. 12b. 17d. 13d. 7c. 20b. 1b. 18d. 3c. 15c. 10d. 6d. 9d.

Look up in your dictionary all the words for which you gave incorrect answers. Only when you have done this should you go on to the next exercise.

EXERCISE 1B

Each word in Word List 1 is used several times in the sentences below to illustrate different meanings or usage. One of the sentences for each word uses the italicized word incorrectly. You are to circle the letter preceding that sentence.

1. (a) There is an *aberration* in the structure which needs to be corrected. (b) In a moment of mental *aberration*, I completely forgot what I wanted to say. (c) Surgeons removed a large *aberration* that had been pressing against the brain.

2. (a) They observed the social *amenities* during their visit but seemed somewhat ill at ease. (b) How pleasant it is to leave the country and enjoy again the *amenities* of the city! (c) The hotel has every *amenity*, including private baths and color television. (d) The ambassador claimed diplomatic *amenity* and could not be arrested.

3. (a) The young man was *benighted* by his king for services to his country. (b) There are some *benighted* souls in the class who question the usefulness of algebra. (c) The president did everything possible to help the *benighted* country, but in vain. (d) What a *benighted* fool I was to agree to such a foolish scheme!

4. (a) After *cerebrating* in the library all day, the scholar needs to relax in the evening. (b) I *cerebrated* that our friend would stay a while, but I was mistaken. (c) The students, their heads bowed in *cerebration,* pondered the examination questions.

5. (a) English, unlike German, does not have a *dative* case. (b) In translating "They gave him bread" into German, one must put "him" into the *dative* case. (c) She assembled all the relevant *dative* before trying to solve the problem. (d) I failed my Latin test because I couldn't remember the *dative* endings.

6. (a) She declined to spend the money and had allowed it to *defalcate* over the years. (b) The treasurer had made off with the money before the *defalcation* was discovered. (c) We know the money was missing but don't know who the *defalcator* might be. (d) When he was entrusted with such large sums, the temptation to *defalcate* was enormous.

7. (a) The sonorous *diapason* of the huge organ echoed through the vast cathedral. (b) He added his small voice to the swelling *diapason* of protest. (c) The sweet *diapason* of their young voices was quite enchanting. (d) The great brass *diapason* reverberated and thundered when it was struck.

8. (a) Her forthrightness *engendered* new respect for her policies. (b) A word may be of masculine, feminine, or neuter *engender.* (c) His lack of experience *engendered* in him a timidity in his new position. (d) It is their belief that crime and lawlessness are *engendered* by poverty.

9. (a) The poor boy found himself in the *fell* clutches of a band of brigands. (b) She helped

us, not out of kindness, but for some dark, *fell* purpose of her own. (c) His prolonged illness had left him looking pale and *fell*. (d) The murderer administered a few drops of the *fell* poison from a small vial.

10. (a) Indian corn is a *hybrid* produced by selective breeding of various strains. (b) The region's *hybrid* culture is a fusion of strong Spanish and French influences. (c) This *hybrid* rose is resistant to insect pests. (d) The guitar player has an almost limitless *hybrid* of tunes.

11. (a) After stealing his dog, they *inveighed* him into offering a reward for its return. (b) It is useless to *inveigh* against this injustice as nothing can be done. (c) She *inveighed* against the terms of the contract, which seemed unduly harsh to her.

12. (a) The insect's *mandible* is used for holding and biting into leaf particles. (b) The lower *mandible* of the pelican is extremely capacious and is used for storing food. (c) Archae-ologists dug up a human *mandible*, with teeth attached, thought to be 5,000 years old. (d) Attendance at the meeting is *mandible* for all freshmen.

13. (a) The cave's *orifice* was hidden by a dense growth of underbrush. (b) Water is *orificed* from the tank by means of a small pump. (c) The clam sucks in seawater through an *orifice* located at the end of a tubelike growth.

14. (a) A human being is a *rational* creature who acts according to the dictates of reason. (b) Please stop raving and explain in a *rational* manner what happened. (c) She has a very *rational* mind and ignores the dictates of the heart. (d) She offered a convincing *rational* of the switch in voter preferences.

15. (a) A *sidereal* year is the time in which the earth completes a revolution of the sun measured with respect to the fixed stars. (b) The study of the stars and nebulas is the province of *sidereal* astronomy. (c) The play has a truly *sidereal* cast, with six Broadway stars in leading roles.

16. (a) The mustard was so *torrid* that it burned my mouth. (b) The novel deals with the *torrid* love affair between a young doctor and her patient. (c) There was no relief from the *torrid* heat of the desert. (d) The earth's *torrid* zone is a band around the equator lying between the tropics.

17. (a) When the *venality* of the judges was exposed, they resigned from office. (b) The fact that some police officers are *venal* should not lead us to condemn them all. (c) The brib-ery of officials and other *venal* practices must be stopped forthwith. (d) The doctor gave the patient an *intravenal* injection of the drug.

EXERCISE 1C

In the construction of English words, we draw most heavily upon Greek and Latin. There is a certain arbitrariness in our choice; in *automobile*, for example, the first part is Greek and the second part Latin in origin.

Here are Latin and Greek roots for five English words:

	Latin	Greek
water	aqua	hydro
star	stell(a)	aster
god	de(us)	the(os)
one	un(us)	mono(s)
good	ben(e)	eu

Complete the italicized words in the sentences below by supplying roots derived from either the Latin or the Greek roots listed above.

1. The fish are kept in a(n) . . . . *rium*.

2. A . . . . *ate* leaf is shaped like a star.

3. The Hindu religion has many . . . . *ities*.

4. The . . . . *oids* are small planets in orbit between Mars and Jupiter.

3

5. .... *phobia* is an abnormal fear of water.

6. He spoke in a(n) .... *tone.*

7. .... *ted* we stand; divided we fall.

8. A(n) .... *isk* is a star-shaped sign used in printing.

9. Her .... *lung* enables her to stay under water a long time.

10. "Passed away" is a(n) .... *phemism* for "died."

11. .... *electric* power is generated by water.

12. An *a* .... *ist* is one who does not believe in God.

13. This project is for the .... *fit* of the whole community.

14. Movie stars usually have .... *phonious* names.

15. A .... *cracy* is a government by priests.

16. A(n) .... *ign* tumor is one that is not harmful.

17. They wanted to .... *ify* him, but he insisted he was no god.

18. The company had a(n) .... *poly* in the sale of salt.

19. A(n) .... *ar* eclipse occurs when one star passes in front of another.

20. A(n) .... *lateral* decision affects one side only.

WORDLY WISE 1

The other common cases, in addition to the DATIVE (indirect object), are: *nominative* (subject), *accusative* (direct object), and *genitive* (possession). Old English, from which modern English evolved, was highly inflected (i.e., had many cases), but position of words in a sentence has largely replaced case-endings to show meaning in modern English. The dative case dropped out of English some five hundred years ago; Chaucer is the last writer known to have employed it.

INVEIGH usually takes the preposition *against* (to inveigh against injustice); don't confuse this word with *inveigle*, which means "to trick" (inveigled into doing something).

RATIONAL is an adjective meaning "reasonable" (a rational explanation) or "endowed with reason" (a rational being). *Rationale* (with the stress on the last syllable) is a noun meaning "an underlying reason" (a person's rationale for doing something).

Etymology

(See the Introduction for an explanation of this term, together with the notes on roots, prefixes, and suffixes.)

Study the roots and prefix given below together with the English words derived from them. Capitalized words are those given in the Word List. You should look up in a dictionary any words that are unfamiliar to you.

Prefix: *ab-* (away from) Latin — Examples: ABERRATION, *ab*sent, *ab*duct

Roots: *gen, gener* (birth) Latin — Examples: EN-GENDER, pro*gen*y, *gener*ate
cerebrum (brain) Latin — Examples: CEREBRATION, *cerebr*al, *cereb*ellum
erra, errat (wander) Latin — Examples: ABERRATION, *err*atic, *err*

Word List 2

ALTERCATION	ECLOGUE	NODULE
ATOLL	EXPEDITIOUS	PARITY
CARTEL	GERMANE	REPERTOIRE
COGNOMEN	INDIGENOUS	THEISM
DECLIVITY	MAELSTROM	UNGUENT
DETRITUS		

Look up the words above in your dictionary. Note that many of them have more than one meaning. When you feel that you know *all* the meanings of *all* the words, go on to the exercises below.

EXERCISE 2A

From the four choices following each phrase or sentence, you are to circle the letter preceding the one that is closest in meaning to the italicized word. Where the same word appears more than once, you should note that it is being used in different senses.

1. a sudden *altercation*
   (a) increase (b) change (c) quarrel (d) move

2. a tiny *atoll*
   (a) one-celled marine animal (b) one-celled marine plant (c) island of volcanic origin (d) ring-shaped coral island.

3. an international *cartel*
   (a) organizations of nations to promote peace (b) group of companies cooperating to control prices (c) identity card permitting free travel across borders (d) law governing the rights of member nations

4. a humorous *cognomen*
   (a) account (b) reply (c) drawing (d) nickname

5. a gentle *declivity*
   (a) manner (b) downward slope (c) refusal (d) rise and fall

6. to examine the *detritus*
   (a) ancient writing material (b) part that remains (c) loose material worn away (d) consequence of an act

7. to compose an *eclogue*
   (a) spirited, patriotic speech (b) short musical piece (c) short pastoral poem (d) long narrative poem

8. *expeditious* methods
   (a) outdated (b) wasteful (c) economical (d) speedy

9. not *germane*
   (a) relevant (b) sufficient (c) possible (d) believable

10. *indigenous* tribes
    (a) wandering freely from place to place (b) lacking all contact with civilization (c) originating naturally in a particular place (d) extremely warlike and hostile

11. to avoid the *maelstrom*
    (a) whirlpool (b) tornado (c) swamp (d) volcano

12. to remove the *nodule*
    (a) nonessential part (b) innermost part (c) outer covering (d) small, rounded lump

13. *parity* with the dollar
    (a) dissatisfaction (b) competition (c) equality (d) satisfaction

14. a large *repertoire*
    (a) book containing pieces by many authors (b) stock of pieces that a person or company can perform (c) company of actors that performs a variety of plays (d) military force combining all of the services

15. a philosophy based on *theism*
    (a) the belief that life is purposeless (b) the belief that life has a purpose (c) a belief in a god or gods (d) a denial of of God's existence

16. a jar of *unguent*
    (a) cleansing paste (b) preserves (c) face powder (d) ointment

Check your answers against the correct ones given below. The answers are not in order; this is to prevent your eye from catching sight of the correct answers before you have had a chance to do the exercise on your own.

3b. 11a. 10c. 12d. 7c. 13c. 2d. 4d. 16d. 14b. 1c. 9a. 6c. 15c. 8d. 5b.

Look up in your dictionary all the words for which you gave incorrect answers. Only when you have done this should you go on to the next exercise.

EXERCISE 2B

Each word in Word List 2 is used several times in the sentences below to illustrate different meanings or usage. One of the sentences for each word uses the italicized word incorrectly. You are to circle the letter preceding that sentence.

1. (a) The cause of the *altercation* was the refusal of either party to give way. (b) The ship made a sudden *altercation* in its course and headed back to port. (c) What began as a reasoned discussion of the issues quickly flared up into an *altercation*.

2. (a) We used to catch trout in the little *atoll* that flowed through the woods. (b) Pacific *atolls* vary in size from less than a mile to over eighty miles in diameter. (c) Kirimati, in the Pacific Ocean, is the largest *atoll* in the world with an area of about 150 square miles. (d) An *atoll* is roughly circular, encloses a lagoon, and is formed of coral.

3. (a) The companies formed a *cartel* with the hope of maintaining high prices for their goods. (b) *Cartels* are not in the consumers' best interests as they replace competition with price-fixing. (c) The customs officer demanded to see my *cartel* before she would allow me into the country.

4. (a) Half a dozen *cognomen* stood at her side awaiting her orders. (b) The townspeople are all related, the McCoy *cognomen* being borne by half of them. (c) "Buffalo Bill" was the *cognomen* adopted by William Frederick Cody.

5. (a) Her home was built on the *declivity* of the farthest side of the hill. (b) The *declivity* of the land continues for several miles before gently rising again. (c) The *declivity* of the river is reduced greatly as it leaves the mountains for the plain. (d) His air of *declivity* charmed all who had the pleasure of meeting him.

6. (a) The hollows have been filled with *detritus* worn away from the rocks. (b) Many of these ballads have been formed from the *detritus* of a long-lost epic. (c) The *detritus* along the shoreline is the result of the sea's pounding against the cliffs. (d) Their remarks are foolish, and I shall continue to ignore such *detritus*.

7. (a) A distinguishing feature of the *eclogue* is the conversation between shepherds on rural topics. (b) She sat down at the piano and played an *eclogue* very softly for us. (c) The *eclogue* was a popular verse form in the sixteenth century.

8. (a) The matter was dealt with efficiently and in her usual *expeditious* manner. (b) Delivery time has been cut in half due to the *expeditiousness* of the workers. (c) She looked *expeditiously* at me when I told him to hurry. (d) Please supply these parts as *expeditiously* as possible as a delay will be costly.

9. (a) We must restrict our discussion to what is *germane* and not get off the subject. (b) I was surprised to hear that they are relatives as I had no idea that they were *germane*. (c) The ideas in their books are always *germane* to the problems facing us.

10. (a) The kangaroo is *indigenous* to Australia. (b) The Native Americans were *indigenous* inhabitants of North America. (c) Certain types of behavior are *indigenous* to human beings. (d) "I don't know what you're talking about," he said *indigenously*.

11. (a) A *maelstrom* sprang up suddenly and blew the ship off course. (b) The small boat was sucked into the dark depths of the *maelstrom*. (c) Possessions, family, all were gone, lost in the *maelstrom* of war.

12. (a) A small bone *nodule* growing on her knee joint was removed by surgeons. (b) The *nodule* of ironstone was crushed to a powder and its constituents analyzed. (c) The space *nodule* containing the two astronauts was recovered exactly on schedule.

13. (a) Lack of *parity* between ability and opportunity is the cause of the discontent. (b) The Canadian dollar must increase 8 cents in value to achieve *parity* with the U.S. dollar. (c) Representatives of both sides protested the *parity* of the country into two halves.

14. (a) She is a skilled pianist but has a rather limited *repertoire*. (b) This season the company has added Shaw's **St. Joan** to its *repertoire*. (c) She is a dedicated singer and is constantly enlarging her *repertoire*. (d) A *repertoire* theater is one that presents a number of different plays over the season.

15. (a) *Theists* believe in a god or gods. (b) *Theist* philosophy teaches that God is the source of all human values. (c) *Theism* is a view of the world as a divinely-ordered sequence of events. (d) A *theist* does not believe that there is a god.

16. (a) The nurse applied an *unguent* to his burns. (b) Jars of *unguents* line the shelves of the apothecary's shop. (c) She smiled in *unguent* fashion when she saw the predicament I was in.

EXERCISE 2C

In each of the sentences below a word is omitted. From the four words provided, select the one that best completes the sentence. Allow ten minutes for this test. If you cannot answer a question, go on to the next without delay. If you have time left over at the end, go back and try to fill in unanswered questions.

18 or over correct:	excellent
14 to 17 correct:	good
13 or under correct:	thorough review of A exercises indicated

1. The inn lacks many of the . . . . of a first-class hotel.
   eclogues cartels cognomens amenities

2. A . . . . day is the time of one revolution of the earth measured against the fixed stars.
   hybrid germane sidereal rational

3. The theater company has added several new plays to its . . . .
   cognomen orifice diapason repertoire

4. The companies formed a . . . . to control prices.
   parity hybrid maelstrom cartel

5. Bribery and other . . . . practices were exposed by the government probe.
   unguent torrid dative venal

6. A mule is a . . . . of a male donkey and a female horse.
   diapason hybrid theism parity

7. The tobacco plant was . . . . to the American continent.
   indigenous benighted engendered unguent

8. It is useless to . . . . against evils that we are powerless to end.
   defalcate engender cerebrate inveigh

9. The . . . . is the case of the indirect object.
   declivity cognomen dative eclogue

10. A . . . . would assert the central importance of a god or gods in human affairs.
    cognomen sidereal hybrid theist

11. The . . . . usually featured a conversation between shepherds.
    declivity eclogue diapason maelstrom

12. The lagoon was protected by the surrounding coral . . . .
    orifice nodule atoll detritus

13. The river flows rapidly here because of the steep . . . . of the land.
    fell amenity declivity repertoire

14. He forgot his own telephone number in a moment of mental ....
cerebration altercation defalcation aberration

15. Only a(n) .... idiot would have agreed to anything so foolish.
torrid germane benighted indigenous

16. Doctors removed a small ....
from the base of the spine.
atoll nodule detritus diapason

17. The colonel's timidity .... a lack of confidence in his troops.
defalcated inveighed engendered cerebrated

18. Although their relative values change, the Canadian and U.S. dollars were once at .... with one another.
parity venal hybrid declivity

19. After much ...., she arrived at a solution to the problem.
cerebration altercation aberration defalcation

20. He richly earned the ....
"Gentleman Jim."
eclogue cognomen altercation mandible

WORDLY WISE 2

A DECLIVITY is a downward slope; an *acclivity* is an upward slope. These two words are antonyms.

Expedite means "to carry out promptly; to accelerate a process or the progress of a task; to facilitate." EXPEDITIOUS is an adjective describing quick or efficient action, and the quality or characteristic of acting expeditiously is denoted by the noun *expeditiousness. Expedition*, although its primary meaning is "journey," can also be used as a synonym for expeditiousness. (He acted with expeditiousness in repairing the roof. Our landlord seldom responds with expedition to our complaints.)

REPERTOIRE and *repertory* can be used interchangeably to describe the list of dramas, songs, etc., which a group or individual is able to perform; *repertoire* is the preferred word, however.

Repertory is the term generally used for a type of theatrical or operatic company that produces a number of different offerings alternately. A repertory company is constantly adding new plays to its repertoire.

Etymology

Study the roots and prefix given below together with the English words derived from them. Capitalized words are those given in the Word List. You should look up in a dictionary any words that are unfamiliar to you.

Prefix: *de-* (down) Latin – Examples: *DE-CLIVITY, de*cline, *de*scend
Roots: *theos* (god) Greek – Examples: *THE*ISM, a*the*ist, *theo*logy
par (equal) Latin – Examples: *PAR*ITY, *par, peer*

Word List 3

ABASE	DELETERIOUS	LAMBENT
ALLERGY	DIVA	MOIETY
ANATHEMA	ESTRANGED	REACTIONARY
BRINDLED	GAFF	TENURE
CITE	IDYLLIC	TUTELAGE
DEBACLE		

Look up the words above in your dictionary. Note that many of them have more than one meaning. When you feel that you know *all* the meanings of *all* the words, go on to the exercises below.

EXERCISE 3A

From the four choices following each phrase or sentence, you are to circle the letter preceding the one that is closest in meaning to the italicized word. Where the same word appears more than once, you should note that it is being used in different senses.

1. to *abase* someone
(a) support (b) destroy (c) suspect (d) humble

2. to have an *allergy*
(a) instinctive understanding of something
(b) suspicious attitude toward something

(c) painful sensitivity to something (d) painful disillusionment with something

3. He is *anathema*.
   (a) a person more than a match for oneself (b) a person cast out and detested (c) a person loved or revered (d) a person who is easily defeated

4. She was the object of their *anathemas*.
   (a) ridiculing remarks (b) practical jokes (c) abuses (d) curses

5. a *brindled* cow
   (a) set aside for breeding purposes (b) de-horned (c) tawny in color with dark streaks (d) black in color with white patches

6. to *cite* Aristotle
   (a) question (b) quote from (c) ignore (d) heed

7. a traffic *citation*
   (a) summons (b) jam (c) detour (d) control device

8. *cited* for bravery
   (a) promoted to officer's rank (b) regarded with awe (c) foolishly condemned (d) mentioned honorably.

9. the causes of the *debacle*
   (a) overwhelming victory (b) bitter quarrel (c) total collapse (d) outbreak of war

10. *deleterious* effects
    (a) beneficial (b) harmless (c) unknown (d) harmful

11. a celebrated *diva*
    (a) female ballet star (b) female author (c) female opera star (d) female sports hero

12. to be *estranged*
    (a) no longer on friendly terms (b) in exile from one's native land (c) locked up in solitary confinement (d) pessimistic concerning the future

13. to use the *gaff*
    (a) large net strung between two boats (b) large hook for landing fish (c) small anchor of sheet metal (d) long sweep-oar used for steering

14. a *gaff*-rigged boat
    (a) fitted with a triangular fore-and-aft mainsail (b) fitted with a triangular traverse mainsail (c) fitted with a four-sided fore-and-aft mainsail (d) fitted with a four-sided traverse mainsail

15. an *idyllic* life
    (a) sadly short (b) unpleasantly painful (c) extremely long (d) wonderfully pleasant

16. a *lambent* surface
    (a) gently undulating (b) softly radiant (c) covered with moisture (d) soft and spongy

17. a *lambent* wit
    (a) deliberately cruel (b) heavy and coarse (c) unintentionally cruel (d) light and brilliant

18. a *moiety* of the estate
    (a) half (b) valuation (c) sale (d) closing up

19. a *reactionary* party
    (a) supported by the military (b) looking toward the future (c) having the support of the people (d) favoring outmoded policies

20. granted *tenure*
    (a) pardon for one's crimes (b) a hearing before the courts (c) forgiveness for one's sins (d) the right to hold a position

21. land *tenure*
    (a) reform (b) enclosure (c) ownership (d) rental

22. a senator's *tenure*
    (a) term of office (b) district represented (c) seniority in the Senate (d) ceremonial functions

23. under his *tutelage*
    (a) reign (b) instruction (c) authority (d) rule

Check your answers against the correct ones given below. The answers are not in order; this is to prevent your eye from catching sight of the correct answers before you have had a chance to do the exercise on your own.

15d. 16b. 4d. 18a. 10d. 19d. 12a. 2c. 14c. 8d. 11c. 7a. 17d. 21c. 1d. 5c. 22a. 3b. 20d. 13b. 9c. 6b. 23b.

Look up in your dictionary all the words for which you gave incorrect answers. Only when you have done this should you go on to the next exercise.

EXERCISE 3B

Each word in Word List 3 is used several times in the sentences below to illustrate different meanings or usage. One of the sentences for each word uses the italicized word incorrectly. You are to circle the letter preceding that sentence.

1. (a) King Lear is *abased* by his evil daughters. (b) The coinage was *abased* by the mixing of cheap metals with the gold and silver. (c) The prisoners were forced to *abase* themselves and plead guilty to the false charges. (d) Her manner was unexpectedly humble, and the reason for this sudden *abasement* was a mystery.

2. (a) Penicillin has amazing curative powers, but some people are *allergic* to it. (b) Doctors have treatments to cope with a wide range of *allergies*. (c) Espionage agents in particular are intensely *allergic* to publicity. (d) One can make an *allergy* between a jet engine and the rapid escape of air from a toy balloon.

3. (a) Whenever a malarial attack threatened, the people dosed themselves heavily with *anathema*. (b) Reducing our military commitments is *anathema* to many senators and representatives. (c) The church *anathematized* him for his acts of heresy. (d) The southern states continued to practice slavery despite the *anathemas* of the abolitionists.

4. (a) The *brindled* Great Dane had a brown coat streaked with black. (b) One of the cows was tawny with dark streaks, and one was gray with dark streaks, but none of the others was *brindled*. (c) The horse *brindled* at the stone wall and refused to jump it.

5. (a) The witness who created the disturbance was *cited* for contempt of court. (b) The *citation* described how the fire fighter had bravely rescued five people from the building. (c) She was able to *cite* from memory all the books she had read on the subject. (d) San Francisco will be the *cite* of the next Republican nominating convention.

6. (a) Napoleon's attempted conquest of Russia was a *debacle* and led to his eventual defeat. (b) Banking and investment laws are designed to prevent a recurrence of the 1929 *debacle*. (c) Rescuers dug through tons of *debacle* in an attempt to reach the buried hikers.

7. (a) The *deleterious* effects of smoking cigarettes are well known. (b) He looked *deleteriously* at me when I accused him of taking the money. (c) Although the fumes smell bad, they are not *deleterious* to health. (d) Heroin and other *deleterious* drugs are outlawed by the federal government.

8. (a) She sang the wonderful *diva* "One Fine Day" from the opera ***Madame Butterfly***. (b) Although she had a very minor role in the opera, she secretly thought herself a *diva*. (c) She is the most renowned *diva* in Italian opera but is not at all temperamental.

9. (a) The *estranged* couple was advised to seek the help of a marriage counselor. (b) The *estrangement* of the artist from the world of science is cause for concern. (c) The father's domination of his children helped to *estrange* them from him. (d) The relationship between them was an *estrange* one.

10. (a) I stood in the stern of the boat ready to *gaff* the fish she had caught. (b) Addressing

Her Majesty as "Queenie" was a terrible social *gaff*. (c) The top of the sail is attached to the *gaff* and the bottom is attached to the boom. (d) Bermuda-rigged boats have triangular sails and are easily distinguished from *gaff*-rigged boats.

11. (a) The edge of the lake is an *idyllic* spot for a picnic. (b) The *idyllic* life of the royal family ended when revolution tore apart the country. (c) Their two-week *idyll* on a tropic island ended all too soon. (d) A utopia is an *idyll* society where everything is perfect.

12. (a) The *lambent* glow of the sky gradually gave way to the velvety blackness of night. (b) The burning logs cast *lambent* shadows on the faces of those gathered around the hearth. (c) With a *lambent* roar, the flood waters burst the banks of the river. (d) The author's *lambent* wit is as quick and light as sunlight on water.

13. (a) There is a *moiety* of the savage in even the most civilized of people. (b) She offered to *moiety* the money equally among the three men. (c) Her son and daughter each claimed a *moiety* of the estate.

14. (a) *Reactionaries* attempted to overthrow the government and restore the former ruler to the throne. (b) *Reactionary* forces are at work undermining the progress of the past few years. (c) To return to the isolationism of the 1920's would be a *reactionary* step. (d) Penicillin can be extremely *reactionary* to those whose systems reject it.

15. (a) *Tenure* lapses if the land is not developed, and ownership then reverts to the government. (b) After six consecutive years with the university, a professor is granted *tenure*. (c) Life in the country continues the even *tenure* of its ways. (d) The president has a four-year *tenure* in the White House.

16. (a) She offered to *tutelage* me in Latin and Greek. (b) He began his political career under the *tutelage* of the Roosevelt New Dealers. (c)

Under the *tutelage* of Rudolf Serkin, she became a fine pianist.

EXERCISE 3C

This exercise is designed to enable you to gain experience in quickly and accurately handling questions dealing with synonyms (an explanation of synonyms is given in the Introduction). It also tests how well you have learned the vocabulary words covered so far.

Underline the word which is most similar in meaning to the capitalized word. Allow only ten minutes for this test. If you cannot answer a question, go on to the next one without delay. If you have time left over at the end, go back and try to fill in unanswered questions.

22 or over correct:	excellent
17 to 21 correct:	good
16 or under correct:	thorough review of **A** exercises indicated

1. HUMBLE
   inveigh engender defalcate cite abase

2. QUARREL
   aberration allergy gaff mandible altercation

3. JAWBONE
   diapason orifice declivity mandible nodule

4. DEFECT
   cerebration hybrid aberration declivity cognomen

5. REASONED
   rational reactionary lambent deleterious brindled

6. EMBEZZLE
   inveigh cite abase cartel defalcate

7. WHIRLPOOL
   maelstrom nodule moiety debacle cognomen

8. IGNORANT
   unguent benighted reactionary indigenous torrid

9. NICKNAME

tutelage diva detritus cognomen diapason

10. CRUEL

venal sidereal fell benighted unguent

11. SPEEDY

reactionary expeditious germane torrid fell

12. THOUGHT

rational aberration altercation cerebration allergy

13. CORRUPT

estranged lambent venal sidereal hybrid

14. OPENING

aberration orifice atoll nodule debacle

15. RANGE

moiety eclogue declivity anathema diapason

16. RELEVANT

estranged benighted idyllic germane indigenous

17. EQUALITY

moiety allergy hybrid anathema parity

18. PRODUCE

fell cite engender defalcate inveigh

19. HARMFUL

benighted unguent indigenous deleterious germane

20. RADIANT

venal dative sidereal brindled lambent

21. HOT

hybrid lambent dative torrid benighted

22. HALF

moiety cognomen tenure gaff parity

23. OWNERSHIP

tutelage cartel eclogue tenure mandible

24. OINTMENT

mandible moiety unguent maelstrom cognomen

25. INSTRUCTION

cerebration altercation theism diapason tutelage

WORDLY WISE 3

ABASE means "to humble; to lower in esteem" (to abase oneself before the king); this word is easily confused with *debase*, which means "to lower the quality of." (You abase yourself by resorting to such methods. Gold coins are debased by the addition of other metals.)

CITE is a verb meaning (1) "to quote," (2) "to summon to court," (3) "to mention honorably." *Site* is a noun and means "location"; it is also a verb meaning "to locate" or "to be located." These two words are homonyms.

Don't confuse GAFF with the word *gaffe*, which means "a social error or blunder." These two words are homonyms.

Etymology

Study the roots and prefix given below together with the English words derived from them. Capitalized words are those given in the Word List. You should look up in a dictionary any words that are unfamiliar to you.

Prefix: *re-* (against) Latin — Examples: *RE*-ACTIONARY, *re*criminate, *re*luctant

Roots: *ten* (hold) Latin — Examples: *TEN*URE, *ten*able, *ten*acity

extraneous (foreign) Latin — Examples: *ESTRANG*ED, *ex*traneous, *strange*

The crossword puzzle for this first chapter has 49 clues. Each clue is a definition of a word from Word Lists 1, 2, and 3. Unless otherwise stated, a word is always used in the form in which it appears on the Word List; each word is used only once.

For every crossword puzzle after the first, review words are included. These are indicated by the number of the Word List from which they are taken appearing after the clue.

ACROSS

1. harmful to health; injurious
4. favoring outmoded policies
8. the jaw, especially the lower jaw
11. a large and violent whirlpool
12. a deviation from what is normal or correct
14. a total collapse, defeat, or disaster
16. originating naturally in a particular place
18. to bring into being
20. a downward slope
24. the case of the indirect object
25. a short, pastoral poem
27. open to or marked by bribery and corruption
28. a salve or ointment
30. acting without delay; speedy
32. attractive features, as of a place
34. a person or thing accursed or detested
36. belief in a god or gods
39. instruction
40. held back by ignorance
44. a mouthlike opening
45. wonderfully pleasant
46. a small, rounded lump
47. to steal or misuse funds entrusted to one;
    to embezzle

DOWN

1. the entire range, as of the voice
2. softly bright or radiant
3. the right to hold an office or position
4. a stock of pieces that a person or group can perform
5. to lower in rank or esteem; to humble
6. intensely hot; scorching
7. an angry dispute or quarrel
9. gray or tan with dark streaks
10. a painful sensitivity to something
13. material worn away or broken off
15. a name, especially a nickname
17. of or relating to the stars
19. of or based on reason
21. a group of companies acting together to control
    prices and production
22. to attack verbally; to speak out against
23. mental activity; thought
26. no longer on friendly terms
29. closely related; relevant
31. equality or value, power, or rank
33. fierce; terrible; wicked
35. of mixed origin, as the offspring of parents of
    different species
37. one of two approximately-equal halves
38. a ring-shaped coral island surrounding a lagoon
41. a large hook for landing fish
42. a female opera star; a prima donna
43. to quote from

Chapter Two

Word List 4

APPRISE	ENTENTE	NEOPHYTE
BOSS	EXECRABLE	PARADIGM
CHECKERED	FAUNA	PENUMBRA
DEVILTRY	IMMANENT	QUONDAM
EGREGIOUS	INSENSATE	TENET
EMETIC	LACHRYMOSE	

Look up the words above in your dictionary. Note that many of them have more than one meaning. When you feel that you know *all* the meanings of *all* the words, go on to the exercises below.

EXERCISE 4A

From the four choices following each phrase or sentence, you are to circle the letter preceding the one that is closest in meaning to the italicized word. Where the same word appears more than once, you should note that it is being used in different senses.

1. to *apprise* someone
   (a) praise (b) criticize (c) shock (d) inform

2. a beautifully-wrought *boss*
   (a) ornamental border (b) criss-cross arrangement (c) support for a column (d) ornamental projection

3. a *checkered* career
   (a) marked by great sacrifice (b) cut off at mid-point (c) marked by changes of fortune (d) with greatly restricted opportunity

4. a *checkered* cloth
   (a) having a pattern of squares (b) having a pattern of stripes (c) having an irregular shape (d) speckled with many colors

5. accused of *deviltry*
   (a) worship of false gods (b) wicked or mischievous acts (c) refusing to believe in God (d) setting oneself up as a god

6. *egregious* errors
   (a) easily spotted (b) pardonable (c) flagrantly bad (d) easily passed over

7. to administer an *emetic*
   (a) substance that calms the nerves (b) substance that relieves constipation (c) substance that induces sleep (d) substance that induces vomiting

8. an *entente* with a foreign power
   (a) exchange of prisoners (b) understanding (c) confrontation (d) undeclared war

9. *execrable* tastes
   (a) questionable (b) worthy of imitation (c) simple (d) detestable

10. the *fauna* of Hawaii
    (a) rocks (b) animals (c) plants (d) people

11. something which is *immanent*
    (a) about to happen (b) present within (c) bound to happen (d) famous

12. to be *insensate*
    (a) rigorously self-denying (b) extremely annoyed (c) lacking awareness of sensation (d) pleasure-loving

13. *lachrymose* pleas
    (a) urgent (b) tearful (c) halfhearted (d) ineffectual

14. a mere *neophyte*
    (a) amateur (b) formality (c) pittance (d) beginner

15. a *paradigm* of animal behavior
    (a) pattern (b) description (c) understanding (d) mystery

16. the area of the *penumbra*
    (a) total lack of light (b) partial airlessness (c) total lack of air (d) partial shadow surrounding a darker center

17. the *penumbra* of consciousness
(a) depths (b) overall totality (c) undefined borderline (d) full awareness

18. my *quondam* associates
(a) loyal (b) treacherous (c) former (d) business

19. a major *tenet*
(a) cause (b) part (c) disaster (d) principle

Check your answers against the correct ones given below. The answers are not in order; this is to prevent your eye from catching sight of the correct answers before you have had a chance to do the exercise on your own.

6c. 15a. 8b. 5b. 16d. 14d. 1d. 9d. 13b. 17c. 2d. 4a. 18c. 12c. 7d. 3c. 11b. 19d. 10b.

Look up in your dictionary all the words for which you gave incorrect answers. Only when you have done this should you go on to the next exercise.

EXERCISE 4B

Each word in Word List 4 is used several times in the sentences below to illustrate different meanings or usage. One of the sentences for each word uses the italicized word incorrectly. You are to circle the letter preceding that sentence.

1. (a) The jeweler examined the ring and *apprised* it at fifty dollars. (b) We were not *apprised* of the facts in this case, so we cannot make a decision. (c) The butler departed to *apprise* the host of our arrival.

2. (a) The shield was of leather, studded with heavy brass *bosses*. (b) The book was a heavy one with *bossed* leather covers. (c) The studs in the belt were the color of *boss* and were brightly polished.

3. (a) He had had a *checkered* career in business, but he provided for his children. (b) A red-and-white *checkered* cloth was spread over the table. (c) The countryside was *checkered* with small patches of woodland. (d) She *checkered* her opponent's attempt to take her rook.

4. (a) Such *deviltries* as pulling away chairs from those about to sit must be stopped. (b) The *deviltry* of the young children is the result of a complete lack of discipline. (c) The barbarian invasion unleashed such *deviltry* on the citizens as to make them long for merciful deaths. (d) The members of the tribe had renounced civilization and had grown savage and *deviltry*.

5. (a) The two politicians who *egregiously* helped themselves to public funds were voted out of office. (b) Entrusting an inexperienced youth with such a delicate task was an *egregious* error. (c) I couldn't help but gasp at such an *egregious* falsehood. (d) He's a very *egregious* person and loves meeting people and going to parties.

6. (a) The doctor gave an *emetic* to the child who had swallowed poison. (b) The lid of the container was *emetically* sealed to prevent air from entering. (c) Brazilian ipecac is useful to medicine because of its *emetic* properties.

7. (a) The *entente* between the two nations was formalized in an alliance of mutual aid. (b) The British government was disturbed by the French-Italian *entente*. (c) Although the government professed peace, it *entented* war.

8. (a) The perpetrator of these *execrable* crimes must be brought swiftly to justice. (b) A couple of poems in this book are acceptable, but the majority are *execrable*. (c) The floodwaters rose slowly and *inexecrably* until they inundated the countryside.

9. (a) We saw only two or three *fauna* on our hike because the dogs made a constant commotion in the woods. (b) Fossil remains give us a clear picture of the *fauna* of the Paleozoic era.

10. (a) A vital force, *immanent* in all organisms, was believed to be the prime cause of evolution. (b) When the car brakes failed, a disaster seemed *immanent*. (c) She believed goodness is *immanent* in all people. (d) Members of that tribe believe that in these objects the spirits of their ancestors are *immanent*.

11. (a) In a moment of *insensate* rage, he struck the old man with his fist. (b) Having lived in the city for so long, they are *insensate* to the beauties of nature. (c) She *insensated* herself into a position of trust within the organization. (d) The woman, alone in her prison cell, addresses her words to the *insensate* stones.

12. (a) They dabbed at their eyes as they concluded their *lachrymose* farewells to each other. (b) The water of the Dead Sea is so *lachrymose* that it is impossible to sink in it. (c) The poems, full of dying heroes and heroines, were indeed *lachrymose*.

13. (a) She is a *neophyte* in the Episcopal church, but she will make a splendid priest when she gains experience. (b) Provision must be made in our prisons to keep the *neophyte* separated from the hardened criminal. (c) To the *neophyte* these two paintings look identical, but the one on the left is a forgery. (d) The painting was so *neophyte* that it had obviously been done by someone with little experience.

14. (a) In grammar, a *paradigm* is a listing of all the forms of a word. (b) Scientists construct *paradigms* to explain recurring patterns of behavior. (c) The view that science is a *paradigm* of all real knowledge is a debatable one. (d) His sad experiences have left him with a *paradigm* view of human nature.

15. (a) He carried a *penumbra* with him at all times, as he believed in always being prepared. (b) A *penumbral* lunar eclipse occurs when the moon passes through the area of partial shadow cast by the earth. (c) The seventeenth century lies in the *penumbra* between the medieval and modern periods. (d) The umbra, or area of total shadow during an eclipse, is surrounded by the *penumbra*, or area of partial shadow.

16. (a) Our *quondam* friends, whom we helped in their need, now turn their backs on us. (b) She was in a terrible *quondam*, since whatever she did would be disastrous. (c) Britain maintains friendly relations with many *quondam* colonies.

17. (a) The principle of equality is a major *tenet* of democracy. (b) The two great *tenets* of science are observation and deduction. (c) It goes against his *tenet* to lend money to anyone.

EXERCISE 4C

Some of the italicized words in the sentences below are used literally; others are used metaphorically (these terms are explained in the Introduction). In the spaces provided write "L" if the word is used literally; if the word is used metaphorically, replace the metaphorical expression with a literal rendering. Be careful not to change the meaning of a sentence.

1. He shot a *tiger* . . . . in the jungles of India.

2. Those arriving late at the theater got *black* . . . . looks from those they disturbed.

3. The corn is still *green* . . . . but should be ripe in a month.

4. The prisoner *hatched* . . . . a clever plan to escape from the prison.

5. She seems *cool* . . . . to the idea now, but she might change her mind later.

6. Many of the players are still pretty *green* . . . . , but they'll improve after a few games.

7. He wore a *black* . . . . armband as a token of his mourning.

8. The new heavyweight champion is a *tiger* . . . . in the ring.

9. The three eggs in the nest *hatched* . . . . yesterday.

10. The doctor's *cool* . . . . hands soothed the patient's fevered brow.

WORDLY WISE 4

APPRISE means "to inform" (apprised of the results); *appraise* means "to estimate the value of" (to appraise the ring).

The British spelling of CHECKERED is *chequered*.

DEVILTRY is sometimes written *devilry;* both forms are correct.

EGREGIOUS means "flagrant" (an egregious error); don't confuse this word with *gregarious*, which means "fond of company; sociable" (a gregarious host). Both words are derived from the Latin *grex, gregis* (herd). In Latin, *egregius* meant "outstanding or distinguished" (literally, "outside the herd"), and had favorable connotations. In current English, "egregious" is only pejorative, and refers to something outstandingly bad.

An ENTENTE is an understanding or agreement between nations marked by goodwill on both sides; a *detente* is an agreement or understanding arrived at between nations where previously there has been hostility or bitterness (A detente was reached between the two nations when they realized that neither could defeat the other).

FAUNA is the general term for the animal life of a region; *flora* is the general term for the plant life. The words are generally used together (the flora and fauna of Alaska).

IMMANENT, *imminent*, and *eminent* are three similar-sounding words with quite different meanings. *Immanent*, the least common of these three words, means "operating within; inherent" (the spirit which is immanent in human beings). *Imminent* means "about to happen" (a disaster was imminent). *Eminent* means "important; outstanding" (an eminent scientist).

Etymology

Study the following roots and prefix together with the English words derived from them. Capitalized words are those given in the Word List. You should look up in a dictionary any words that are unfamiliar to you.

Prefix: *para-* (beside; like) Greek – Examples: *PARA*DIGM, *para*llel, *para*phrase
Roots: *neo* (new) Greek – Examples: *NEO-*PHYTE, *neo*lithic, *neo*classic
umbra (shadow) Latin – Examples: PEN*UMBRA*, *umbra*lla, *umbr*age
pene (almost) Latin – Examples: *PENE*UMBRA, *pen*insula, *pen*ultimate

Word List 5

ACUMEN	EMOLUMENT	LIBATION
ATONE	EQUITY	NUPTIAL
BUCOLIC	EXEGESIS	PATRIMONY
CODICIL	FETISH	PRECEDENT
DISSENSION	INCURSION	SOBRIQUET
EGRESS	ITINERANT	YAW

Look up the words above in your dictionary. Note that many of them have more than one meaning. When you feel that you know *all* the meanings of *all* the words, go on to the exercises below.

EXERCISE 5A

From the four choices following each phrase or sentence, you are to circle the letter preceding the one that is closest in meaning to the italicized word. Where the same word appears more than once, you should note that it is being used in different senses.

1. to show *acumen*
   (a) great interest (b) lack of ability (c) slight interest (d) keenness of mind

2. to *atone* for something
   (a) disclaim responsibility (b) refuse to pay (c) make amends (d) take credit

3. *bucolic* poetry
   (a) pastoral (b) religious (c) humorous (d) patriotic

4. to read the *codicil*
   (a) terms of the contract (b) ancient manuscript (c) addition to a will (d) final draft of a speech or book

5. to create *dissension*
   (a) fervor (b) quarreling (c) harmony (d) apathy

6. looking for the *egress*
   (a) rare, plumed bird (b) way in (c) baby eagle (d) way out

7. a large *emolument*
   (a) group (b) undertaking (c) salary (d) tomb

8. to achieve *equity*
   (a) understanding (b) satisfaction (c) victory (d) fairness

9. an *exegesis* of the passage
   (a) committing to memory (b) reading aloud (c) critical interpretation (d) translation into a foreign language

10. to wear a *fetish*
    (a) small crown symbolizing royalty (b) oak-leaf cluster symbolizing victory (c) object believed to have magical properties (d) coarse, one-piece woolen garment

11. The automobile has become a *fetish*.
    (a) expensive item (b) symbol of progress (c) status-symbol (d) object of excessive devotion

12. an *incursion* by a foreign power
    (a) offer to negotiate (b) sudden invasion (c) offer of help (d) internal collapse

13. an *itinerant* teacher
    (a) devout (b) aged (c) stern (d) traveling

14. a *libation* to the gods
    (a) act of submission (b) human sacrifice (c) poured offering (d) animal sacrifice

15. the *nuptial* day
    (a) wedding (b) judgment (c) first (d) last

16. a small *patrimony*
    (a) state absorbed into a larger one (b) book containing wise sayings (c) sacrifice made for one's country (d) estate inherited from one's father

17. to look for a *precedent*
    (a) cause that is not immediately apparent (b) act used to justify a later one (c) person willing to accept the blame (d) indication as to how things will develop

18. *precedent* causes
    (a) earlier (b) direct (c) indirect (d) unknown

19. an appropriate *sobriquet*
    (a) form of dress (b) message of greeting (c) bedside manner (d) assumed name

20 The ship began to *yaw*.
    (a) sink lower into the water (b) swing off course (c) fill up with water (d) rise and fall with a rocking motion

Check your answers against the correct ones given below. The answers are not in order; this is to prevent your eye from catching sight of the correct answers before you have had a chance to do the exercise on your own.

10c. 18a. 4c. 16d. 5b. 19d. 12b. 2c. 14c. 8d. 11d. 7c. 17b. 1d. 15a. 3a. 13d. 9c. 6d. 20b.

Look up in your dictionary all the words for which you gave incorrect answers. Only when you have done this should you go on to the next exercise.

EXERCISE 5B
Each word in Word List 5 is used several times in the sentences below to illustrate different meanings or usage. One of the sentences for each word uses the italicized word incorrectly. You are to circle the letter preceding that sentence.

1. (a) A real test of the governor's *acumen* is deciding which candidate to support. (b) He had done foolish things in his youth, but he

grew more *acumen* as he got older. (c) I had thought her a woman of rare *acumen,* but her recent blunders cause me to wonder.

2. (a) They were prepared to do anything to *atone* for their thoughtlessness. (b) She accepted her self-reproach as sufficient *atonement* for her cruelty. (c) Vivid descriptive passages do little to *atone* for the book's lack of plot. (d) The poet *atoned* the words of the ode in a high, monotonous voice.

3. (a) The baby has a touch of *bucolic* and wants its stomach rubbed. (b) The *"Bucolics"* of Theocritus are simple poems celebrating life in the country. (c) She retired to the country and now leads a *bucolic* life on her farm. (d) The paintings are *bucolic* renderings of milkmaids, hayfields, and other rural subjects.

4. (a) A meeting of the *codicil* has been called for this evening to discuss future plans. (b) In a *codicil* drafted just before his death, the father disinherited his son. (c) The lawyer read the will proper before going on to read the *codicils* to it.

5. (a) The *dissension* among the crew members is caused by the poor food and harsh discipline. (b) We must end *dissension* within the ranks of the party if we are to move ahead. (c) Those who disagreed formed a separate *dissension* and broke away from the main group.

6. (a) We found ourselves in a large cave whose only *egress* was the hole we had entered by. (b) Crowds following the sign that said "This Way to the *Egress*" found themselves outside. (c) This compound is suitable for keeping cattle in provided that an *egress* to the pasture is constructed. (d) She *egressed* for a moment from her prepared speech and spoke briefly of her childhood.

7. (a) His *emolument* consisted of a small wage supplemented by generous tips. (b) What would you consider a fair *emolument* for this job? (c) Rub a little *emolument* into the skin where it is sore.

8. (a) She was prompted by considerations of *equity* to honor claims that lacked strictly legal validity. (b) The courts strive to maintain *equity* and avoid favoring one side over the other. (c) She offered to *equity* those who felt they had been unfairly treated. (d) This seems to be the most *equitable* way of dividing the money.

9. (a) The work of generations of *exegetes* enables us to understand fully these once obscure passages. (b) Her *exegesis* of a difficult passage in Chaucer earned her the respect of literary scholars. (c) The poem is supplied with an *exegesis* so that its more obscure passages can be understood without difficulty. (d) The curve on the graph reaches its *exegesis* at this point and then flattens out.

10. (a) These wooden carvings are *fetishes* believed by the natives to have magical powers. (b) An aborigine might make a *fetish* out of a bunch of feathers while another person might make one out of the picture of a saint. (c) The army made a *fetish* of discipline. (d) The natives in the jungle are still *fetish*, never having seen a missionary.

11. (a) Nightly *incursions* across the border by armed bands may soon lead to war. (b) The U.S. *incursion* into Cambodia created a storm of protest. (c) The surgeon made a six-inch *incursion* just below the patient's rib cage.

12. (a) *Itinerant* agricultural workers move into the area for the harvest and then move on. (b) He enjoyed the life of an *itinerant*, traveling from town to town with his goods for sale. (c) *Itinerant* lecturers took culture to people in rural areas. (d) "Do whatever you think best," she *itineranted.*

13. (a) The Greeks poured a little of the oil on the ground as a *libation* to Zeus. (b) After copious *libations* of claret, the fat, red-faced man fell into a sound sleep. (c) The wine was poured into a *libation* and passed among the group.

14. (a) The bride and groom busied themselves with preparations for the approaching *nuptials*. (b) A *nuptial* was hastily summoned to perform the marriage ceremony. (c) During the mating season, male birds are glorious in their *nuptial* plumage. (d) Over a hundred guests toasted the newly married couple at the *nuptial* feast.

15. (a) Cordelia's open rebelliousness against her father cost her her *patrimony*. (b) An investment of ten thousand dollars yields a yearly *patrimony* of five hundred dollars. (c) The son owed so much money that his *patrimony* was swallowed up paying off his debts.

16. (a) The convention broke *precedent* in electing an actor as chairperson. (b) The mass movement of people to the cities is *unprecedented* in our history. (c) The motion to adjourn was *precedent* to the others and will be voted on first. (d) She was elected *precedent* of the society by unanimous vote.

17. (a) The nurse applied a *sobriquet* to his arm to stop the bleeding. (b) The rowdies of the frontier town had such colorful *sobriquets* as "Wild Bill" and "Six-Gun Pete." (c) His fight against civic corruption earned him the *sobriquet* "Honest John."

18. (a) A sudden *yaw* of the ship may occur if the propeller rises out of the water. (b) The torpedo ripped a jagged *yaw* along the side of the ship. (c) The plane shows no tendency to roll, pitch, or *yaw*. (d) The woman at the helm struggled with the wheel as the ship *yawed* to starboard.

EXERCISE 5C

From the five numbered choices, complete the analogies below by underlining the word that stands in the same relationship to the third word as the second word does to the first. (An explanation of analogies is given in the Introduction.)

1. flora:fauna::plant: (1) root (2) leaf (3) grow (4) animal (5) rear

2. frigid:torrid::cold: (1) temperature (2) icy (3) ice (4) freezing (5) hot

3. solar:sun::sidereal: (1) earth (2) planets (3) moon (4) stars (5) time

4. forward:progressive::backward: (1) moiety (2) precedent (3) incursion (4) entente (5) reactionary

5. genitive:possession::dative: (1) direct object (2) subject (3) indirect object (4) predicate (5) nominative

6. annex:building::codicil: (1) agreement (2) seize (3) testimony (4) illness (5) will

7. good:beneficent::harm: (1) bucolic (2) itinerant (3) deleterious (4) expeditious (5) quondam

8. frigid:warmth::insensate: (1) cold (2) speech (3) fear (4) feeling (5) numb

9. spectrum:colors::diapason: (1) music (2) notes (3) sights (4) pictures (5) feelings

10. coward:courage::neophyte: (1) expert (2) timidity (3) boast (4) beginner (5) experience

WORDLY WISE 5

An EGRESS is an exit; the antonym of this word is *ingress*, which means "entrance." Either word may be used for the means by which one enters or leaves or for the act of entering or leaving.

EQUITY has a legal meaning in addition to those given in the exercises. The value of property beyond the amount owed on it is the equity. If a person owes twenty thousand dollars on a house worth fifty thousand, his or her equity in that house would be thirty thousand dollars.

Etymology

Study the following roots and prefixes together with the English words derived from them. Capitalized words are those given in the Word List. You should look up in a dictionary any words that are unfamiliar to you.

Prefixes: *pre-* (before) Latin – Examples: *PRECE-DENT*, *pre*decessor, *pre*destined

dis- (apart) Latin – Examples: *DIS-SENSION*, *dis*sociate, *dis*tant

Roots: *patri* (father) Latin – Examples: *PATRI*MONY, *pater*nal, *pater*nity

cedo (go) Latin – Examples: *PRECE-DENT*, re*cede,* se*cede*

curr, curs (run) Latin – Examples: IN-*CURS*ION, *curr*ent, dis*curs*ive

---

Word List 6

APOCRYPHAL	ENJOIN	MACHETE
BLUDGEON	EULOGY	PALPABLE
CACOPHONY	EXTRUDE	PECCADILLO
DEPOSITION	GIGOLO	PROGENY
DIVINE	INHIBIT	STENTORIAN
ÉLAN	JOCOSE	ZEPHYR

Look up the words above in your dictionary. Note that many of them have more than one meaning. When you feel that you know *all* the meanings of *all* the words, go on to the exercises below.

EXERCISE 6A

From the four choices following each phrase or sentence, you are to circle the letter preceding the one that is closest in meaning to the italicized word. Where the same word appears more than once, you should note that it is being used in different senses.

1. an *apocryphal* story
   (a) highly comical (b) undoubtedly true (c) deeply tragic (d) of doubtful authenticity

2. a heavy *bludgeon*
   (a) short club (b) professional fighter (c) supporting beam (d) balancing weight

3. a sudden *cacophony*
   (a) piece of good fortune (b) surprise attack (c) harsh, jarring sound (d) change of fortune

4. a servant's *deposition*
   (a) willingness to serve another (b) generally negative attitude toward life (c) expectation of receiving an inheritance (d) written testimony given under oath

5. a king's *deposition*
   (a) right to rule (b) line of succession (c) removal from power (d) right to choose a successor

6. *divine* power
   (a) without limit (b) based on military might (c) limited (d) coming from God

7. to *divine* the truth
   (a) hide (b) figure out (c) reject (d) have respect for

8. a Puritan *divine* of the seventeenth century
   (a) saint (b) holy relic (c) religious belief (d) member of the clergy

9. *divine* pastry
   (a) heavy (b) unsweetened (c) excellent (d) moist

10. to show *élan*
    (a) great enthusiasm (b) great fear (c) undue pessimism (d) undue optimism

11. to *enjoin* someone
    (a) associate oneself with (b) derive pleasure from (c) obey (d) command

12. a long *eulogy*
    (a) closing speech in a play (b) column of mourners (c) speech of praise (d) gay musical composition

13. molten rock is *extruded*
    (a) deeply buried (b) forced out (c) quickly cooled (d) freely flowing

14. a young *gigolo*
    (a) man guided and helped by another man (b) man financially supported by a woman (c) man hired to teach his employer's children (d) man hired to commit a crime

15. to *inhibit* growth
    (a) observe (b) measure (c) increase (d) check

21

16. an *inhibited* person
    (a) bold (b) weak (c) wealthy (d) shy

17. a *jocose* manner
    (a) serious (b) jesting (c) tearful (d) excited

18. to carry a *machete*
    (a) heavy knife (b) heavy club (c) leather whip
    (d) flaming torch

19. a *palpable* object
    (a) that increases in size (b) that is too small to
    be seen (c) that can be touched (d) that gives
    off light

20. a *palpable* lie
    (a) clever (b) harmful (c) harmless (d) obvious

21. to ignore the *peccadillo*
    (a) indirect suggestion (b) official order (c)
    posted warning (d) minor fault

22. her *progeny*
    (a) plea (b) expectation (c) offspring (d) wish

23. a *stentorian* voice
    (a) pleading (b) hoarse (c) cultured (d) loud

24. a soft *zephyr*
    (a) mild rebuke (b) downy bed (c) gentle
    breeze (d) easy life

Check your answers against the correct ones
given below. The answers are not in order; this is to
prevent your eye from catching sight of the correct
answers before you have had a chance to do the
exercise on your own.

3c. 11d. 19c. 10a. 18a. 12c. 7b. 20d. 22c. 4d. 2a.
17b. 13b. 23d. 9c. 1d. 14b. 16d. 5c. 8d. 15d. 6d.
21d. 24c.

Look up in your dictionary all the words for
which you gave incorrect answers. Only when you
have done this should you go on to the next
exercise.

Each word in Word List 6 is used several times
in the sentences below to illustrate different
meanings or usage. One of the sentences for each
word uses the italicized word incorrectly. You are
to circle the letter preceding that sentence.

1. (a) The story of George Washington chopping
   down the cherry tree is probably *apocryphal*.
   (b) The expert's task is to separate the
   apocryphal from the authentic. (c) The doctor
   answered *apocryphally* when I asked whether
   my condition was serious. (d) The *Apocrypha*
   is a collection of fourteen books excluded
   from the Protestant Bible because of their
   doubtful authenticity.

2. (a) She had *bludgeoned* into a trap from
   which there was no escape. (b) The victim had
   been *bludgeoned* to death and thrown into a
   doorway. (c) When I saw the *bludgeon* in my
   assailant's hand, I turned and ran. (d) A
   rapierlike wit disconcerts an opponent more
   than *bludgeoning* him or her with masses
   of statistics.

3. (a) Their voices rose *cacophonously* as they
   struggled to finish the song. (b) A *cacophony*
   of cries filled the air as the gulls fought over
   the food scraps. (c) He has composed a
   cacophony for violin and full orchestra. (d) I
   was disturbed by the shrieks of *cacophonous*
   laughter from the next room.

4. (a) The judge accepted the *deposition* of the
   witness who was unable to come to court. (b)
   Following the *deposition* of the king, a military council ruled the country. (c) The president was *deposed* in a bloodless coup organ-
   ized by the army. (d) She has a somewhat surly
   deposition, so I avoid her as much as possible.

5. (a) We must bow before the *divine* will. (b)
   The road *divines* its way along the bank of the
   river. (c) I think I have *divined* the cause of
   her unhappiness. (d) She thought that Eliza-
   beth Barrett Browning's poems were *divine*.

6. (a) As she grew older, she became even more
   élan than she had been as a youth. (b) She

performed with great dash and *élan*. (c) He took an army of dispirited soldiers and filled them with *élan*. (d) The *élan* of the Gay Nineties is now beyond recall.

7. (a) The jury was sternly *enjoined* from discussing the case. (b) He was bound to avenge his father; the gods *enjoined* it. (c) The two ends were *enjoined* so neatly that no break could be seen.

8. (a) A close friend of the deceased delivered the *eulogy* at the funeral. (b) In *eulogistic* tones he praised the efforts of his predecessor. (c) She has been *eulogized* by so many that there is little left to add. (d) The long *eulogy* of mourners filed past the coffin.

9. (a) *Extruded* parts are formed by forcing them through specially designed openings after they have been heated. (b) These *extrusions* were formed when molten rock was forced through cracks in the earth. (c) It was rude of him to *extrude* his way into your house without an invitation.

10. (a) She could play the flute and the *gigolo* with almost professional skill. (b) Many women disdain other women who support *gigolos*. (c) I called him a *gigolo*, but he insisted there was nothing wrong with being a paid escort for a wealthy woman.

11. (a) His shyness *inhibited* him from speaking in class. (b) The house is *inhibited* by a woman and her three children. (c) He had no *inhibitions* and was game for anything.

12. (a) The candidate's speech consisted of sly *jocosities* directed at his opponent. (b) She made a few *jocose* remarks that had the audience laughing uproariously. (c) His constant *jocosity* seems inappropriate in a judge. (d) I didn't think that you would take my little *jocose* seriously.

13. (a) With our trusty *machetes*, we hacked our way through the jungle. (b) The workers sharpened their *machetes* and set to work chopping down the sugar cane. (c) With our sharp knives, we cut a narrow *machete* through the jungle.

14. (a) The patient's spleen is *palpably* enlarged. (b) To suggest that I took the money is a *palpable* absurdity. (c) There was a *palpable* dampness in the air that chilled us to the bone. (d) If the car causes an accident, the registered owner is *palpable*.

15. (a) The biography alludes briefly to the *peccadilloes* of her youth but gives us no details. (b) The *peccadillo* they have at the zoo is a most curious creature. (c) He kept his confession brief as he did not want to bore the priest with his every *peccadillo*.

16. (a) The man and woman were proud of their *progeny*. (b) She was so weak and *progeny* from old age that she rarely left her room. (c) The *progeny* resulting from combining these two strains is a hard, winter wheat.

17. (a) In *stentorian* tones she called out to us across the lake. (b) A *stentorian* trumpet blast shattered the silence. (c) He was a *stentorian* in the imperial Roman guard.

18. (a) He grew a few *zephyrs* in the window box and tended them with loving care. (b) We lay in the sunshine, a cool *zephyr* blowing gently over us. (c) A gentle *zephyr* sprang up, barely filling the sails of the boat.

EXERCISE 6C

This exercise is divided into two parts: Part A deals with synonyms; Part B, with antonyms. (These terms are explained in the Introduction.) Allow only fifteen minutes for this test. If you cannot answer a question, go on to the next one without delay. If you have time left over at the end, go back and try to fill in unanswered questions.

26 or over correct: excellent
22 to 25 correct: good
21 or under correct: thorough review of A
                       exercises indicated

Part A (Synonyms)

Underline the word which is most similar in meaning to the capitalized word.

1. PATTERN
   zephyr fetish penumbra peccadillo paradigm

2. TRAVELING
   neophyte precedent apocryphal itinerant nuptial

3. FLAGRANT
   apocryphal bucolic checkered immanent egregious

4. ENTHUSIASM
   deviltry penumbra tenet sobriquet élan

5. FORMER
   quondam palpable jocose exegesis immanent

6. TANGIBLE
   stentorian precedent itinerant palpable mandible

7. INFORM
   inveigh engender apprise atone extrude

8. PASTORAL
   nuptial bucolic itinerant apocryphal jocose

9. OFFSPRING
   fauna zephyr progeny neophyte codicil

10. INHERENT
    lambent emetic lachrymose immanent venal

11. FAULT
    anathema atoll sobriquet tenet peccadillo

12. TEARFUL
    egregious emetic bucolic brindled lachrymose

13. FAIRNESS
    allergy progeny moiety equity eulogy

14. UNDERSTANDING
    incursion codicil quondam entente emolument

15. SALARY
    quondam emolument patrimony libation equity

Part B (Antonyms)

Underline the word which is most nearly opposite in meaning to the capitalized word.

16. ENTRANCE
    zephyr bludgeon incursion paradigm egress

17. GENUINE
    apocryphal checkered germane egregious reactionary

18. ADMIRABLE
    nuptial torrid execrable apocryphal hybrid

19. QUIET
    fell sobriquet fetish divine stentorian

20. STUPIDITY
    deposition élan exegesis acumen gaff

21. HONEST
    estranged quondam unguent execrable venal

22. ENCOURAGE
    cite inhibit yaw atone defalcate

23. SENTIENT
    rational stentorian neophyte insensate immanent

24. UPLIFT
    abase inveigh enjoin apprise inhibit

25. BENEFICIAL
    itinerant bucolic apocryphal deleterious palpable

26. AGREEMENT

patrimony   dissension   libation   incursion
lachrymose

27. COLD

lachrymose quondam lambent torrid brindled

28. EXPERT

hybrid quondam neophyte sobriquet codicil

29. HARMONY

maelstrom   paradigm cognomen zephyr
cacophony

30. SOLEMN

jocose hybrid sidereal nuptial expeditious

WORDLY WISE 6

ÉLAN is a French word; it has not been Anglicized to the point where the acute accent (´) can be dropped.

ENJOIN takes the preposition "to" when it means "to command" (enjoined by the gods to avenge his father); it is frequently followed by "from" when its meaning is "to forbid; to prohibit" (enjoined from revealing clients' names). *Enjoinder* and *injunction*, nouns formed from the same root as *enjoin*, both mean either "command" or "prohibition," depending on context.

The plural of PECCADILLO is *peccadillos* or *peccadilloes*.

Stentor, a Greek warrior in *The Iliad*, was famed for his powerful voice. His name has added the word STENTORIAN, "loud-voiced," to the language.

Zephyrus was the personification of the west wind in Greek mythology. Other winds were Boreas (north), Notus (south), and Eurus (east). According to the myths they were kept confined in a mountain-top cave by Aeolus, god of the winds. From these names are derived ZEPHYR, now any soft, gentle breeze; *boreal*, meaning "northern; cold and wintry," and *aeolian*, referring to something which gives forth a sound produced by or sounding like the wind (the aeolian voices of the trees).

Etymology

Study the roots given below together with the English words derived from them. Capitalized words are those given in the Word List. You should look up in a dictionary any words that are unfamiliar to you.

Roots: *eu* (well) Greek – Examples: *EULOGY, euphony, euphemism*
phone (sound) Greek – Examples: *CACOPHONY, telephone, phonograph*
palpa (feel) Latin – Examples: *PALPABLE, palpitate*

ACROSS
1. tearful; melancholy
5. to inform; to notify
12. a recent convert; a beginner
13. of shepherds and the country; pastoral
15. a critical interpretation of a word or passage
16. written testimony given under oath
17. to force or push out
18. to hold back; to check
19. strife; quarreling
20. detestable
21. of marriage or a wedding
23. all the animals of a region
30. to make up for; to make amends
34. former
36. a west wind; a gentle breeze
37. a salve or ointment (2)
38. a substance that induces vomiting
39. a minor sin; a petty offense
40. remaining or operating within; inherent
41. a man paid to be a woman's escort
46. a way out; an exit
47. an estate inherited from one's father
48. an assumed name
50. a short, heavy club
51. a protruding ornament or stud
52. to figure out
53. great ardor and enthusiasm
54. gain from employment; salary
55. of doubtful authenticity
56. to swing off course, as a ship or plane

DOWN
1. an offering of wine or oil to the gods
2. harsh, jarring sounds
3. a heavy knife used for cutting sugar cane
4. very loud; deafening
6. an earlier act used to justify a later one
7. lacking feeling
8. to command; to prohibit
9. a separate addition to a will
10. traveling from place to place
11. partial shadow, as in an eclipse
14. softly bright or radiant (3)
22. keenness of mind; shrewdness
24. to lower in rank or esteem (3)
25. an example, pattern, or model
26. a small, rounded lump (2)
27. an understanding between nations
28. a principle or belief held to be true
29. marked by changes of fortune
31. a speech of praise
32. plainly or flagrantly bad
33. reckless mischief
35. a small-scale, sudden invasion; a raid
39. that can be touched or felt
42. children; offspring
43. given to jokes or jesting
44. fairness; justice
45. an object believed to have magical powers
49. fierce; terrible; cruel (1)

Chapter Three

Word List 7

APLOMB	ICONOCLASTIC	PUSILLANIMOUS
APOGEE	INCUBUS	RISIBLE
BOLUS	LONGEVITY	SEDULOUS
COMATOSE	MINCE	SYCOPHANTIC
DISSIPATE	OBDURATE	TURBID
FECUND	PATINA	

Look up the words above in your dictionary. Note that many of them have more than one meaning. When you feel that you know *all* the meanings of *all* the words, go on to the exercises below.

EXERCISE 7A

From the four choices following each phrase or sentence, you are to circle the letter preceding the one that is closest in meaning to the italicized word. Where the same word appears more than once, you should note that it is being used in different senses.

1. done with *aplomb*
   (a) poise (b) much fumbling (c) much hesitation (d) speed

2. the moon's *apogee*
   (a) point farthest from the earth (b) point closest to the earth (c) path around the earth (d) speed in relation to the earth

3. the *apogee* of a political party's power
   (a) beginning (b) low point (c) end (d) high point

4. to swallow the *bolus*
   (a) indignity heaped upon one (b) draught of ale or beer (c) story that is obviously false (d) soft mass of chewed food

5. to administer a *bolus* to an animal
   (a) sound thrashing (b) large pill (c) shot with a needle (d) stern rebuke

6. to be *comatose*
   (a) highly inflammable (b) explosively unstable (c) in an aggressive mood (d) in a sleeplike state

7. to *dissipate* one's wealth
   (a) add to (b) store up (c) spend wastefully (d) divide equally

8. to *dissipate* the fumes
   (a) penetrate (b) disperse (c) avoid (d) condense

9. The fog *dissipated* after sunrise.
   (a) became warmer (b) became more dense (c) turned to rain (d) vanished

10. a *fecund* female
    (a) dull (b) fertile (c) malicious (d) talkative

11. an *iconoclastic* person
    (a) given to vulgar displays of religious piety (b) given to servile flattery of those in authority (c) given to attacking established beliefs and institutions (d) given to exaggerating one's own importance

12. a terrible *incubus*
    (a) punishment (b) dilemma (c) nightmare (d) crime

13. the *incubus* of high office
    (a) burden (b) dignity (c) reward (d) pursuit

14. a hoped-for *longevity*
    (a) period of peace (b) general agreement (c) long ocean cruise (d) long life

15. to *mince* meat
    (a) eat delicately (b) eat hungrily (c) chop finely (d) pound heavily

16. to *mince* words
    (a) hesitate over (b) misuse (c) learn the meanings of (d) choose carefully for a polite effect

17. a *mincing* step
    (a) militarily correct (b) affectedly dainty (c) gracefully light (d) ponderously heavy

18. to be *obdurate*
    (a) stubborn (b) stupid (c) easily led (d) unconscious

19. the *patina* of old age
    (a) slowness (b) wisdom (c) aches and pains (d) surface appearance

20. the *patina* of copper
    (a) stains (b) heat conductivity (c) maker's hallmark (d) greenish film

21. a *pusillanimous* person
    (a) brilliant (b) aggressive (c) fainthearted (d) slow-witted

22. *risible* behavior
    (a) arousing concern (b) arousing pity (c) arousing contempt (d) arousing laughter

23. *sedulous* efforts
    (a) diligent (b) halfhearted (c) underhanded (d) futile

24. a *sycophantic* manner
    (a) overbearingly loud (b) servilely flattering (c) deceptively mild (d) graciously self-assured

25. a *turbid* stream
    (a) clear (b) swift (c) muddy (d) swollen

Check your answers against the correct ones given below. The answers are not in order; this is to prevent your eye from catching sight of the correct answers before you have had a chance to do the exercise on your own.

10b. 19d. 11c. 3d. 24b. 18a. 12c. 7c. 20d. 22d. 4d. 2a. 25c. 17b. 13a. 23a. 9d. 1a. 14d. 16d. 5b. 8b. 15c. 6d. 21c.

Look up in your dictionary all the words for which you gave incorrect answers. Only when you have done this should you go on to the next exercise.

EXERCISE 7B

Each word in Word List 7 is used several times in the sentences below to illustrate different meanings or usage. One of the sentences for each word uses the italicized word incorrectly. You are to circle the letter preceding that sentence.

1. (a) She completed the difficult task with her usual *aplomb* and reported for a fresh assignment. (b) Although this was his first public appearance, he performed with the *aplomb* of a veteran. (c) She *aplombed* their attempts to improve the community.

2. (a) Dutch genre painting reached its *apogee* in the work of Jan Vermeer (1632-1675). (b) The plane went into an uncontrolled *apogee* when its engine failed. (c) The moon at its *apogee* is 252,710 miles from the earth. (d) The satellite put into orbit yesterday has an *apogee* of 820 miles.

3. (a) The cowboys on the Pampas bring down steers by hurling *boluses* at their legs. (b) The autopsy revealed that the woman choked to death when a *bolus* of food stuck in her windpipe. (c) The veterinarian forced the horse to swallow the *bolus*.

4. (a) The patient was *comatose* on arrival at the hospital and never regained consciousness. (b) They *comatosed* their days in idle chatter and desultory card games. (c) Broadway has been *comatose* for too long, and serious playwrights now look to the provincial theater.

5. (a) Let us not *dissipate* our energies in foolish quarrels among ourselves. (b) She had led a life of such *dissipation* that at the age of forty she looked like an old woman. (c) By applying heat to the solution, we *dissipate* the salts out of it. (d) He was a compulsive gambler and had *dissipated* his patrimony in less than a year.

6. (a) The first settlers were delighted by the mildness of the climate and the *fecundity* of the soil. (b) Dr. Seuss's *fecund* imagina-

tion was responsible for children's books. (c) The people in these parts are notably *fecund*, and families of ten or more are common. (d) His locks, once a rich chestnut brown, were now *fecund* with age.

7. (a) Audiences were stunned by the *iconoclastic* plays of George Bernard Shaw. (b) H.L. Mencken, noted writer and *iconoclast*, disturbed the complacencies of America. (c) A cheerful *iconoclasm* runs through the pages of this irreverent little magazine. (d) This material is highly *iconoclastic* and is guaranteed not to stretch out of shape.

8. (a) The eggs are placed in the *incubus* and hatch in ten to twelve days. (b) The U.N. Security Council, free from the *incubus* of the veto, acted decisively. (c) Shortly after waking up, she remembered the horrible *incubus* of the previous night.

9. (a) The *longevity* of these steel bearings is due to their high molybdenum content. (b) The one-party system of the South enabled politicians from that region to achieve remarkable *longevity* in office. (c) The *longevity* of the wharf is being increased to accommodate more boats. (d) Her *longevity* confounded the doctor's predictions that she would not survive her first birthday.

10. (a) I'm afraid that the person you asked to do the job has made a real *mince* of it. (b) An overdressed young fop came *mincing* into the room and asked me please to wait. (c) I shall tell her exactly what I think, and I won't *mince* words. (d) The meat is first *minced*, and then the onion and other flavorings are added.

11. (a) I've begged and pleaded with her to change her mind, but she remains *obdurate*. (b) The settlers were hard put to eke out a living from the *obdurate* soil of the uplands. (c) He is an *obdurate* old man, utterly incapable of mending his ways. (d) She is an honest woman and *obdurates* all forms of hypocrisy.

12. (a) She took her chair outside and sat in the *patina* of the old oak tree for a while. (b) The copper-covered dome of the state capitol has acquired a fine *patina* over the years. (c) Fine old leather has a *patina* that no artificial process can duplicate.

13. (a) "I'd like to help you, but I have to consider my position," he said *pusillanimously*. (b) They complain constantly but are too *pusillanimous* to try to improve conditions. (c) The *pusillanimous* policy of appeasement toward Hitler was savagely denounced by Winston Churchill. (d) Her heartbeat was so *pusillanimous* that I thought she had died.

14. (a) The *risible* courtroom antics of the defense attorney aroused the judge's displeasure. (b) I fail to see the *risibility* of a person's slipping on a banana skin. (c) The submarine's periscope is *risible* to a height of fifteen feet.

15. (a) The fine quality of these products is the result of *sedulous* workmanship. (b) The soil is so *sedulous* that it is possible to grow two crops a year. (c) Doctor Johnson's every utterance was *sedulously* recorded by Boswell. (d) Both candidates *sedulously* avoided taking a stand on the issues.

16. (a) Ministers were chosen for their *sycophantic* airs rather than for any political acumen. (b) The bootlicking *sycophancy* of the emperor's court disgusted foreign visitors. (c) She surrounds herself with *sycophants* who tell her only what she wishes to hear. (d) When she blew into the trumpet, nothing came out but a *sycophantic* squeak.

17. (a) His *turbid* mind is full of dark fancies and half-formulated longings. (b) Her thumb is still *turbid* where she hit it with the hammer. (c) The *turbidity* of the river is caused by the soils washed into it by the heavy rains.

EXERCISE 7C

The English language is constantly refreshing itself by discarding words no longer needed and acquiring new words to meet new needs. A dead language is one that no longer changes; classical Latin, for example, has not changed in almost two thousand years. Sometimes a need is met by giving an old word additional meanings; conversely a word may survive although it loses one or more of its several original meanings. *Skyscraper* was once the word for the topmost sail of a clipper ship.

Look carefully over the words listed below. Circle the ten words that have come into the language during the past one hundred years; strike out the five words that have passed out of current usage and are now archaic or obsolete.

transistor	laser
launderette	varlet
typewriter	beldam
bionics	democracy
electricity	heliport
penicillin	automobile
tobacco	yclept
herdic	element
curricle	coach
smog	computerized

WORDLY WISE 7

The point at which an orbiting body is at its greatest distance from earth is its APOGEE; its *perigee* is the point at which it is closest to the earth. *Apogee* is used also to mean "the highest point" (the apogee of her career).

A BOLUS is (1) a soft ball of food that is swallowed, (2) a large pill administered by veterinarians. A *bola* (plural *bolas*) is a weapon consisting of two or more stone or iron balls attached to the ends of a cord and used for throwing at and bringing down animals.

Iconoclasts were those who took part in the 8th and 9th century movement to put down the use of images or pictures (*icons*) in the Eastern Christian church. The term was revived and applied in the 16th and 17th century to Protestants who practiced a similar destruction of images in the churches. By metaphorical application, ICONOCLAST now refers to anyone who attacks cherished beliefs on the ground that they are erroneous or harmful.

LONGEVITY is pronounced with a soft *g* (lon-JEV-ə-ti).

Etymology

Study the roots and prefixes given below together with the English words derived from them. Capitalized words are those given in the Word List. You should look up in a dictionary any words that are unfamiliar to you.

Prefixes: *apo-* (from; away) Greek – Examples: APOGEE, *apo*stle, *apo*cryphal

ob- (against) Latin – Examples: OBDURATE, *ob*jection, *ob*jurgate

Roots: *rid, ris* (laugh) Latin – Examples: RISIBLE, *rid*icule, de*ride*

dur (hard) Latin – Examples: OB*DU*RATE, *dur*able, en*dure*

Word List 8

ACCRETION	IMMOLATE	REMISS
BIER	INGRATE	ROCOCO
CANARD	LUCENT	SONIC
DASTARD	MULCT	SYLVAN
ENDEMIC	OLFACTORY	UNANIMITY
FERAL	PERSPICACIOUS	

Look up the words above in your dictionary. Note that many of them have more than one meaning. When you feel that you know *all* the meanings of *all* the words, go on to the exercises below.

EXERCISE 8A

From the four choices following each phrase or sentence, you are to circle the letter preceding the one that is closest in meaning to the italicized word. Where the same word appears more than once, you should note that it is being used in different senses.

1. the *accretion* of particles
   (a) microscopic size (b) slow wearing away (c) gradual coming together (d) controlled acceleration

2. the *accretion* of knowledge
   (a) process of writing down (b) process of transmitting (c) entire scope (d) process of growth by accumulation

3. a flag-draped *bier*
   (a) political convention hall (b) stand for a public speaker (c) stand for a coffin (d) float in a parade

4. to believe the *canard*
   (a) statement put out by the government (b) solemn affirmation of one's intentions (c) absurd report spread as a hoax (d) person known to be an obdurate liar

5. a *dastardly* knight
   (a) cowardly (b) foolhardy (c) chivalrous (d) foppish

6. *endemic* diseases
   (a) caused by living in the tropics (b) that respond easily to treatment (c) restricted to a particular area (d) that do not respond to treatment

7. *feral* behavior
   (a) worthy of imitation (b) gentle (c) peculiar (d) beastlike

8. to *immolate* the animal
   (a) tether the legs of (b) strip the hide from (c) kill as a sacrifice (d) spare the life of

9. to be an *ingrate*
   (a) social outcast (b) unknown quantity (c) ungrateful person (d) disreputable person

10. *lucent* prose
    (a) bombastic (b) cryptic (c) ornate (d) clear

11. a *lucent* surface
    (a) sticky (b) luminous (c) speckled (d) slippery

12. to *mulct* someone
    (a) intimidate by making threats (b) flatter in an insincere way (c) offer help and encouragement to (d) get money from by fraud

13. *olfactory* organs
    (a) of the sense of smell (b) of the sense of touch (c) of the sense of taste (d) of the sense of hearing

14. very *perspicacious*
    (a) selfish (b) astute (c) uncomfortable (d) finicky

15. How *remiss* of you!
    (a) foolish (b) cruel (c) considerate (d) negligent in performing a duty

16. *rococo* architecture
    (a) classically simple (b) elaborately ornamental (c) ultra-modern (d) oriental

17. *sonic* waves
    (a) sound (b) light (c) radio (d) ocean

18. a *sylvan* scene
    (a) sunlight (b) wooded (c) wintry (d) seaside

19. *unanimity* of purpose
    (a) lack of agreement (b) lack of discussion (c) thorough discussion (d) complete agreement

Check your answers against the correct ones given below. The answers are not in order; this is to prevent your eye from catching sight of the correct answers before you have had a chance to do the exercise on your own.

10d. 18b. 4c. 16b. 5a. 12d. 2d. 14b. 8c. 19d. 11b. 7d. 17a. 1c. 15d. 3c. 13a. 9c. 6c.

Look up in your dictionary all the words for which you gave incorrect answers. Only when you have done this should you go on to the next exercise.

EXERCISE 8B

Each word in Word List 8 is used several times in the sentences below to illustrate different meanings or usage. One of the sentences for each word uses the italicized word incorrectly. You are to circle the letter preceding that sentence.

1. (a) A number of myths have *accreted* around the lives of the Brontë sisters. (b) A war of *accretion* is one marked by large scale death and destruction of both sides. (c) Every culture is a complex *accretion* of rules, laws,

customs, and habits. (d) The cannon had been under water for two hundred years, and the *accretion* of mineral deposits had made it almost unrecognizable.

2. (a) The coffin was lifted off the *bier* and lowered gently into the grave. (b) Mourners filed past the *bier*, paying their last respects to the dead person. (c) The people in the *bier* garden sat drinking pots of ale and talking among themselves.

3. (a) Don't believe anything that mischievous old *canard* tells you. (b) The *canard* that flying saucers had landed in Central Park was picked up by several newspapers. (c) You surely don't believe that old *canard* that Roosevelt knew of the impending Japanese attack on Pearl Harbor.

4. (a) Is this the *dastard* who committed this cowardly and despicable crime? (b) These four hulking men attacked in *dastardly* fashion one defenseless old woman. (c) With a graceful *dastard*, followed by a sudden lunge, the swordsman disarmed his opponent.

5. (a) She had come from that world of country clubs and expensive cars where snobbery is *endemic*. (b) Malaria is *endemic* in tropical countries. (c) The marsupials, such as the kangaroo, are *endemic* in Australia. (d) The influenza *endemic* spread quickly throughout the area.

6. (a) The animal bared its teeth in a *feral* snarl. (b) With a single shot she felled the *feral* that had been terrorizing the district. (c) The case of the *feral* child who had been brought up by wolves attracted much attention. (d) The homeless dogs soon became *feral*.

7. (a) The calf was led to the altar and swiftly *immolated* as an offering to the gods. (b) The Buddhist monk *immolated* himself as a protest against the repressive government. (c) The *immolation* of youth in war is a terrible tragedy. (d) He *immolates* himself in his books for hours at a time.

8. (a) After I took him into my home and fed him, the *ingrate* made off with my silver. (b) You must think me an *ingrate* for rushing off without thanking you. (c) How *ingrate* of her to accept your help and then turn against you.

9. (a) John Milton speaks of "the sun's *lucent* orb." (b) The brooch had a large uncut *lucent* in the center, surrounded by tiny brilliants. (c) The *lucency* of the underwater world cannot be described, only experienced. (d) She writes in a sensible and *lucent* prose that carries the reader along effortlessly.

10. (a) A *mulct* of peat is spread over the soil to enrich it. (b) The treasurer has been *mulcting* the company of thousands of dollars. (c) The widower was *mulcted* of his fortune by unscrupulous swindlers.

11. (a) If the *olfactory* lobe in the brain is damaged, the sense of smell is lost. (b) *Olfactometry* is the science of testing and measuring the sensitivity of the sense of smell. (c) Garlic is so *olfactory* that good cooks use only a tiny amount of it in any recipe.

12. (a) How *perspicacious* of you to figure out the meaning of this difficult poem. (b) In solving the problem so quickly, you show great *perspicacity*. (c) If you find trigonometry too *perspicacious*, you should drop it for another subject.

13. (a) I *remissed* paying my bills, and now my creditors are hounding me. (b) I'm afraid the guards were *remiss* in their duties and allowed the prisoner to escape. (c) If you are *remiss* in attending to your correspondence, your friends will just stop writing to you.

14. (a) *Rococo* is marked by elaborately fanciful and frivolous ornamentation. (b) *Rococo* music, art, architecture, and literature flourished in the early eighteenth century. (c) His *rococo* writing style is better suited to the society pages than to financial reporting. (d) A stone *rococo* had fallen from one of the ornamental cornices of the roof.

15. (a) A *sonic* boom is caused when a plane exceeds the speed of sound. (b) A *sonic* mine is activated by the sounds from a ship overhead. (c) Following the examination, the doctor told her that her heart was perfectly *sonic*.

16. (a) We watched the squirrels scamper for the trees as we strolled along the *sylvan* paths. (b) Fawns and other *sylvan* creatures roamed freely in the woods. (c) The log cabin, with its lovely *sylvan* setting, was the subject of many paintings. (d) The oak tree had stood there for two hundred years and was now *sylvan* with age.

17. (a) There was complete *unanimity* among us as to the importance of Harriet Beecher Stowe in American history. (b) The book was written *unanimously*, and the identity of the author was never discovered. (c) The resolution was passed *unanimously*.

EXERCISE 8C

In each of the sentences below a word is omitted. From the four words provided, select the one that best completes the sentence. Allow ten minutes for this test. If you cannot answer a question, go on to the next one without delay. If you have time left over at the end, go back and try to fill in unanswered questions.

18 or over correct:	excellent
14 to 17 correct:	good
13 or under correct:	thorough review of A exercises indicated

1. Atheistic communism is . . . . to those who believe in God.
   itinerant bucolic apocryphal anathema

2. The door was of heavy oak, studded with iron . . . .
   fells gaffs bosses tenets

3. Her acts of . . . . get her into a lot of trouble.
   extrusion exegesis deviltry declivity

4. The court accepted the . . . . of the witness who was unable to appear.
   diapason apogee canard deposition

5. I love the . . . . that this old furniture has.
   rococo élan debacle patina

6. The aircraft is capable of flying at super- . . . . speeds.
   sidereal sonic sylvan sedulous

7. His . . . . nerve is damaged, and he has no sense of smell.
   apocryphal incubus obdurate olfactory

8. The story you were told is a long-discredited . . . .
   bolus yaw canard gaff

9. The . . . . didn't even thank me for my help.
   ingrate jocose canard cognomen

10. The veterinarian forced the . . . . down the horse's throat.
    zephyr quondam orifice bolus

11. Her scathing social criticism made her reputation as a(n) . . . .
    cognomen iconoclast peccadillo sycophant

12. I didn't . . . . words but told him exactly what I thought of him.
    abase mince inveigh remiss

13. Were you able to . . . . his intention?
    fell aplomb mulct divine

14. A close friend of the deceased delivered the funeral . . . .
    eulogy olfactory apogee repertoire

15. A . . . . bore the sailboat gently across the lake.
    bucolic diva sylvan zephyr

16. The son was urged to spend his . . . .
wisely.
progeny patrimony aberration entente

17. The . . . . knot was tied, and the
happy couple left the church.
neophyte fecund nuptial feral

18. She gives a thorough. . . . . .of this
difficult passage.
tenet penumbra exegesis incubus

19. She believes that goodness is . . . .
in every human heart.
germane itinerant risible immanent

20. She had had a(n) . . . . career,
winning and losing several fortunes.
expeditious lucent checkered stentorian

WORDLY WISE 8

Both *dastardly* and *pusillanimous* (Word List 7) are synonyms for *cowardly*. *Pusillanimous* specifically suggests a contemptible lack of spirit, whereas *dastardly* suggests behavior which combines cowardice with treachery (a dastardly surprise attack on unarmed settlers). Thus a DASTARD is often a villain as well as a coward.

ENDEMIC, *pandemic*, and *epidemic* are three words that are easily confused. *Endemic* is an adjective and means "restricted or indigenous to a particular area" (sleeping sickness is endemic in certain parts of Africa). *Epidemic* is a noun and means "a disease that is prevalent and spreading rapidly"; it may also be used as an adjective to convey the same meaning (influenza was of epidemic proportions). *Pandemic* is an adjective and means "affecting many people" (fear of war was pandemic). As a noun it refers to an epidemic of major and uncontrollable proportions.

Etymology

Study the following roots together with the English words derived from them. Capitalized words are those given in the Word List. You should look up in a dictionary any words that are unfamiliar to you.

Roots: *dem, demos* (people) Greek — Examples: EN*DEM*IC, epi*dem*ic, pan*dem*ic, *demo*cracy

unus (one) Latin — Examples: *UNA*-NIMITY, *uni*form, *uni*ted

animus (mind) Latin — Examples: UN*A*-N*IM*ITY, magn*anim*ous, pusill*anim*ous

gratus (thankful) Latin — Examples: IN*GRATE*, *grat*itude, *grate*ful

---

Word List 9

BILATERAL	LARGO	REINCARNATION
CAPARISON	LUMINARY	SALUBRIOUS
DICTUM	NOTARY	SUNDER
EXPEDIENT	OPTOMETRIST	TRUMPERY
FORENSIC	PREVARICATE	WROTH
INCIPIENT		

Look up the words above in your dictionary. Note that many of them have more than one meaning. When you feel that you know *all* the meanings of *all* the words, go on to the exercises below.

EXERCISE 9A

From the four choices following each phrase or sentence, you are to circle the letter preceding the one that is closest in meaning to the italicized word. Where the same word appears more than once, you should note that it is being used in different senses.

1. a *bilateral* agreement
(a) voluntarily entered into (b) binding on one side only (c) imposed on the parties involved (d) affecting both sides equally

2. the horse's *caparison*
(a) richly dressed rider (b) head harness (c) ornamental covering (d) companion in harness

3. to dispute the *dictum*
(a) formal statement of opinion (b) verdict rendered by a jury (c) decision made by a referee (d) disposition of property in a will

4. an *expedient* course of action
(a) recklessly neglectful of the consequences

(b) hastily arrived at and executed (c) forced upon one by circumstances (d) advantageous without necessarily being right or proper

5. a *forensic* skill
(a) medical (b) debating (c) intellectual (d) athletic

6. the *incipient* stages
(a) developed (b) hidden (c) beginning (d) final

7. to be played *largo*
(a) in bright and lively fashion (b) with a plucking of strings (c) in a freely improvised manner (d) in a slow and stately manner

8. a theatrical *luminary*
(a) rank beginner (b) leading figure (c) convention (d) illusion

9. an artificial *luminary*
(a) source of food (b) source of life (c) source of heat (d) source of light

10. to swear before a *notary*
(a) official authorized to administer an estate (b) official authorized to validate legal documents (c) lawyer appointed by the courts to defend the accused (d) lawyer appointed by the city to prosecute in court

11. to see an *optometrist*
(a) doctor specializing in surgery of the eye (b) doctor specializing in diseases of the ear, nose, and throat (c) person who grinds eyeglass lenses to a prescription (d) person who diagnoses eye defects and prescribes corrective lenses

12. to *prevaricate* shamelessly
(a) avoid telling the truth (b) overstate the case (c) accept bribes (d) make flattering remarks

13. a belief in *reincarnation*
(a) transference of thoughts between persons (b) the influence of the stars on human lives

(c) rebirth of the spirit in another physical body (d) the literal truth of the Koran

14. *salubrious* effects
(a) unexpected (b) predictable (c) beneficial (d) harmful

15. to *sunder* the nation
(a) lead (b) curse (c) split (d) unite

16. *trumpery* articles
(a) plain but well-made (b) cheap and showy (c) richly ornamented (d) classically simple

17. a speech filled with *trumpery*
(a) metaphors and similes (b) factual details (c) emotional appeal (d) worthless nonsense

18. a collection of *trumpery*
(a) musical instruments of the Middle Ages (b) trivial or useless items (c) fine china (d) antique furniture

19. to be *wroth*
(a) full of self-pity (b) genuinely repentant (c) extremely angry (d) extremely lazy

Check your answers against the correct ones given below. The answers are not in order; this is to prevent your eye from catching sight of the correct answers before you have had a chance to do the exercise on your own.

10b. 11d. 3a. 7d. 12a. 4d. 2c. 17d. 13c. 18b. 9d. 1d. 14c. 16b. 5b. 8b. 15c. 6c. 19c.

Look up in your dictionary all the words for which you gave incorrect answers. Only when you have done this should you go on to the next exercise.

EXERCISE 9B

Each word in Word List 9 is used several times in the following sentences to illustrate different meanings or usage. One of the sentences for each word uses the italicized word incorrectly. You are to circle the letter preceding that sentence.

1. (a) The United States will negotiate *bilaterally* with each country in turn. (b) One of the warring nations broke away from its allies and signed a *bilateral* treaty with the enemy. (c) The roof is slightly *bilateral* and should be raised an inch at this end.

2. (a) The king, mounted on his richly *caparisoned* horse, rode at the head of his troops. (b) There is no *caparison* between the performance of athletes forty years ago and those of today. (c) Autumn *caparisons* the trees in glorious reds, browns, and golds.

3. (a) A professor must heed the *dictum* "Publish or Perish" if he or she wishes to succeed. (b) I listened to the critic's *dicta* as to what ails modern art, and I disagree with them all. (c) The general overthrew the legal government and set up a *dictum* of his own.

4. (a) Finding the bridge collapsed, we had to devise some *expedient* for crossing the river. (b) They found it *expedient* to say nothing when the hoax was discovered. (c) *Expediency,* rather than morality, guides nations in their dealings with others. (d) She loves all sports but is most *expedient* in tennis and golf.

5. (a) The *forensic* skills of the defense lawyer greatly impressed the jury. (b) All students interested in debating should sign up for the *forensics* program. (c) *Forensic* medicine is the scientific application of medical facts to legal problems. (d) In a fit of *forensic* rage, she hurled the heavy doorstop across the room.

6. (a) Aspirin, lots of fluids, and rest are effective in checking an *incipient* cold. (b) The soup had an *incipient* taste, but we drank it as there was nothing else. (c) Appeals for law and order are useless once the riots have passed the *incipient* stage.

7. (a) Handel's "Largo" is a musical composition of great stateliness and dignity. (b) The passage in the opera in which the sovereign kneels in prayer is played *largo*. (c) He moved in such a *largo* manner that I thought he was drugged.

8. (a) The clock had *luminary* hands and figures so that one could tell the time in the dark. (b) The dinner was given to honor a number of *luminaries* of the legal profession. (c) The stars, considered as *luminaries*, afford a negligible amount of light.

9. (a) The *notary* put her stamp on the document and signed her name over it. (b) He *notaried* in his diary everything he did each day. (c) The document is not legally valid until it has been *notarized*. (d) The statement was sworn to, signed, and witnessed before a *notary*.

10. (a) I got headaches after reading for a while, so I decided to see an *optometrist*. (b) The university offers a course of study leading to a degree in *optometry*. (c) His eyes are slightly *optometrist* but not enough to require corrective lenses. (d) An *optometrist* may prescribe and fit corrective lenses but may not prescribe drugs or perform surgery.

11. (a) The river follows a *prevaricating* course with numerous twists and turns. (b) "Don't *prevaricate*, sir!" the judge thundered. "Let us have a straight answer to the question." (c) She was honest and straightforward and answered the questions without *prevarication*.

12. (a) Hindus believe that after many *reincarnations* the human soul reaches a state of perfection. (b) She believed that she was the *reincarnation* of a seventeenth century queen. (c) A belief in *reincarnation* is more common in India than in Western countries. (d) The money, after being missing for some time, was *reincarnated* in the lining of the jacket.

13. (a) Her criticism was merciless toward the cheap and second rate and had a *salubrious* effect on American literature. (b) The *salubrious* climate of California draws many people there from other states. (c) A strict diet and lots of rest will have you feeling *salubrious* again.

14. (a) Riots threaten to rip *asunder* the fabric of our society. (b) A strategically-placed stick of dynamite *sundered* the rock. (c) The nation was *sundered* by religious and political differences. (d) The old man fumed and *sundered*, but his partner refused to give in to him.

15. (a) Beads, baubles, and other *trumpery* were given to the Native Americans in exchange for their land. (b) Many believe that the pomp of kings and bishops is mere *trumpery* in the eyes of God. (c) The critic heaped scorn on the *trumpery* pathos of television soap operas. (d) A cry of *trumpery* rose from the crowd as their champion defeated his opponent.

16. (a) He feared the *wroth* of his parents if he admitted the theft. (b) She was *wroth* when she saw that her orders had been disobeyed. (c) The *wrothful* waves dashed the boat repeatedly against the rocks.

EXERCISE 9C

This exercise combines synonyms and antonyms. You are to underline the word which is *either* most similar in meaning *or* most nearly opposite in meaning to the capitalized word. Underline only one word for each question after deciding that it is either a synonym or an antonym and write A (for antonym) or S (for synonym) after the capitalized word. Allow only fifteen minutes for this test. If you cannot answer a question, go on to the next one without delay. If you have time left over at the end, go back and try to fill in unanswered questions.

26 or over correct: excellent
22 to 25 correct: good
21 or under correct: thorough review of A
                        exercises indicated

1. WOODED . . . .
   forensic sylvan sonic rococo feral

2. QUOTE . . . .
   dissipate notary cite sunder immolate

3. PERIGEE . . . .
   aplomb eclogue apocryphal apogee largo

4. BEGINNING . . . .
   olfactory endemic obdurate salubrious incipient

5. BARREN . . . .
   fecund comatose expedient immanent palpable

6. CELEBRITY . . . .
   hybrid peccadillo neophyte luminary canard

7. NIGHTMARE . . . .
   patina diva incubus reincarnation canard

8. WIDE-AWAKE . . . .
   apocryphal incipient salubrious comatose lucent

9. AGREEMENT . . . .
   anathema unanimity trumpery patrimony detritus

10. COWARD . . . .
    caparison sycophantic ingrate gigolo dastard

11. POISE . . . .
    patina rococo bolus élan aplomb

12. RUBBISH . . . .
    bludgeon cacophony peccadillo notary trumpery

13. HOARD . . . .
    enjoin divine extrude dissipate egress

14. SPLIT . . . .
    paradigm gaff sunder entente atone

15. BEASTLIKE . . . .
    feral palpable mandible risible execrable

16. HARMFUL . . . .
    incipient salubrious forensic olfactory sedulous

17. FLATTERER . . . .
gigolo canard rococo sycophant zephyr

18. DILIGENT . . . .
quondam egregious deleterious lucent sedulous

19. PRINCIPLE . . . .
patina tenet tenure quondam parity

20. STUPID . . . .
perspicacious pusillanimous endemic expedient salubrious

21. ACCUMULATION . . . .
bier mulct accretion debacle stentorian

22. IRRELEVANT . . . .
wroth forensic sedulous germane feral

23. LAUGHABLE . . . .
feral turbid germane lambent risible

24. ANGRY . . . .
wroth stentorian venal expeditious fell

25. OPAQUE . . . .
sedulous risible lucent sonic endemic

26. CONCILIATORY . . . .
insensate obdurate perspicacious sedulous comatose

27. SACRIFICE . . . .
tutelage extrude reincarnate canard immolate

28. CLEAR . . . .
sylvan salubrious turbid incipient lambent

29. NEGLIGENT . . . .
perspicacious jocose pusillanimous remiss rococo

30. SPIRITED . . . .
feral fecund stentorian divine pusillanimous

WORDLY WISE 9

The plural of DICTUM is *dicta*; *dictums* is also correct.

EXPEDIENT is both an adjective and a noun. Each frequently has a disparaging connotation, suggesting something advantageous but not necessarily right or proper. In addition, the noun "expedient" means "a makeshift device, especially something devised in an emergency." Do not confuse these words with *expeditious* (Wordly Wise 2) which means "prompt; speedy."

An OPTOMETRIST is a person qualified to test for defects of vision and to prescribe corrective lenses.

An *ophthalmologist* is a medical doctor specializing in diseases of the eye and qualified to perform operations upon the eye.

An *optician* is a person who grinds lenses to prescription and sells glasses and other optical items.

Oculist is a now outdated term that can refer variously to an optometrist or an ophthalmologist.

Modern dictionaries are descriptive rather than prescriptive, that is, they record the predominant meanings of a word as actually used, and do not merely determine what a word *ought* to mean. Authorities in the past, for example, have pointed out that PREVARICATE means "to evade telling the truth by quibbling or confusing the issue" (he could prevaricate no longer and finally admitted that the accusation was correct), but Webster's *Third International Dictionary* has recognized our growing tendency to use *prevaricate* as a euphemism for *lie*.

SALUBRIOUS means "healthful; wholesome" (a salubrious climate). *Salutary* has somewhat the same meaning with the suggestion of something being beneficial without being pleasant of itself (showing photographs of accident victims to careless drivers has a salutary effect).

Etymology

Study the roots and prefixes given below together with the English words derived from them. Capitalized words are those given in the Word List. You should look up in a dictionary any words that are unfamiliar to you.

bi (two) Latin – Examples: *BI*LATERAL, *bi*cycle, *bi*nary
latus (side) Latin – Examples: BI*LATERAL*, multi*lateral*, *lateral*
dict (say) Latin – Examples: *DICT*UM, *dict*ate, pre*dict*

ACROSS

1. to avoid telling the truth
4. an ungrateful person
7. resembling a wild beast; brutal
9. diligent; industrious
11. elaborately ornamental
13. one who has achieved distinction in his or her field
15. to kill as a sacrifice
17. advantageous without being right or proper
18. a gradual coming together or growth
19. self-possession; poise
20. just beginning to appear or develop
24. a troublesome burden; a nightmare
28. to get money from by fraud
29. one who diagnoses eye defects and prescribes corrective lenses
30. a temporary or small scale invasion (5)
33. servilely flattering
34. to make up for; to make amends (5)
35. to use up wastefully; to scatter
36. moved to intense anger; wrathful
38. in a sleeplike state; lethargic
39. an ornamental covering, as for a horse
41. of or relating to woodland; wooded
46. complete agreement
47. a deviation from what is correct (1)
48. an addition to a will (5)
49. a formal statement of opinion
50. stubborn and obstinate
51. beneficial to health; healthful

DOWN

1. cowardly; fainthearted
2. restricted or native to a particular area
3. thick with sediment
4. given to attacking established beliefs
5. the point in orbit farthest from earth
6. great ardor and enthusiasm (6)
7. capable of producing; fertile
8. glowing with light; luminous
10. long life
12. relating to the stars (1)
14. the belief in spiritual rebirth in another body
16. showing neglect or inattention
21. a greenish film formed on bronze or copper
22. showy but worthless
23. of or relating to the sense of smell
25. affecting both sides equally
26. of or relating to sound
27. showing keenness of judgment; astute
31. an official authorized to validate legal documents
32. of or relating to public debate
35. one who shrinks from danger; a coward
37. causing laughter; ridiculous
38. an absurd story spread as a joke
40. to split or break apart
42. in music, slow and stately
43. to act or speak with affected delicacy
44. a soft mass of chewed food
45. a stand on which a coffin rests

Chapter Four

Word List 10

AMATORY	ECLECTIC	OBELISK
APOTHEOSIS	ENCOMIUM	PELLUCID
ATTENUATE	ESPOUSE	PREDILECTION
CAMBRIC	GASTRONOMY	SCHISM
CLARION	INTRANSIGENT	
CURIA	MINUTIAE	

Look up the words above in your dictionary. Note that many of them have more than one meaning. When you feel that you know *all* the meanings of *all* the words, go on to the exercises below.

EXERCISE 10A

From the four choices following each phrase or sentence, you are to circle the letter preceding the one that is closest in meaning to the italicized word. Where the same word appears more than once, you should note that it is being used in different senses.

1. *amatory* verses
   (a) nonsensical (b) richly humorous (c) dealing with love (d) dealing with war

2. the *apotheosis* of the emperor
   (a) divine right to rule (b) line of descent (c) removal from the throne (d) elevation to a godlike state

3. the *apotheosis* of armed might
   (a) voluntary restraints (b) inevitable failure (c) ultimate expression (d) uncertain reliability

4. to *attenuate* radio signals
   (a) transmit (b) strengthen (c) receive (d) weaken

5. *attenuated* fibers
   (a) absorbant (b) thin (c) tough (d) flexible

6. made of *cambric*
   (a) finely-woven linen (b) finely-woven wool (c) finely-woven silk (d) finely-woven gold thread

7. a *clarion* sound
   (a) booming (b) muffled (c) brilliantly clear (d) prolonged

8. a meeting of the *Curia*
   (a) Communist International (b) governing body of the Council of Europe (c) governing body of the United Nations (d) governing body of the Roman Catholic Church

9. an *eclectic* philosopher
   (a) whose views are narrowly defined (b) who selects from various doctrines (c) who views people as inherently evil (d) who views people as inherently good

10. many *encomiums*
    (a) units of housing (b) sums of money (c) rival groups (d) expressions of praise

11. to *espouse* someone
    (a) marry (b) divorce (c) betray (d) trust

12. to *espouse* a cause
    (a) suspect (b) abandon (c) attack (d) support

13. a book on *gastronomy*
    (a) the art of good eating (b) disorders of the stomach (c) the art of predicting human events (d) disorders of the nervous system

14. They were *intransigent*.
    (a) unable to understand (b) unwilling to compromise (c) unable to move (d) unwilling to stay

15. preoccupied with the *minutiae*
    (a) preliminary negotiations (b) records of the meeting (c) petty details (d) microscopic pond-life

16. a carved *obelisk*
    (a) flat stone tablet with a rounded top (b) tall, four-sided stone monument (c) pointed stone arch (d) round base supporting a statue

17. *pellucid* water
   (a) greenish-blue (b) turbulent (c) muddy (d) transparent

18. *pellucid* writing
   (a) obscure (b) muddled (c) ambiguous (d) clear

19. a *predilection* for something
   (a) preference (b) abhorrence (c) advance payment (d) firm offer

20. The Great *Schism*
   (a) rebirth of learning (b) breakdown of the empire (c) split in the Church (d) rise of the city-state

Check your answers against the correct ones given below. The answers are not in order; this is to prevent your eye from catching sight of the correct answers before you have had a chance to do the exercise on your own.

11a. 7c. 17d. 1c. 15c. 3c. 20c. 13a. 9b. 6a. 10d. 18d. 4d. 16b. 5b. 19a. 12d. 2d. 14b. 8d.

Look up in your dictionary all the words for which you gave incorrect answers. Only when you have done this should you go on to the next exercise.

EXERCISE 10B

Each word in Word List 10 is used several times in the sentences below to illustrate different meanings or usage. One of the sentences for each word uses the italicized word incorrectly. You are to circle the letter preceding that sentence.

1. (a) The young couple kept stealing *amatory* glances at each other during the talk. (b) The young plants need tender *amatory* care if they are to flourish. (c) In an *amatory* outburst, Romeo expresses his love for Juliet.

2. (a) Helen of Troy is the *apotheosis* of female beauty. (b) The *apotheosis* of Alexander the Great was a source of secret amusement to him. (c) A feeling of acute *apotheosis* gripped him, turning his knees to rubber.

3. (a) Disease had greatly *attenuated* the ranks of the general's army. (b) The air at these high altitudes is extremely *attenuated*. (c) The *attenuated* limbs of the children are an indication of severe malnutrition. (d) After much struggle, he finally *attenuated* his lifelong goal.

4. (a) A cotton fabric with a glazed finish that resembles linen is sold as *cambric*. (b) Their table linen was made of finest *cambric*. (c) He wore a fine linen *cambric* with ruffles at the throat and wrists.

5. (a) The bugle's *clarion* call roused us from our beds at daybreak. (b) The song of the birds rang out *clarion* clear in the still of the evening. (c) The vultures fed on the dead deer and other *clarion*.

6. (a) The cardinal formerly held a high position in the *Curia*. (b) Among his collection of *curias* was a carved wooden idol from Malaya. (c) The *Curia*, once a highly conservative body, is slowly becoming more liberal.

7. (a) Her taste in music is *eclectic*, ranging from Bach to the latest rock sound. (b) His philosophy lacks a unified wholeness and has been criticized for its *eclecticism*. (c) She is one of our most *eclectic* authors and admits to being influenced by most of the great literary figures of our time. (d) She grinned *eclectically* at me when the results were announced.

8. (a) The settlers built an *encomium* around the village to keep away marauders. (b) She revelled in the *encomiums* of her admirers. (c) I stood up and added my *encomium* to the praise already showered on him.

9. (a) The *espousal* of the farmer's son to his neighbor's daughter was an occasion for much rejoicing. (b) He was in his sixties while his *espouse* was barely half his age. (c) She had *espoused* the cause of civil rights long before it was popular to do so.

10. (a) The book is a *gastronomical* guide to the foods of the Orient. (b) He has a *gastronomical* ulcer and must eat only bland foods. (c) *Gastronomy* is nurtured most lovingly by the gourmets of France. (d) The meal was a *gastronomer's* delight with each dish prepared to perfection.

11. (a) The road to peace is blocked by the *intransigence* of the enemy leaders. (b) The strike is in its tenth day, but both management and labor are *intransigent*. (c) The road is under repair and is *intransigent* to all vehicular traffic. (d) The *intransigents* among the opposition consider a willingness to negotiate a sign of weakness.

12. (a) A single drop of water contains thousands of *minutiae*, invisible except under a microscope. (b) A good general does not neglect the *minutiae* of battle plans. (c) The teacher's comments seemed to ignore the thesis of my paper and concentrate on such *minutiae* as spelling and punctuation.

13. (a) The best known *obelisk* in the United States is the Washington Monument. (b) An *obelisk* is a tall, four-sided stone monument that tapers as it rises and terminates in a pyramid. (c) One glance from the *obelisk*, a mythical lizardlike creature, was supposed to be fatal.

14. (a) Through the *pellucid* water of the lagoon, we watched the fish swimming far below (b) Her firm, *pellucid* handwriting contrasted greatly with her husband's irregular scrawl. (c) The *pellucidity* of her prose makes it a delight to read. (d) The pendant consisted of a white *pellucid* suspended on a gold chain.

15. (a) A *predilection* was held to determine which candidate was to represent the party. (b) Her *predilection* for bluntly speaking her mind sometimes gets her into trouble. (c) Those with a *predilection* for military history should certainly visit Gettysburg.

16. (a) The Great *Schism* was the split in the Roman Catholic Church between the years 1378 and 1417. (b) Church authorities punished those who expressed *schismatic* opinions. (c) His get-rich-quick *schisms* never seem to amount to anything. (d) The widening *schism* between science and the arts is the subject of tonight's talk.

EXERCISE 10C

It is possible for two words to be fairly close synonyms and yet express quite different attitudes because of their different emotional content. Bertrand Russell expresses this neatly: I am firm; you are obstinate; he is pig-headed.

Complete each sentence below by selecting the word that expresses a *favorable* attitude toward the subject or object and striking out the other word.

1. "I don't know what you mean," she said (cautiously/evasively).

2. His soldiers are a (loyal/servile) bunch who will follow him anywhere.

3. She is so (miserly/thrifty) that she walks five miles to work each day to save a dime.

4. The cabin is in a very (lonely/secluded) spot.

5. I saw her (gloat/smile) when it was announced that she had won the contest.

6. He has a very (subtle/devious) mind.

Complete each sentence below by selecting the word that expresses an *unfavorable* attitude and striking out the other word.

7. That was the most (bombastic/eloquent) speech I have ever heard.

8. "My family has owned this land for three hundred years," she said (proudly/arrogantly).

9. This is their way of showing their (disloyalty/independence).

10. Charging the enemy single-handed was a (foolhardy/daring) thing to do.

11. A heavy bombardment compelled the troops to (retreat/withdraw).

12. He dealt (ruthlessly/firmly) with those who disagreed with him.

WORDLY WISE 10

AMATORY and *amorous* are similar in meaning; both are synonymous with *loving* but *amatory* specifically refers to the affection between lovers. (A mother bestows loving care on her child. Lovers exchange amatory (or amorous) glances.)

The plural of ENCOMIUM is *encomiums* or *encomia*.

MINUTIAE means "unimportant details"; the singular form of this word, rarely used, is *minutia*.

An OBELISK is a tall, four-sided monument with a pyramidal top; a *basilisk* is a mythical creature whose glance was believed by the ancients to be fatal. These two words sound sufficiently alike to cause possible confusion.

Etymology

Study the roots and prefix given below together with the English words derived from them. Capitalized words are those given in the Word List. You should look up in a dictionary any words that are unfamiliar to you.

Prefix: *ec-* (out of) Greek — Examples: *EC-LECTIC, ecstasy, eccentric*
Roots: *gastro* (stomach) Greek — Examples: *GASTRONOMY, gastric*
lux, luc (light) Latin — Examples: *PEL-LUCID, lucid, translucent*
clarus (clear) Latin — Examples: *CLARION, clarify, clarity*

Word List 11

AEON	DESPOIL	LUCUBRATE
ANCILLARY	ELIDE	MOOT
ARGOT	ENCROACH	OCHER
BAWDY	EXACTING	PERFUNCTORY
CHIMERICAL	GENUFLECT	QUERULOUS
COVERT	IDEALIZE	TIER

Look up the words in List 11 in your dictionary. Note that many of them have more than one meaning. When you feel that you know *all* the meanings of *all* the words, go on to the exercises below.

EXERCISE 11A

From the four choices following each phrase or sentence, you are to circle the letter preceding the one that is closest in meaning to the italicized word. Where the same word appears more than once, you should note that it is being used in different senses.

1. an *aeon* ago
   (a) year and a day (b) period of fourteen days (c) immeasurably short split-second (d) indefinitely long period of time

2. *ancillary* measures
   (a) emergency (b) primary (c) secondary (d) ineffectual

3. thieves' *argot*
   (a) honor (b) stolen property (c) slang (d) method of working

4. a *bawdy* tale
   (a) historically authentic (b) heroically inspiring (c) vulgarly improper (d) childishly simple

5. *chimerical* notions
   (a) practical (b) idealistic (c) dangerous (d) unrealistic

6. with *covert* satisfaction
   (a) smug (b) open (c) concealed (d) enormous

7. to *despoil* the countryside
   (a) litter (b) beautify (c) plunder (d) dislike

8. to *elide* a passage
   (a) underline (b) read aloud (c) strike out (d) dictate

9. to *elide* the vowel
   (a) mispronounce (b) emphasize (c) write out (d) slur over

10. to *encroach* upon
(a) lie (b) trespass (c) exist (d) settle

11. an *exacting* employer
(a) lax (b) strict (c) unfair (d) generous

12. to *genuflect*
(a) salute one's opponent before battle (b) give serious thought to the consequences of an act (c) bend the knee in worship (d) study diligently

13. to *idealize* someone
(a) regard as perfect (b) think constantly of (c) suggest the name of (d) suspect

14. to *lucubrate*
(a) take one's case (b) study laboriously (c) exercise regularly (d) offer or accept bribes

15. a *moot* question
(a) direct (b) difficult (c) indirect (d) debatable

16. to *moot* the topic
(a) dismiss (b) raise (c) forbid (d) question

17. a point made *moot* by subsequent events
(a) devoid of practical significance (b) historically inaccurate (c) highly relevant (d) very mysterious

18. red *ocher*
(a) wood noted for its hardness (b) artificial food coloring (c) cloth made from wool fibers (d) pigment used in paints

19. a *perfunctory* manner
(a) zealous (b) mechanically routine (c) suspicious (d) cheerful and carefree

20. a *querulous* person
(a) in uncertain health (b) of indeterminate age (c) given to asking questions (d) given to complaining

21. the top *tier*
(a) row (b) half (c) story (d) sail

Check your answers against the correct ones given below. The answers are not in order; this is to prevent your eye from catching sight of the correct answers before you have had a chance to do the exercise on your own.

15d. 1d. 17a. 7c. 11b. 3c. 20d. 13a. 9d. 6c. 21a. 8c. 14b. 2c. 12c. 19b. 10b. 18d. 4c. 16b. 5d.

Look up in your dictionary all the words for which you gave incorrect answers. Only when you have done this should you go on to the next exercise.

EXERCISE 11B

Each word in Word List 11 is used several times in the sentences below to illustrate different meanings or usage. One of the sentences for each word uses the italicized word incorrectly. You are to circle the letter preceding that sentence.

1. (a) Hydrogen *aeons* are formed when salts are dissolved in water. (b) Evolution has continued its course through countless *aeons* of time. (c) The supply of oxygen on Mars was used up *aeons* ago.

2. (a) The main factory is served by several *ancillary* plants. (b) He *ancillaried* the charge against him by pleading "not guilty." (c) She served in an *ancillary* capacity to several of our nation's leaders.

3. (a) The detective had spent so much time among criminals that he spoke the *argot* of the underworld. (b) In the *argot* of teenagers, "boss" means "excellent; very good." (c) The gold is melted down and cast into *argots* for easier storage.

4. (a) The soldiers in the barracks entertained themselves with tales filled with *bawdry*. (b) Such *bawdy* talk offended the guests who were expecting polite conversation. (c) The *bawdiness* of several of Chaucer's **Canterbury Tales** surprises many readers. (d) "Don't *bawdy* words with me, young man!" said the manager sternly.

5. (a) His *chimerical* notions of running away and becoming a painter annoyed his family. (b) The *chimera*, a mythical beast with a lion's head, goat's body, and serpent's tail, symbolizes unrealistic ideas. (c) To work for such obviously unrealistic goals is to pursue a *chimera*. (d) It was *chimerical* of her to get into an argument over something so trivial.

6. (a) She glanced *covertly* at her fiancé to see how he was taking the news. (b) The stag hid in a *covert* in an attempt to elude its pursuers. (c) Such support as was forthcoming was offered in a very *covert* fashion. (d) Some people think it is wrong to *covert* what is not yours.

7. (a) The Goths poured into Italy and *despoiled* the city of Rome. (b) Under Henry VIII the monasteries were *despoiled* of their treasures. (c) The soldiers bore away tapestries, gold ornaments, and other *despoils* of war. (d) The senator deplores the strip-mining methods which *despoil* the countryside of its beauty.

8. (a) He *elided* certain passages that he thought might prove embarrassing to him. (b) The plane *elided* over the field and landed safely. (c) Changes of pronunciation are brought about by people's *eliding* certain sounds. (d) "There is" becomes "There's" by a process of *elision*.

9. (a) You are free to do as you please provided you do not *encroach* on the rights of others. (b) Green belts should be established around urban areas to halt the *encroachment* of the city upon the countryside. (c) I hesitate to *encroach* the subject, but when do you plan to leave?

10. (a) The most *exacting* conditions must be met if the experiment is to be a success. (b) Because of the *exacting* demands of this work, you will be given frequent rest periods. (c) When we added the salt solution, the mixture began *exacting* just as I had predicted.

11. (a) He *genuflected* before the altar and quietly left the church. (b) Candidates for office in Communist countries are expected to *genuflect* before Marxist ideology. (c) There was a *genuflection* of sorrow in her voice as she spoke. (d) The picture shows the martyr in an attitude of *genuflection* before the cross.

12. (a) He tried to *idealize* what the house would look like when it was finished. (b) She tends to *idealize* her friends and is disappointed when they fail to live up to her expectations. (c) This is an *idealized* portrait of Joan of Arc and does not pretend to be an exact likeness in every detail.

13. (a) After long and earnest *lucubration*, I arrived at the solution. (b) She spread her books out on the table, and by the light of a candle *lucubrated* far into the night. (c) A little powdered graphite is used to *lucubrate* the moving parts.

14. (a) The question of her guilt or innocence seems a *moot* one since she will never be brought to trial. (b) He looked *mootly* at me when I asked him where he had been. (c) A *moot* court is a series of mock trials in which law students argue hypothetical cases. (d) A change of policy toward Latin America was first *mooted* some years ago.

15. (a) *Ocher,* varying in color from red to yellow, is a pigment derived from iron-rich clay. (b) Yellow *ocher* is favored by artists because of its permanence and richness of hue. (c) A pair of carved ivory *ochers* stood on the shelf.

16. (a) His speech was so lifeless and *perfunctory* that the attention of the audience soon began to wander. (b) She greeted me *perfunctorily* when I walked in. (c) She entered the results in a *perfunctory* manner as though her thoughts were elsewhere. (d) He was a minor *perfunctory* in some government department.

17. (a) "What are you doing now?" she asked *querulously*. (b) The only way we can tolerate

his *querulousness* is by ignoring him when he starts complaining. (c) With her unceasingly *querulous* demands and questions, the old woman made her daughter's life a misery. (d) The action to be taken must remain *querulous* until a decision is made.

18. (a) The hall has thirty *tiers* of seats banked steeply in order to give everyone a good view. (b) The calf's legs were *tiered* together to prevent it from escaping. (c) A magnificent three-*tiered* wedding cake occupied the center of the table.

EXERCISE 11C

Complete the analogies below by underlining the numbered pair of words that stand in the same relationship to each other as do the first pair of words.

1. covert:overt:: (1) later:earlier (2) secret:hidden (3) seek:find (4) hide:seek (5) hidden:open

2. bier:beer:: (1) barrel:wine (2) thirst:drink (3) principle:tenet (4) interest:principal (5) principal:principle

3. rococo:classical:: (1) Italy:Greece (2) architecture:sculpture (3) ornate:simple (4) modern:ancient (5) Greece:Rome

4. unilateral:bilateral:: (1) first:second (2) one:half (3) one:two (4) one:many (5) complete:unfinished

5. predilection:liking:: (1) lucubration:thought (2) aberration:feel (3) cerebration:feel (4) cerebration:thought (5) aberration:thought

6. feel:hear:: (1) see:sight (2) palpable:audible (3) touch:palpable (4) hear:audible (5) palpable:solid

7. ingrate:gratitude:: (1) neophyte:experience (2) neophyte:beginner (3) neophyte:expert (4) expert:beginner (5) experience:age

8. real:chimerical:: (1) spirit:reincarnation (2) wise:perspicacious (3) stubborn:obdurate (4) live:longevity (5) authentic:apocryphal

9. risible:laugh:: (1) olfactory:sob (2) chimerical:tear (3) ancillary:weep (4) lachrymose:cry (5) comatose:awaken

10. elide:elision:: (1) remnant:remainder (2) egress:digression (3) add:omission (4) addition:subtraction (5) enjoin:injunction

WORDLY WISE 11

AEON may also be spelled *eon*; the former spelling is the more common and is preferred.

ARGOT can be pronounced *AR-got* but is more commonly pronounced with the *t* silent (*AR-go*).

BAWDY is an adjective and means "vulgarly improper." It can also be a noun meaning "vulgarly improper language" or "the quality of being bawdy," and in this meaning only is usually written *bawdry*.

COVERT is an adjective and means "hidden" (covert glances); it is also a noun meaning "a hiding place." Don't confuse this word with *covet*, which is a verb and means "to desire what does not belong to one."

ENCROACH is generally followed by the preposition *on* or *upon* (to encroach upon the rights of others).

Etymology

Study the roots given below together with the English words derived from them. Capitalized words are those given in the Word List. You should look up in a dictionary any words that are unfamiliar to you.

Roots: *genu* (knee) Latin — Examples: *GENUFLECT*

flect, *flex* (bend) Latin — Examples: GENU*FLECT*, *flex*ible, re*flect*

queri (complain) Latin — Examples: *QUERU*LOUS, *quar*rel

Word List 12

ABROGATE	DRAGOON	IMPERIOUS
ANNULAR	EMOLLIENT	MENSURATION
ARRANT	EQUANIMITY	NATAL
BEHEMOTH	FRENETIC	OLEAGINOUS
CITRUS	GAINSAY	REFECTORY
CUPIDITY	GRATIS	VAGARY

Look up the words above in your dictionary. Note that many of them have more than one meaning. When you feel that you know *all* the meanings of *all* the words, go on to the exercises below.

EXERCISE 12A

From the four choices following each phrase or sentence, you are to circle the letter preceding the one that is closest in meaning to the italicized word. Where the same word appears more than once, you should note that it is being used in different senses.

1. to *abrogate* a right
   (a) abolish (b) establish (c) exercise (d) neglect

2. *annular* growths
   (a) irregular (b) yearly (c) stunted (d) circular

3. an *arrant* fool
   (a) comical (b) wise (c) apparent (d) complete

4. to stare at the *behemoth*
   (a) sheet of mountain ice (b) creature of great size (c) creature of incredible ugliness (d) problem of enormous complexity

5. a *citrus* grove
   (a) of grape vines used in winemaking (b) of pear, apple, and related trees (c) of orange, lemon, and related trees (d) of olive and related plants

6. to show *cupidity*
   (a) love for one particular person (b) love for all mankind (c) a greedy desire for wealth (d) unbridled ambition

7. a young *dragoon*
   (a) mounted soldier (b) military bandsman (c) military policeman (d) naval officer

8. to *dragoon* them
   (a) persuade (b) compel (c) ask (d) aid

9. to use an *emollient*
   (a) soothing ointment (b) threat of force (c) promise of reward (d) suitable pretext

10. with complete *equanimity*
    (a) fairness to all concerned (b) disregard for what is right (c) calmness of mind (d) disregard for one's own safety

11. a *frenetic* pace
    (a) leisurely (b) measured (c) irregular (d) hectic

12. *frenetic* cries
    (a) faint (b) pitiful (c) frantic (d) melodious

13. to *gainsay* her
    (a) support (b) speak against (c) overtake (d) speak for

14. to *gainsay* the report
    (a) suppress (b) accept (c) broadcast (d) deny

15. They supplied it *gratis.*
    (a) promptly (b) on request (c) without charge (d) at cost

16. an *imperious* manner
    (a) friendly (b) domineering (c) soothing (d) shy

17. the *mensuration* of the earth
    (a) traveling around (b) motion (c) encirclement (d) measuring

18. the *natal* day
    (a) of birth (b) of coming to manhood (c) of retirement (d) of death

19. *oleaginous* substances
    (a) fibrous (b) crystalline (c) oily (d) powdery

20. an *oleaginous* manner
    (a) briskly efficient (b) deeply concerned (c) smoothly bland (d) pleasantly relaxed

21. to enter the *refectory*

    (a) private chapel (b) sleeping quarters (c) open courtyard (d) dining hall

22. the *vagaries* of fashion

    (a) leaders (b) unpredictable whims (c) followers (d) centers

Check your answers against the correct ones given below. The answers are not in order; this is to prevent your eye from catching sight of the correct answers before you have had a chance to do the exercise on your own.

11d. 7a. 17d. 1a. 15c. 6c. 9a. 21d. 13b. 20c. 3d. 8b. 14d. 2d. 12c. 22b. 19c. 10c. 18a. 4b. 16b. 5c.

Look up in your dictionary all the words for which you gave incorrect answers. Only when you have done this should you go on to the next exercise.

EXERCISE 12B

Each word in Word List 12 is used several times in the sentences below to illustrate different meanings or usage. One of the sentences for each word uses the italicized word incorrectly. You are to circle the letter preceding that sentence.

1. (a) The collapse of the empire was a direct result of the *abrogation* of its moral values. (b) By decision of the president, all treaties between the two countries are now *abrogated*. (c) These are fundamental human rights and are not to be *abrogated* at the whim of any government. (d) He *abrogated* to himself the right to decide who should be spared.

2. (a) The annual rings of a tree trunk are usually *annular*. (b) An *annular* eclipse occurs when a thin, outer ring of the sun is visible around the disc of the moon as the moon passes between the sun and the earth. (c) Meetings are held *annularly* on the first Friday in November.

3. (a) "Why, thou art an *arrant* knave," quoth the knight, drawing his sword. (b) Her proposal is a piece of *arrant* nonsense and should be ignored. (c) A knight *arrant* was one who travelled far and wide in search of adventure.

4. (a) The linesmen on the football team were *behemoths* who terrified the opposition. (b) The *Behemoth* mentioned in the Bible (Job 40:15-24) was probably the hippopotamus. (c) The great blue whale, the *behemoth* of the sea, is in danger of becoming extinct. (d) Each side was trying to *behemoth* the other into surrendering.

5. (a) Lemons and limes are extremely rich in *citrus*. (b) A bumper crop of oranges was harvested, although other *citrus* fruits will be in short supply. (c) All *citruses* are rich in vitamin C.

6. (a) By promising to make them rich overnight, he appealed to their *cupidity*. (b) The ravaged landscape is a monument to the *cupidity* of the strip-mining companies. (c) Reports of the discovery of gold inflamed the *cupidity* of the people who flocked west. (d) The question of who thought of the idea first is a mere *cupidity*.

7. (a) The colonel sent a company of *dragoons* to put down the rebellion. (b) The mounted soldiers *dragooned* the townspeople into building fortifications. (c) He was *dragooned* into accompanying them to the railroad station. (d) She *dragooned* herself out of bed and rubbed her eyes sleepily.

8. (a) Workers on the project receive an *emollient* of sixteen dollars a day. (b) This jar of *emollient* cream is good for soothing and softening the skin. (c) Her soft words acted as an *emollient* and soothed their ruffled feelings.

9. (a) When he realized the gravity of the news, his *equanimity* broke and he began sobbing. (b) She received the news with *equanimity* and even managed to make a little joke. (c) The *equanimity* of the Florida climate is what attracts people to that state. (d) The most

vicious insults and personal attacks failed to disturb her *equanimity*.

10. (a) In *frenetic* activity on the stock exchange yesterday over seven million shares were traded. (b) The man waved his arms *frenetically as* taxi after taxi sped past him. (c) A noisy and *frenetic* celebration followed the announcement of the end of the war. (d) The pain from the wound was so *frenetic* that she almost fainted.

11. (a) It cannot be *gainsaid* that victory would have been impossible without our allies. (b) You cannot *gainsay* the truth of what I have said. (c) No one *gainsays* your right to speak your mind, but you must allow others the same right. (d) She was able to *gainsay* the hundred dollars into a fortune in less than two years.

12. (a) If you buy two cans of dog food, you get a third one *gratis*. (b) An iron *gratis* covered the opening to the sewer. (c) Admission is fifty cents for adults; children under eighteen are allowed in *gratis*.

13. (a) She glared *imperiously* at the headwaiter and demanded a better table. (b) The *imperious* crown was worn by the emperor only on state occasions. (c) His *imperious* manner offended his co-workers, who felt that he should be more tolerant.

14. (a) *Mensuration* of the region for mapping purposes is carried out by teams of surveyors. (b) In *mensuration* of astronomical distances, the light year is the standard unit. (c) The amount of payment is in direct *mensuration* with the work done.

15. (a) July 4th, 1776, was the *natal* day of our nation. (b) The *natal* death rate refers to the percentage of babies who die at birth. (c) The tobacco plant is *natal* to the American continent.

16. (a) Olive oil or some similar *oleaginous* substance is used in this recipe. (b) If the two angles are *oleaginous* with each other, the adjacent sides must be equal in length. (c) The fixed smile and *oleaginous* manner of the master of ceremonies repelled me.

17. (a) If the children continue to be *refectory*, you should punish them. (b) A *refectory* table is a long, narrow table used for dining. (c) Meals at the college are served in the *refectory* at the hours posted.

18. (a) The time taken for the transatlantic voyage depends on the *vagaries* of the weather. (b) The *vagaries* of the stock market should not deter you from buying some shares. (c) The river follows a *vagary* course as it winds its way to the sea. (d) Louisa May Alcott's novels deal with the *vagaries* of growing up in small town America.

EXERCISE 12C

This exercise combines synonyms and antonyms. You are to underline the word which is *either* most similar in meaning *or* most nearly opposite in meaning to the capitalized word. Underline only one word for each question after deciding that it is either an antonym or a synonym and write A (for antonym) or S (for synonym) after the capitalized word. Allow only fifteen minutes for this test. If you cannot answer a question, go on to the next one without delay. If you have time left over at the end, go back and try to fill in unanswered questions.

26 or over correct:	excellent
22 to 25 correct:	good
21 or under correct:	thorough review of A exercises indicated

1. OILY . . . .
amatory eclectic pellucid oleaginous lucubrate

2. STRENGTHEN . . . .
arrant covert attenuate genuflect dragoon

3. SUPPORT . . . .
prevaricate mince encroach apprise espouse

4. FREE . . . .

insensate fetish gratis salubrious sylvan

5. MUDDY . . . .

bawdy pellucid natal unguent indigenous

6. GREED . . . .

gratis cupidity argot mensuration intransigence

7. FANTASTIC . . . .

lachrymose execrable sonic iconoclastic chimerical

8. LOVING . . . .

salubrious sedulous apocryphal amatory eulogy

9. FONDNESS . . . .

predilection altercation aberration chimera equanimity

10. OPEN . . . .

risible emollient idyllic bucolic covert

11. LOUD . . . .

clarion stentorian cacophony trumpery gratis

12. ESTABLISH . . . .

apprise idealize inveigh yaw abrogate

13. TRESPASS . . . .

defalcate inhibit sunder dissipate encroach

14. SPLIT . . . .

incubus schism obelisk egress cacophony

15. UNCOMPLAINING . . . .

querulous reactionary deleterious frenetic annular

16. SALVE . . . .

rococo behemoth emollient paradigm exegesis

17. STUDY . . . .

sobriquet engender caparison elide lucubrate

18. DEBATABLE . . . .

lucent pellucid nuptial moot itinerant

19. LAX . . . .

quondam venal exacting emollient turbid

20. UTTER . . . .

feral bilateral bucolic arrant brindled

21. MEASUREMENT . . . .

progeny moiety canard mensuration curia

22. SLANG . . . .

curia behemoth zephyr argot hybrid

23. PERTURBATION . . . .

exegesis lachrymose genuflection refectory equanimity

24. COMPEL . . . .

atone gaff prevaricate mince dragoon

25. LEISURELY . . . .

intransigent rococo frenetic reactionary execrable

26. HUMBLE . . . .

itinerant neophyte olfactory imperious sedulous

27. AGE . . . .

patina aeon élan atoll apogee

28. WHIM . . . .

vagary diapason cognomen luminary trumpery

29. SECONDARY . . . .

ancillary annular arrant apocryphal expeditious

30. ADMIT . . . .

espouse atone idealize arrant gainsay

WORDLY WISE 12

Don't confuse ABROGATE, which means "to abolish" (to abrogate a law), with *arrogate*, which means "to take or seize without right." (She arrogated to herself the right to speak for all of us.)

ANNULAR means "like or forming a ring." *Annual* means "yearly." The annual rings of a tree are so named because a new one is formed every year. These growths are annular because they are in the form of a ring.

ARRANT means "complete; utter" and is somewhat archaic (an arrant knave); *errant* means "wrong; erring" (his errant ways) or "wandering" (a knight errant).

In the early 1600s a *dragoon* was a musket that "breathed fire" like a dragon. Mounted soldiers armed with these muskets soon became known as DRAGOONS, and the term was later generalized to mean any cavalrymen, but especially of certain historically important regiments. The verb *dragoon* meant "to set upon with dragoons" or "to use dragoons to force (someone)" and now means simply to force someone or extort something by rigorous or harassing measures.

An EMOLLIENT is an ointment or salve; don't confuse this word with *emolument* (Word List 5), which means "salary; payment."

IMPERIOUS means "domineering" (the manager's imperious manner); *imperial* means "of or resembling an emperor or empire" (the imperial city of Rome; the imperial crown of the emperor).

Etymology

Study the roots given below together with the English words derived from them. Capitalized words are those given in the Word List. You should look up in a dictionary any words that are unfamiliar to you.

Roots: *aequus* (even) Latin — Examples: *EQUA-NIMITY*, *equi*nox, *equa*ble

noct, nox (night) Latin — Examples: equi*nox*, *noct*urnal, *noct*urne

ACROSS

1. a strong liking or preference
7. sharp and clear; shrill
9. a fine, closely woven linen cloth
10. to study laboriously
13. anything odd or unpredictable; a whim
14. fretful and complaining
16. without charge; free
18. existing only in the imagination
19. to use up wastefully (7)
20. to swing off course suddenly (5)
22. to speak against; to deny
23. lacking interest or enthusiasm
26. elevation to a godlike state
29. open to question; debatable
30. a greedy desire for wealth
31. a dining hall, especially in a religious institution
33. to trespass or intrude
34. to look upon as being perfect
37. to bend the knee in worship
38. to lend support to
39. of or relating to birth
42. the art of good eating
43. selecting or selected from various sources
45. soothing; mollifying
47. an object believed to have magical powers (5)
48. domineering; overbearing
49. secondary; subsidiary; subordinate
50. refusing to compromise
51. wildly excited; hectic; frantic

DOWN

1. transparently clear
2. an expression of praise
3. making severe demands; strict
4. a yellow or reddish earth pigment
5. a tall, four-sided stone monument tapering to a pyramidal top
6. petty details
7. hidden; concealed
8. a particular vocabulary of a specialized group
11. anything huge, especially a creature of great size
12. calmness of mind; composure
15. vulgarly improper
16. a large hook for landing fish (3)
17. an indefinitely long period of time
19. to compel by force or threats
21. complete; thoroughgoing
24. to make thin; to weaken
25. a lemon, lime, orange, or similar fruit
26. to put an end to; to abolish
27. of or relating to love between the sexes
28. a division or split, especially in the church
29. measurement; measuring
32. smoothly bland; oily in manner
35. to strip of belongings or possessions
36. like or forming a ring
40. any one of a series of rows or layers
41. keenness of mind; shrewdness (5)
44. the governing body of the Roman Catholic Church
45. to slur over; to omit
46. a principle or belief held to be true (4)

Chapter Five

Word List 13

CARNAL	LAUD	RETROGRADE
CONTUMACIOUS	MOUNTEBANK	SIMIAN
DIALECTIC	NEPOTISM	SUPPLICATE
FULSOME	PERIPHERY	UNCTUOUS
IMPUTE	PORCINE	
JADED	PROVENDER	

Look up the words above in your dictionary. Note that many of them have more than one meaning. When you feel that you know *all* the meanings of *all* the words, go on to the exercises below.

EXERCISE 13A

From the four choices following each phrase or sentence, you are to circle the letter preceding the one that is closest in meaning to the italicized word. Where the same word appears more than once, you should note that it is being used in different senses.

1. *carnal* pleasures
   (a) fleeting (b) forbidden (c) spiritual (d) fleshly

2. a *contumacious* person
   (a) ridiculous (b) rebellious (c) pitiable (d) sick

3. an expert in *dialectic*
   (a) foreign languages (b) church history (c) logical argument (d) church law

4. *fulsome* praise
   (a) richly deserved (b) unintended (c) offensively excessive (d) fit and proper

5. to *impute* the blame
   (a) escape (b) remove entirely (c) spread among many people (d) attribute accusingly

6. to be *jaded*
   (a) worried (b) satiated (c) annoyed (d) excited

7. to *laud* him
   (a) praise (b) revile (c) need (d) listen to

8. She is a *mountebank*.
   (a) assault soldier (b) wealthy businessperson (c) unscrupulous faker (d) champion athlete

9. to practice *nepotism*
   (a) a form of medicine based on bone manipulation (b) the custom of having several wives at once (c) favoritism to relatives in filling jobs (d) belief in a multiplicity of gods

10. on the *periphery*
    (a) highest point (b) list of applicants (c) agenda of the meeting (d) outer edge

11. *porcine* features
    (a) sharp (b) piglike (c) aristocratic (d) ferret-like

12. a supply of *provender*
    (a) small-arms ammunition (b) warm winter clothing (c) feed for livestock (d) firewood

13. measures that are *retrograde*
    (a) effective earlier (b) tending to make things worse (c) imposed by force (d) firmly established

14. *retrograde* motion
    (a) dancelike (b) circular (c) directed downward (d) directed backward

15. *simian* characteristics
    (a) apelike (b) catlike (c) doglike (d) horselike

16. to *supplicate*
    (a) die from lack of air (b) answer evasively (c) exercise one's limbs (d) beg humbly

17. an *unctuous* manner
    (a) pleasantly at ease (b) brisk and efficient (c) showing false concern (d) showing deep concern

18. an *unctuous* substance
    (a) rubbery (b) evil smelling (c) medicinal (d) oily

Check your answers against the correct ones given below. The answers are not in order; this is to prevent your eye from catching sight of the correct answers before you have had a chance to do the exercise on your own.

3c. 11b. 10d. 12c. 7a. 13b. 17c. 2b. 4c. 16d. 14d. 1d. 9c. 6b. 15a. 8c. 5d. 18d.

Look up in your dictionary all the words for which you gave incorrect answers. Only when you have done this should you go on to the next exercise.

EXERCISE 13B

Each word in Word List 13 is used several times in the sentences below to illustrate different meanings or usage. One of the sentences for each word uses the italicized word incorrectly. You are to circle the letter preceding that sentence.

1. (a) On stage, players smudge their lower lashes with a stick of *carnal* to make their eyes look larger. (b) The Victorian novelist stressed the superiority of the spiritual and eternal over the *carnal.*

2. (a) The teacher demanded that the *contumacious* student be ousted from the class. (b) The people's refusal to pay taxes was an act of *contumacy* that no government could tolerate. (c) The fruit had been left too long on the trees and was slightly *contumacious.* (d) Troops were dispatched to the riot area to bring the *contumacious* mobs under control.

3. (a) "Yourn" is *dialectic* for "yours." (b) The comedies of George Bernard Shaw are noted for subtle ironies and brilliant *dialectics.* (c) Let us use a *dialectical* approach in our discussions and not descend to name calling. (d) Her speech provided a lesson for the audience in the art of *dialectic.*

4. (a) He praised her *fulsomely* for her efforts on his behalf. (b) The queen gloried in the *fulsome* compliments of her courtiers. (c) The author frequently gets carried away and lapses into a *fulsome* prose style. (d) The child was attractive and *fulsomely* plump with a fine, laughing sense of humor.

5. (a) I *imputed* her visit to a desire to gloat over my misfortunes. (b) I resent the *imputation* that I encouraged him in his wrongdoing. (c) How dare you *impute* such monstrous motives to me! (d) I have a message to *impute* to you when we are alone.

6. (a) The Roman crowds demanded ever bloodier spectacles to satisfy their *jaded* lust for violence. (b) The metal had been *jaded* to a fine greenish-blue patina. (c) This is an excellent wine that is sure to stimulate your *jaded* palate.

7. (a) The editors of this magnificent volume should be *lauded* for their efforts. (b) She made a *laudable* attempt to make good her error. (c) In *laudatory* terms he praised the governor for her efforts on behalf of the poor. (d) He was an English *laud* and felt that this entitled him to special treatment.

8. (a) The fort was placed atop a high *mountebank* and was virtually impregnable. (b) He accused the congressman of being a rogue and a *mountebank* and said he should resign immediately. (c) The medicine he bought from a *mountebank* at the fair turned out to be colored water.

9. (a) The prime minister denied *nepotism* existed and claimed that all positions were filled strictly on merit. (b) The new office holders were expected to be *nepotists* as they had so many relatives out of work. (c) She was appointed chief *nepot* in the new government.

10. (a) Surgeons removed part of the patient's *periphery* in an emergency operation

yesterday. (b) Objects beyond the *periphery* of vision cannot be seen. (c) Cultural questions were regarded as *peripheral,* and discussion of them was postponed indefinitely. (d) A point near the *periphery* of a revolving circle travels faster than one nearer the center.

11. (a) His snoutlike nose and tiny eyes gave him a *porcine* appearance. (b) She killed the *porcine* and hung it up to let the blood drain from it. (c) The empress *porcinely* glutted herself on fine foods while her subjects starved in the streets. (d) The section on *porcine* diseases lists everything a pig is likely to get.

12. (a) There is enough *provender* to last the cattle through the winter. (b) Grain, oats, and other *provender* can be bought at the feed store in town. (c) She showed great *provender* in choosing her allies from among the most powerful leaders in the Senate.

13. (a) To increase taxes would be a *retrograde* step that would greatly lower incentives. (b) The order was dated March 14th, but was *retrograde* to January 1st. (c) The terrible wars of this century indicate that we are *retrograding* rather than advancing.

14. (a) Although it has many *simian* characteristics, this creature is not a monkey. (b) The chimpanzees are kept apart from the other *simians.* (c) His pronounced stoop and drooping arms gave him a *simian* gait. (d) These statues are carved from *simian* that is dug up in the nearby quarries.

15. (a) We fell on our knees and *supplicated* Allah to have mercy on us. (b) The refugees *supplicate* the consul to give them visas. (c) Her leg muscles were gently *supplicated* by a skilled masseur. (d) The *supplicant* knelt and begged the king to spare his life.

16. (a) Her *unctuous* manner annoyed us because we knew she was not being sincere. (b) The jar contained an *unctuous* preparation that is rubbed into aching muscles. (c) The train leaves *unctuously* every hour on the hour. (d) "I wish every one of us could have won," the boy who had come in first said *unctuously* to the others.

EXERCISE 13C

Many words have connotations that are private to us and are the result of our personal experiences. Certain connotations, however, have by convention become attached to certain words, and we read into these words more than their denotative meaning (these terms are explained in the Introduction).

Match the qualities in the column below against the italicized names of animals and colors that, by convention, connote these qualities.

1. Are you a man or a *mouse*? (   )
2. crazy like a *fox* (   )
3. What a *pig* you are! (   )
4. They fought like *lions.* (   )
5. a *bull* of a man (   )
6. You're *yellow*! (   )
7. a *green* ball player (   )
8. I saw *red.* (   )
9. He felt so *blue*! (   )
10. born to the *purple* (   )

inexperience	anger
depressed	courage
royalty	cowardice
strength	cunning
timidity	greed

WORDLY WISE 13

The noun form of CONTUMACIOUS is *contumacy.*

The adjectives *dialectical* and *dialectic* are related to the noun DIALECTIC and mean "of or pertaining to logical argument." *Dialectal* is the adjective to use for "of or pertaining to dialects or regional speech variations" (Professor Henry Higgins had studied the dialectal peculiarities of various regions and could pinpoint a person's birthplace by hearing him or her speak).

Two adjectives, quite different in meaning, are derived from the verb LAUD: *laudable* means "worthy of praise" (a laudable attempt); *laudatory* means "expressing praise; commendatory" (laudatory comments).

MOUNTEBANK is from the Italian *montimbanco*, "mounted on a bench." The Elizabethans used the term to refer to travelling sellers of quack medicines who would speak from a platform and attract a crowd with juggling, stories, and tricks. It now refers to anyone who impudently pretends to have skill or knowledge and who resorts to degrading means to attract notice.

Etymology

Study the roots and prefixes given below together with the English words derived from them. Capitalized words are those given in the Word List. You should look up in a dictionary any words that are unfamiliar to you.

Prefixes: *peri-* (around) Greek — Examples: *PERI*PHERY, *peri*meter, *peri*patetic

retro- (backward) Latin — Examples: *RETRO*GRADE, *retro*active, *retro*spective

Roots: *carn* (flesh) Latin — Examples: *CARN*AL, in*carn*ate, *carn*ivorous

puta (think) Latin — Examples: IM*PUTE*, com*pute*, *puta*tive

---

Word List 14

ANNEAL	JUNTO	REDUNDANT
CHIAROSCURO	LEVY	SANGUINE
CRESCENDO	NADIR	SPLENETIC
DORY	NIHILISM	TAUTOLOGY
GARROTE	PERMEATE	UNMITIGATED
INGRATIATE	PRELATE	

Look up the words above in your dictionary. Note that many of them have more than one meaning. When you feel that you know *all* the meanings of *all* the words, go on to the exercises below.

EXERCISE 14A

From the four choices following each phrase or sentence, you are to circle the letter preceding the one that is closest in meaning to the italicized word. Where the same word appears more than once, you should note that it is being used in different senses.

1. to *anneal* metal
   (a) bond together in layers (b) beat into a paper-thin leaf (c) draw out into fine wire (d) toughen by heating and then cooling

2. vivid *chiaroscuro*
   (a) pictorial use of exaggeration (b) pictorial use of light and shade (c) pictorial use of color (d) pictorial use of line

3. Play it *crescendo*.
   (a) in a stately manner (b) with decreasing loudness (c) at a barely audible level (d) with increasing loudness

4. to reach a *crescendo*
   (a) quiet passage (b) turning point (c) peak of intensity (d) point of no return

5. a fisher's *dory*
   (a) heavy weatherproof coat (b) flat-bottomed boat (c) private fishing area (d) colored floating marker

6. to *garrote* someone
   (a) execute by beheading (b) execute by burning alive (c) execute by stoning (d) execute by strangling

7. to *ingratiate* oneself
   (a) congratulate (b) quietly remove (d) deliberately deceive (d) win favor for

8. the members of the *junto*
   (a) firing squad (b) court of military law (c) group of political plotters (d) panel of distinguished lawyers

9. to *levy* charges
   (a) reduce (b) increase (c) forego (d) impose

10. to *levy* war
    (a) wage (b) abhor (c) outlaw (d) love

11. the *levy* of troops
(a) training (b) feeding (c) disbanding (d) conscription

12. to reach the *nadir*
(a) starting point (b) highest point (c) lowest point (d) finishing point

13. a complete *nihilism*
(a) acceptance of what fate has in store (b) rejection of all established beliefs (c) withdrawal from all human contact (d) abandonment to sensual pleasures

14. to *permeate* something
(a) go around (b) break up (c) spread through (d) link up with

15. a *prelate* of the church
(a) major tenet (b) high dignitary (c) early form (d) general meeting

16. to be *redundant*
(a) used up (b) necessary (c) not needed (d) duplicated

17. to be *sanguine*
(a) cheerful (b) despondent (c) excitable (d) bloodthirsty

18. a *sanguine* complexion
(a) ruddy (b) swarthy (c) pale (d) sallow

19. to be *splenetic*
(a) in good health (b) easily irritated (c) mentally ill (d) unjustifiably optimistic

20. to point out the *tautology*
(a) inevitable consequence of an act (b) absurdity of something (c) contradictory statement (d) needless repetition of ideas

21. *unmitigated* folly
(a) unprecedented (b) unamusing (c) absolute (d) universal

Check your answers against the following correct ones. The answers are not in order; this is to prevent your eye from catching sight of the correct answers before you have had a chance to do the exercise on your own.

10a. 18a. 4c. 16c. 21c. 5b. 19b. 12c. 2b. 14c. 8c. 11d. 7d. 17a. 1d. 15b. 3d. 20d. 13b. 9d. 6d.

Look up in your dictionary all the words for which you gave incorrect answers. Only when you have done this should you go on to the next exercise.

EXERCISE 14B
Each word in Word List 14 is used several times in the sentences below to illustrate different meanings or usage. One of the sentences for each word uses the italicized word incorrectly. You are to circle the letter preceding that sentence.

1. (a) They *anneal* the steel by heating it in furnaces and then allowing it to cool. (b) The judge may *anneal* the contract if it can be proved that the facts were misrepresented. (c) *Annealed* glass is much stronger and tougher than ordinary glass.

2. (a) He's a *chiaroscuro* fellow, happy one minute and despondent the next. (b) She did a quick charcoal sketch of the scene in *chiaroscuro*. (c) She was a master of the interplay of highlight and deep shadow called *chiaroscuro*.

3. (a) With a deafening *crescendo*, the symphony came to a dramatic end. (b) The gale reached a *crescendo* by evening when winds of 60 miles an hour were recorded. (c) The *crescendo* passages were played with great force by the tympanist. (d) The *crescendo* swept through the town, destroying everything in its path.

4. (a) *Dories* are used chiefly by the fishers of the New England coast. (b) He went fishing for *dory* but met with little success. (c) The *dory* is a flat-bottomed fishing boat with high sides and a sharp bow.

5. (a) The band struck up a tune, and the dancers flung themselves into a lively *garotte*. (b) The

murder victim seems to have been *garotted* with a rope by someone from behind. (c) Prisoners in Spain were executed by means of the *garotte*, an iron collar, which was tightened around the neck.

6. (a) She smiled *ingratiatingly* and offered to help in any way she could. (b) His *ingratiating* manner won him many friends. (c) You must think me very *ingratiate* to have left without thanking you. (d) She tried to *ingratiate* herself with them by doing little jobs.

7. (a) The military *junto* exiled the former president as soon as they were in power. (b) Members of the *junto* were arrested when the queen received word of the conspiracy. (c) After seizing power, he made himself supreme *junto* of the country.

8. (a) The country is very poor and is in no condition to *levy* war on its neighbors. (b) A *levy* of five dollars was made on the members to pay for the damage to the clubhouse. (c) Troops were *levied* from the towns because the country folk were needed on the farms. (d) The swollen river broke through the *levy* and flooded the countryside.

9. (a) The point of the celestial sphere directly opposite to the zenith is called the *nadir* and is vertically downward from the observer. (b) He was dressed in rich robes as befitted the son of an Arabian *nadir*. (c) The *nadir* of his misfortunes occurred when his last five dollars was stolen from him.

10. (a) The *Nihilists* of 19th-century Russia believed that all human institutions should be destroyed. (b) Today's young people seem to be more *nihilistic* than their parents were. (c) No attempt was made to replenish the soil and it grew *nihilistic* within a few years. (d) Their *nihilism* had its roots in the deplorable social conditions of the time.

11. (a) The air was *permeated* by the smell of rotten eggs. (b) Water easily *permeates* the layers of limestone. (c) Shells from the largest guns can *permeate* six-inch steel plates with ease. (d) The poem is *permeated* with a childlike delight at the coming of spring.

12. (a) The archbishop is meeting with other *prelates* of the church at his residence this morning. (b) The coronation of the young sovereign was attended by all the *prelates* and royalty of the land. (c) He was *prelated* to the bishopric at the early age of 43.

13. (a) The workers were declared *redundant* and found themselves out of work. (b) In the sentence "I locked it myself" the word "myself" is *redundant*. (c) She writes a clean, hard prose free of *redundancies*. (d) There was a *redundant* thud as his head struck the overhead beam.

14. (a) The struggle was brief but *sanguine*, and the deck was awash with blood before it ended. (b) Despite numerous setbacks, she retains her *sanguine* approach to life. (c) The *sanguine* glow of burning cedar logs lit up the cabin.

15. (a) The *splenetic* tone of her book is at odds with her claims of objectivity. (b) "Get out of here! All of you!" she roared *splenetically*. (c) He spent his money so *splenetically* that he soon found himself penniless.

16. (a) At the university she majored in *tautology* and sociology. (b) "A beginner who has just started" is a *tautology*. (c) In the phrase "audible to the ear," "to the ear" is *tautological*.

17. (a) He is an *unmitigated* bore, and that is why I shun his company. (b) Her *unmitigated* conceit leads her to think that her every remark is important. (c) The new opera is an *unmitigated* triumph for its composer. (d) The judge *unmitigated* the charges when the circumstances of the case were revealed.

In each of the sentences below a word is omitted. From the four words provided, select the one that best completes the sentence. Allow ten minutes for this test. If you cannot answer a question, go on to the next one without delay. If you have time left over at the end, go back and try to fill in unanswered questions.

18 or over correct:	excellent
14 to 17 correct:	good
13 or under correct:	thorough review of A exercises indicated

1. Cleanliness is a . . . . with him.
   prelate tautology fetish junto

2. The enemy . . . . was easily repulsed by the border guards.
   ancillary incursion mountebank refectory

3. The clearing in the forest made an . . . . setting for our picnic.
   oleaginous idyllic eclectic endemic

4. Stand by to . . . . the fish as I reel it in.
   moot dory mulct gaff

5. Last week we lost 18-0, and this Saturday's game will be another . . . .
   behemoth nadir debacle dictum

6. They took a vow of poverty to . . . . for their past sins.
   gainsay supplicate atone abrogate

7. She was accused of trying to . . . . the state of thousands of dollars.
   impute anneal espouse mulct

8. The horse wore a rich . . . . of embroidered cloth.
   patina chiaroscuro periphery caparison

9. The . . . . of the Roman emperor was a futile attempt to give the godless Romans someone to worship.
   unanimity accretion mensuration apotheosis

10. I deal with the broader issues, and my assistant handles the . . . .
    chimera curia apocrypha minutiae

11. Certain passages that might have given offense were . . . . from the speech.
    espoused sundered elided despoiled

12. Christmas Island was so named because it was discovered on Christ's . . . . day.
    apocryphal notary annular natal

13. After appointing all her relatives to high office, she had the gall to deny that there had been any . . . .
    sycophancy eclecticism nepotism redundancy

14. We'll deal only with the main item and not allow ourselves to be sidetracked by . . . . matters.
    incipient frenetic emollient peripheral

15. . . . . was provided for the cattle.
    largo provender argot quondam

16. The storm reached a(n) . . . . just before dawn and then quickly died down.
    penumbra crescendo apogee nadir

17. He slipped a cord around his victim's neck and tried to . . . . him.
    garrote supplicate abrogate caparison

18. "Visible to the eye" is a . . . . expression.
    bilateral peripheral tautological splenetic

19. He's a most important man, a . . . . of the church.
    prelate laud junto curia

20. The leader's . . . . was "Honesty is the best policy."
    espousal chimera genuflection dictum

WORDLY WISE 14

The plural of CRESCENDO is *crescendoes* or *crescendos*.

GARROTE may also be spelled *garotte*.

JUNTO is also written *junta*; either form is correct.

Don't confuse LEVY, which has several meanings as outlined in the exercises, with *levee*, which means (1) "a raised embankment to prevent flooding," and (2) "a reception or assembly in honor of some person." These two words are homonyms.

The point on the celestial sphere lying directly beneath the observer is the NADIR; its opposite point, lying directly above the observer, is the *zenith*; these two words are antonyms; both are used generally to refer to a low point or a high point. (Her career reached its zenith when she was awarded the Nobel Prize. Her misfortunes reached their nadir when she lost her job.)

Etymology

Study the root and prefix given below together with the English words derived from them. Capitalized words are those given in the Word List. You should look up in a dictionary any words that are unfamiliar to you.

Prefix: *per-* (through, throughout) Latin — Examples: PERMEATE, *per*functory, *per*vade

Root: *nihil* (nothing) Latin — Examples: NIHILISM, an*nihil*ate

---

Word List 15

ADJURE	KINETIC	REGIME
CONCATENATION	LITIGATION	SAVANT
DESCRY	NATATION	SUBVERSIVE
FACTIOUS	OROTUND	UBIQUITOUS
IMBIBE	PERSPICUOUS	VERNAL
ISTHMUS	PRISTINE	

Look up the words above in your dictionary. Note that many of them have more than one meaning. When you feel that you know *all* the meanings of *all* the words, go on to the following exercises.

EXERCISE 15A

From the four choices following each phrase or sentence, you are to circle the letter preceding the one that is closest in meaning to the italicized word. Where the same word appears more than once, you should note that it is being used in different senses.

1. to *adjure* someone
   (a) unreservedly admire (b) shamelessly abandon (c) violently detest (d) solemnly command

2. a bewildering *concatenation*
   (a) medley of sounds (b) mixture of unknown ingredients (c) chain of events (d) variety of choices

3. to *descry* something
   (a) condemn (b) give an account of (c) praise (d) catch sight of

4. *factious* disputes
   (a) between relatives (b) between nations (c) caused by children (d) caused by a group of quarrelsome dissenters

5. to *imbibe*
   (a) object (b) drink (c) sleep (d) relax

6. to *imbibe* knowledge
   (a) spread (b) stifle (c) venerate (d) absorb

7. a long *isthmus*
   (a) projecting landmass almost entirely surrounded by water (b) narrow strip of land connecting two large landmasses (c) chain of islands connecting two large landmasses (d) crescent-shaped coral reef surrounding a tropical island.

8. *kinetic* energy
   (a) of the sun (b) of the atom (c) of motion (d) of position

9. to engage in *litigation*
   (a) acrimonious debate (b) armed conflict (c) delicate maneuvering (d) legal action

10. experts in *natation*
    (a) swimming (b) horseback riding (c) archery
    (d) boxing

11. an *orotund* voice
    (a) high-pitched (b) gruff (c) resonant (d)
    pleading

12. *orotund* verses
    (a) comical (b) nonsensical (c) pompous (d)
    unpretentious

13. a *perspicuous* report
    (a) disjointed (b) wide-ranging (c) unintelligible (d) easily understood

14. in its *pristine* state
    (a) most recent (b) earliest (c) most developed
    (d) final

15. *pristine* beauty
    (a) unspoiled (b) unappreciated (c) short-lived
    (d) enduring

16. an unpopular *regime*
    (a) dictatorial ruler (b) decision of the court
    (c) topic of study (d) system of government

17. a famous *savant*
    (a) warrior (b) scholar (c) prose work (d)
    legendary figure

18. *subversive* activities
    (a) healthful to mind or body (b) conducted
    in stealth or secrecy (c) tending to undermine
    or destroy (d) tending to support or build up

19. to be *ubiquitous*
    (a) downright wicked (b) extremely wise (c)
    present everywhere (d) harmful to health

20. *vernal* flowers
    (a) spring (b) summer (c) autumn (d) tropical

Check your answers against the following correct ones. The answers are not in order; this is to prevent your eye from catching sight of the correct answers before you have had a chance to do the exercise on your own.

10a. 18c. 4d. 16d. 5b. 3d. 20a. 13d. 9d. 6d. 11c. 7b. 17b. 1d. 15a. 19c. 12c. 2c. 14b. 8c.

Look up in your dictionary all the words for which you gave incorrect answers. Only when you have done this should you go on to the next exercise.

EXERCISE 15B

Each word in Word List 15 is used several times in the sentences below to illustrate different meanings or usage. One of the sentences for each word uses the italicized word incorrectly. You are to circle the letter preceding that sentence.

1. (a) The judge *adjured* the case for two weeks at the request of the defense attorney. (b) I reminded her that she was under oath and *adjured* her to speak the truth. (c) He refused to heed his parents' *adjurations* that he complete his studies.

2. (a) The detective unraveled the complicated *concatenation* of events that led to identifying the murderer. (b) The witches muttered weird *concatenations* as they danced around the caldron. (c) It is not a coincidence that these events are *concatenated* so closely.

3. (a) A shout of joy arose when one of the shipwrecked sailors *descried* a sail on the horizon. (b) The two escaped prisoners were *descried* crossing the river a mile from the prison camp. (c) In speaking in support of pure research I do not mean to *descry* applied research.

4. (a) These *factious* disputes threaten to tear the organization apart. (b) We shall vigorously oppose these measures without being in any way *factious* or divisive. (c) A teething baby easily grows *factious* and should be given extra attention at this time.

5. (a) After *imbibing* several cups of coffee, we set out on our journey. (b) Plants *imbibe*

nourishment through their leaves as well as through their roots. (c) She was *imbibed* from expressing her true feelings by her friend's presence. (d) He *imbibed* these principles of honesty and fairness from his parents.

6. (a) A narrow *isthmus* connects the peninsula to the mainland. (b) The patient suffers from *isthmus* and has great difficulty breathing. (c) The *isthmus* of Panama connects South America to Central and North America.

7. (a) The faster a moving body travels, the greater the *kinetic* energy it possesses. (b) The dance has a *kinetic* force quite overpowering to audiences. (c) The engine has only four *kinetic* parts; thus friction is reduced to a minimum. (d) The *kinetic* energy of moving air powers the windmill.

8. (a) The *litigant* was persuaded to drop her lawsuit and agreed to settle out of court. (b) No case can be *litigated* beyond the Supreme Court. (c) Because of heavy legal costs, *litigation* should be resorted to only when all else has failed. (d) The review board allowed the *litigation* of his prison sentence from five years to three.

9. (a) She was the first woman *natator* to swim the channel. (b) Swans, ducks, and other *natational* birds make their nests around the lake. (c) She proved her dexterity at *natation* by swimming three lengths of the pool. (d) The *natation* period, from conception to birth, of a human baby is nine months.

10. (a) The *orotund* tones of the speaker lent a rolling majesty to her words. (b) His political campaign was marked by *orotund* utterances that, when analyzed, meant nothing. (c) A chubby-faced, *orotund* man appeared and beckoned us to follow.

11. (a) How very *perspicuous* of you to spot the error. (b) This report is not as *perspicuous* as one would wish and readily lends itself to misunderstanding. (c) The *perspicuity* of her argument left us with no doubts as to her grasp of the subject.

12. (a) We marvelled at the *pristine* beauty of the snowclad Himalayas. (b) The poem harks back to a *pristine* world, uncorrupted by human hands. (c) The house has been recently *pristined* in an attempt to recapture its former beauty. (d) The state forest has been preserved in all its *pristine* wildness.

13. (a) The Nazi *regime* inflicted unimaginable horrors on Germany and the rest of Europe. (b) The democratic government was overthrown, and a military *regime* established. (c) After making himself *regime* of the country, he imprisoned all his political opponents.

14. (a) The queen summoned the wisest *savants* of the land to help her solve the problem. (b) "I think it better that I don't get involved," he said *savantly*. (c) The conference, which attracted *savants* from the universities as well as artists from all fields, was a great success.

15. (a) Such inflammatory publications have a *subversive* effect on impressionable minds. (b) The attorney general is empowered to investigate groups believed to be *subversive*. (c) The government arrested the students on the grounds that they were *subversives* plotting to overthrow the government. (d) The parts were stuck together and proved *subversive* to all attempts to separate them.

16. (a) Not even on buses and subways can one escape the *ubiquitous* transistor radio. (b) "Keep half for yourself, and give her the other half," he said *ubiquitously*. (c) It is hard to believe that the *ubiquitous* paperback was almost unknown thirty years ago. (d) Only by returning to America can one escape the *ubiquitous* American tourist.

17. (a) He loved April, the month whose *vernal* freshness gave hope to the year. (b) The *vernal* equinox occurs on March 21, when the sun crosses the equator and day and night are of

equal length. (c) The bribery of officials and other *vernal* practices must be stopped forthwith.

EXERCISE 15C

This exercise combines synonyms and antonyms. You are to underline the word which is *either* most similar in meaning *or* most nearly opposite in meaning to the capitalized word. Underline only one word for each question after deciding that it is either an antonym or a synonym and write A (for antonym) or S (for synonym) after the capitalized word. Allow only fifteen minutes for this test. If you cannot answer a question, go on to the next one without delay. If you have time left over at the end, go back and try to fill in unanswered questions.

26 or over correct: excellent
22 to 25 correct: good
21 or under correct: thorough review of A
                        exercises indicated

1. ABSTRUSE . . . .
retrograde redundant amatory perspicuous perspicacious

2. REVILE . . . .
permeate levy laud sunder gainsay

3. IMPOSE . . . .
levy genuflect mulct adjure supplicate

4. SCHOLAR . . . .
behemoth savant junto simian dragoon

5. PIGLIKE . . . .
simian fulsome olfactory eclectic porcine

6. OBEDIENT . . . .
annular endemic sanguine ubiquitous contumacious

7. QUARRELSOME . . . .
kinetic jaded forensic factious perfunctory

8. FLESHLY . . . .
oleaginous intransigent porcine carnal splenetic

9. WEAKEN . . . .
attenuate supplicate prevaricate litigate caparison

10. GLOOMY . . . .
simian chiaroscuro pusillanimous ocher sanguine

11. PLAUDIT . . . .
predilection notary dialectic levy encomium

12. ABSOLUTE . . . .
retrograde orotund unmitigated sedulous immanent

13. EXCESSIVE . . . .
intransigent sedulous orotund fulsome perspicuous

14. ABOLISH . . . .
sunder imbibe descry abrogate genuflect

15. DRINK . . . .
mulct laud natation imbibe lucubrate

16. SLOW . . . .
fulsome pellucid orotund itinerant largo

17. EVEN-TEMPERED . . . .
ubiquitous retrograde splenetic palpable bucolic

18. HEALTHFUL . . . .
pristine pellucid arrant kinetic salubrious

19. DETAILS . . . .
curia rococo chiaroscuro minutiae vagaries

20. PROGRESSIVE . . . .
contumacious retrograde pristine expedient imperious

21. PLUNDER . . . .
natation crescendo despoil extrude abase

63

22. SEE . . . .
    atone anneal adjure gainsay descry

23. UNSPOILED . . . .
    vernal unctuous annular sylvan pristine

24. OLEAGINOUS . . . .
    carnal porcine unctuous frenetic luminary

25. ZENITH . . . .
    nihilism nepotism periphery nadir
    mountebank

26. APELIKE . . . .
    fecund simian carnal kinetic bawdy

27. SPRINGLIKE . . . .
    chimerical vernal simian pristine sylvan

28. OMNIPRESENT . . . .
    ubiquitous unmitigated perspicuous risible
    pusillanimous

29. BEG . . . .
    garrote prevaricate anneal abrogate supplicate

30. NEEDED . . . .
    redundant factious sedulous salubrious
    perspicuous

DESCRY means "to catch sight of" (to descry something on the horizon). Don't confuse this word with *decry*, which means "to denounce" (to decry the habit of rushing into print with half-formulated views).

OROTUND and *rotund* both mean "round; full." But note that *orotund* generally refers to sounds or voices (an orotund voice), while *rotund* refers to form (a rotund figure).

PERSPICUOUS and perspicacious (Word List 8) are easily confused. *Perspicuous* means "easily understood; clear." *Perspicacious* means "having keen judgment; shrewd." The noun form of *perspicuous* is *perspicuity*; the noun form of *perspicacious* is *perspicacity*.

Etymology

Study the roots given below together with the English words derived from them. Capitalized words are those given in the Word List. You should look up in a dictionary any words that are unfamiliar to you.

Roots: *bib* (drink) Latin – Examples: IM*BIBE*, *bib*ulous

kinein (move) Greek – Examples: *KI-NETIC*, *cine*ma

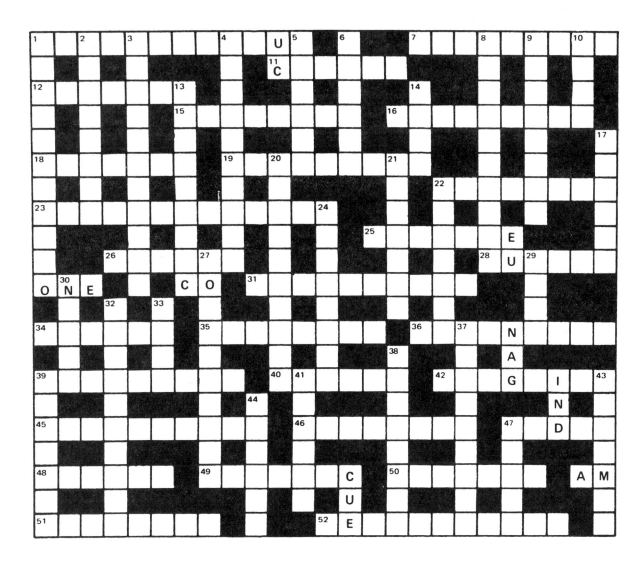

ACROSS

1. showing resistance to authority
7. an increase in volume or intensity
11. of the flesh; sensual
12. a narrow strip of land connecting two large landmasses
15. to penetrate or spread throughout
16. the external boundary or edge of something
18. a mouthlike opening (1)
19. a needless repetition of ideas or words
22. causing or produced by strife
23. a connected series, as of events
25. a high dignitary of the church
26. a political or other ruling system or group
28. a speech of praise (6)
31. the engaging in a lawsuit; legal action
34. to command solemnly
35. favoritism to relatives in securing jobs
36. not needed; unnecessary
39. dry food for livestock
40. of or like an ape or monkey
42. cheerful; optimistic
45. going back to a worse state
46. of the earliest times; unspoiled
47. dulled by surfeit or excess
48. to take in; to drink
49. of or resulting from motion
50. resonant and full-voiced
51. to bring into being (1)
52. easily understood; clear

DOWN

1. the pictorial use of light and shade
2. the art or action of swimming
3. unrelieved; absolute
4. to seek or find favor
5. a learned person; a scholar
6. to toughen by heating and slowly cooling
8. to beg humbly
9. selecting or selected from various sources (10)
10. a flat-bottomed fishing boat with high sides
13. easily irritated; quick to anger
14. to impose, as a tax or fine
17. to catch sight of; to notice
20. present everywhere
21. to execute or murder by strangling
22. offensive because excessive or insincere
24. the rejection of all established beliefs
27. an unscrupulous cheat; a charlatan
29. to sing the praises of; to extol
30. the lowest point
32. tending to undermine or destroy
33. an indefinitely long period of time (11)
37. logical debate or argument
38. making a false show of concern
39. piglike; of or suggesting swine
41. to attribute accusingly
43. restricted or native to a particular area (8)
44. of or occurring in the spring
47. a group of political plotters

65

Chapter Six

Word List 16

ABRADE	EXPATRIATE	QUARANTINE
APPENDAGE	GENOCIDE	RESUSCITATE
BEGET	INCUBATE	STRICTURE
CALCIFY	LIAISON	TENABLE
COAGULATE	OBLOQUY	TRUNCATED
COUP	PHILANDER	

Look up the words above in your dictionary. Note that many of them have more than one meaning. When you feel that you know *all* the meanings of *all* the words, go on to the exercises below.

EXERCISE 16A

From the four choices following each phrase or sentence, you are to circle the letter preceding the one that is closest in meaning to the italicized word. Where the same word appears more than once, you should note that it is being used in different senses.

1. to *abrade* the surface
   (a) decorate (b) scrape away (c) cover up (d) smooth

2. a worthless *appendage*
   (a) argument (b) title (c) performance (d) attachment

3. to *beget* children
   (a) bring up (b) abhor (c) assign rights to (d) become the father of

4. to *calcify*
   (a) dissolve into a solution (b) become hard and stony (c) crumble into dust (d) become soft and spongy

5. *calcified* methods
   (a) effective (b) flexible (c) inflexible (d) ineffective

6. to *coagulate*
   (a) clot (b) separate (c) dissolve (d) waver

7. a brilliant *coup*
   (a) highly successful stroke or stratagem (b) gathering of distinguished people (c) blood-red precious stone (d) display of histrionics

8. to be an *expatriate*
   (a) person who gives his life for his country (b) person who chooses to live in exile (c) person who plots against his country (d) person who travels the world

9. accused of *genocide*
   (a) inciting a person to commit a murder (b) killing someone who is painfully and incurably ill (c) systematically killing off an entire race (d) the murder of a head of state

10. to *incubate*
    (a) protect oneself by lying low (b) protect until ready for hatching (c) involve others in one's misfortune (d) recover slowly from a disease

11. poor *liaison*
    (a) knowledge of enemy troop movements (b) spirit among soldiers (c) support from one's allies (d) intercommunication between units

12. to discover the *liaison*
    (a) illicit love affair (b) plot to overthrow the government (c) underlying cause of something (d) person ultimately responsible

13. to utter *obloquy*
    (a) mild protests (b) confusing remarks (c) condemnatory statements (d) laudatory comments

14. to live in *obloquy*
    (a) uncertainty (b) retirement (c) fear (d) disgrace

15. to *philander*
    (a) be unable to make up one's mind (b) show

cowardice in battle (c) love lightly and insincerely (d) rob and pillage in time of war

16. kept in *quarantine*
(a) ignorance of another's intentions (b) unaccustomed luxury (c) an imposed isolation (d) a military stockade

17. to *resuscitate* someone
(a) inflict pain upon (b) deliberately antagonize (c) put to death by choking (d) revive from near death

18. to ignore the *stricture*
(a) sharp pain (b) critical remark (c) open break (d) broken bone

19. *strictures* upon private enterprise
(a) scholarly books (b) heavy taxes (c) narrow restraints (d) legislative debates

20. a *tenable* position
(a) highly unstable (b) that can be reversed easily (c) that is extremely uncomfortable (d) that can be maintained

21. a *truncated* version
(a) shortened (b) revised (c) falsified (d) extended

Check your answers against the correct ones given below. The answers are not in order; this is to prevent your eye from catching sight of the correct answers before you have had a chance to do the exercise on your own.

11d. 7a. 17d. 1b. 15c. 6a. 9c. 13c. 20d. 3d. 21a. 8b. 14d. 2d. 12a. 19c. 10b. 18b. 4b. 16c. 5c.

Look up in your dictionary all the words for which you gave incorrect answers. Only when you have done this should you go on to the next exercise.

EXERCISE 16B

Each word in Word List 16 is used several times in the following sentences to illustrate different meanings or usage. One of the sentences for each word uses the italicized word incorrectly. You are to circle the letter preceding that sentence.

1. (a) She *abraded* the skin of her arms and legs when she fell down the cliff face. (b) *Abraded* yarns are yarns which have had their surfaces roughened. (c) These constant insults *abraded* his spirit so much that he just gave up. (d) The teacher *abraded* the student before the whole class for coming in late.

2. (a) The testing was done in a small shed set up as a kind of *appendage* to the main building. (b) Courses in fine arts should be regarded as essential and not as mere *appendages* to high school education. (c) She *appendaged* a final chapter to her book in which is summed up her findings.

3. (a) We must attack poverty since it is poverty that *begets* crime. (b) Andrew Marvell's poem speaks of love "*begotten* by despair/Upon impossibility." (c) She continued with her plan although she knew it would *beget* her into trouble. (d) We are told in the Bible that Jacob *begot* many children.

4. (a) Deposits of calcium carbonate cause the bones to *calcify* in old age. (b) Organizations *calcify* as they get older and become resistant to change and fearful of outside interference. (c) She *calcified* the odds so that they were in her favor.

5. (a) Certain substances in the blood cause it to *coagulate* when exposed to the air. (b) She *coagulated* when I questioned her and refused to give any straight answers. (c) Vague feelings of dissatisfaction finally *coagulated* into the certainty that something was wrong. (d) Rennet is a *coagulant* and is used to cause milk to clot.

6. (a) Disraeli's greatest *coup* was his unauthorized purchase for England of a controlling interest in the Suez Canal. (b) The king was overthrown in a palace *coup* and replaced by

his younger brother. (c) She drove up in a sporty looking two-door *coup* she had just bought.

7. (a) She *expatriated* herself because of her deep dissatisfaction with her native land. (b) The salesclerk *expatriated* at length on what a bargain I was getting. (c) Gertrude Stein, a well-known woman of literature, was part of a group of American *expatriates* living in Paris. (d) He returned to this country from Brazil after many years of *expatriation*.

8. (a) The patient's wounds were bathed in a mild *genocidal* solution. (b) The Nazi extermination of the Jews was an act of *genocide*. (c) The gas chamber was but one of the *genocidal* weapons employed by the Nazis. (d) Another act of *genocide* was the wholesale destruction of the Carib Indians of Hispaniola by the Spanish.

9. (a) The period between the catching of a disease and the appearance of the first symptoms is known as the *incubation* period. (b) The plan slowly *incubated* in her mind as she traveled to and from work. (c) The eggs are *incubated* for twenty-one days and are then ready to hatch. (d) He is *incubating* from a serious disease and is at present on an ocean cruise.

10. (a) A *liaison* officer's job is to establish and maintain lines of communication between the various units. (b) She offered to *liaison* me as far as the border, at which point I would be on my own. (c) His numerous *liaisons* with different women gave him a bad reputation in some circles. (d) The farmers and small business people share the same goals, but there is little *liaison* between them.

11. (a) Hamlet's most famous *obloquy* is the one beginning "To be, or not to be." (b) No one came forward to defend me when *obloquy* was heaped upon my good name. (c) She lived out her last days in the *obloquy* of one who had betrayed her country.

12. (a) It's true they like to *philander*, but one of these days they'll marry and settle down. (b) She started with many advantages, but she has *philandered* every opportunity she has had. (c) The newcomer at the club soon developed a reputation as a *philanderer*. (d) "Your *philandering* ways will get you in trouble with your spouse," the friend warned.

13. (a) A four-masted *quarantine* flying the Spanish flag hove into view and commenced firing. (b) Animals brought into the country must be kept in *quarantine* for six months. (c) Only four African countries refused to support the the diplomatic *quarantine* of South Africa during its apartheid rule. (d) He was *quarantined* in his room until the nature of the disease could be ascertained.

14. (a) Mouth-to-mouth *resuscitation* consists of breathing air into the lungs of a person whose breathing has stopped. (b) Her dynamic leadership did much to *resuscitate* the Liberal Party. (c) Efforts to *resuscitate* the drowning victim proved unsuccessful. (d) The money was *resuscitated* from a secret drawer where it had lain hidden for years.

15. (a) By placing *strictures* upon purchases abroad, government hoped to stem the outflow of its gold reserves. (b) The referee stuck to his decision and ignored the *strictures* of the crowd. (c) Such unpopular measures are sure to arouse the *strictures* of the opposition. (d) The earthquake opened up a deep *stricture* in the earth's surface.

16. (a) These scholarships are *tenable* at any approved four-year college. (b) Her theory is a *tenable* one, but I will reserve a final judgment until all the facts are in. (c) Their position was no longer *tenable*, and they ceased their attempts to hold it. (d) Objects of art and other valuable *tenables* can be imported free of duty.

17. (a) A *truncated* line of verse is one lacking an expected final syllable. (b) Such a *truncated* quotation does not do justice to her full

argument. (c) They *truncated* their way around Europe with not a care in the world. (d) A *truncated* pyramid is one which has had its apex removed.

EXERCISE 16C

What does *mean* mean?

Most words have specific meanings which can be located in a dictionary and about which there can be no argument. If you declare that a quadruped is a four-footed animal, no one will argue the point with you. Some words, however, do cause intense argument as to exactly what their meanings are. Much of the world's troubles and misunderstandings are caused by people's having different ideas as to what such words as *freedom, communism,* and *democracy* mean.

Write out in the spaces provided how each of the following people might define *freedom.*

1. a poor, homeless person . . . .

. . . .

. . . .

2. a person serving time in jail . . . .

. . . .

. . . .

3. a slave in pre–Civil War days . . . .

. . . .

. . . .

4. a teenager whose parents maintain strict discipline . . . .

. . . .

Suggest how each of the following might define *democracy.*

5. a professor of political science . . . .

. . . .

. . . .

6. a citizen of fifth-century B.C. Athens . . . .

. . . .

. . . .

7. a person rebelling against a dictator . . . . . .

. . . .

. . . .

8. a ruler who has absolute power . . . .

. . . .

. . . .

WORDLY WISE 16

Don't confuse ABRADE, which means "to scrape away the surface of," with *upbraid,* which means "to scold; to reproach."

The French word COUP (pronounced *koo*) literally means "a blow"; it occurs in a couple of common phrases also taken from the French; a *coup d'etat* (pronounced *koo-day-TA*) is a sudden unseating of an established government; a *coup de grace* (pronounced *koo də GRAS*) is a death blow, an act or event that puts a merciful end to something.

To EXPATRIATE oneself is to go into voluntary exile from one's native land. To *expatiate* (pronounced *ex-PAY-shee-ate*) is to speak or write at length. (The expatriates expatiated at length on their reasons for leaving their native land.)

Etymology

Study the following roots and prefix together with the English words derived from them. Capitalized words are those given in the Word List. You should look up in a dictionary any words that are unfamiliar to you.

Prefix: *ex-* (out) Latin – Examples: *EX*PATRI-
ATE, *ex*pel, *ex*trude

Roots: *patri* (country) Latin – Examples: EX-
*PATRI*ATE, *patri*ot

philo (loving) Greek – Examples: *PHI-*
LANDER, anglo*phile*, *philo*sophy

Word List 17

ADIPOSE	FACTITIOUS	RAREFIED
ARPEGGIO	IMPUGN	SENTIENT
BEHOOVE	INDENT	SUTURE
CANON	LORGNETTE	TERCENTENARY
COHERE	OBSTREPEROUS	VENIAL
DESUETUDE	PLENITUDE	

Look up the words above in your dictionary.
Note that many of them have more than one
meaning. When you feel that you know *all* the
meanings of *all* the words, go on to the exercises
below.

EXERCISE 17A

From the four choices following each phrase
or sentence, you are to circle the letter preceding
the one that is closest in meaning to the italicized
word. Where the same word appears more than
once, you should note that it is being used in
different senses.

1. *adipose* tissue
(a) fatty (b) bone (c) scar (d) muscle

2. to play the *arpeggio*
(a) musical piece for two performers (b)
musical accompaniment (c) stringed instrument resembling a harp (d) notes of a chord
played in quick succession

3. It *behooves* us to leave.
(a) is unnecessary for (b) is fitting for (c) is
inconvenient for (d) beckons

4. the Chaucer *canon*
(a) literary period (b) verse form (c) style of
writing (d) complete works

5. a *canon* of democracy
(a) fervent supporter (b) important principle
(c) sworn enemy (d) brief period

6. to be made a *canon*
(a) priest serving a country district (b) army
officer in charge of artillery (c) navy officer
specializing in gunnery (d) member of the
clergy attached to a cathedral

7. the church *canon*
(a) body of law (b) tower housing the bells (c)
religious center (d) bell rung on special occasions

8. to *cohere*
(a) end (b) help (c) stick (d) separate

9. fallen into *desuetude*
(a) evil ways (b) grievous error (c) disuse (d)
a sleeplike state

10. a *factitious* quality
(a) genuine (b) artificial (c) nonexistent (d)
actual

11. to *impugn* his honesty
(a) vigorously defend (b) believe in (c) vividly
demonstrate (d) call into question

12. to *indent* the line
(a) underline the words of (b) capitalize the
words of (c) space in from the margin (d)
make a space above and below

13. a jewelled *lorgnette*
(a) medallion worn as a queen's symbol of
office (b) pair of eyeglasses with a handle (c)
hinged brooch containing a miniature picture
(d) crown worn as a symbol of royalty

14. to be *obstreperous*
(a) abysmally stupid (b) ill at ease (c) stubbornly defiant (d) fiendishly clever

15. the *plenitude* of deer
(a) abundance (b) scarcity (d) habits (d)
habitat

16. *rarefied* air
(a) lacking warmth (b) extremely dry (c)
extremely humid (d) lacking density

17. to move in *rarefied* circles

(a) monotonously commonplace (b) severely limited (c) stiflingly closed in (d) socially select

18. *sentient* beings

(a) lacking in feeling (b) lacking powers of movement (c) having feelings (d) possessing supernatural powers

19. to *suture* the wound

(a) clean (b) stitch (c) probe (d) cover

20. to celebrate the *tercentenary*

(a) fiftieth anniversary (b) two hundredth anniversary (c) three hundredth anniversary (d) five hundredth anniversary

21. a *venial* offense

(a) deadly (b) unmentionable (c) unpardonable (d) forgivable

Check your answers against the correct ones given below. The answers are not in order; this is to prevent your eye from catching sight of the correct answers before you have had a chance to do the exercise on your own.

3b. 11d. 19b. 10b. 18c. 12c. 7a. 21d. 20c. 13b. 17d. 2d. 4d. 16d. 1a. 9c. 6d. 15a. 8c. 5b. 14c.

Look up in your dictionary all the words for which you gave incorrect answers. Only when you have done this should you go on to the next exercise.

EXERCISE 17B

Each word in Word List 17 is used several times in the sentences below to illustrate different meanings or usage. One of the sentences for each word uses the italicized word incorrectly. You are to circle the letter preceding that sentence.

1. (a) The surgeon had to cut through layers of *adipose* tissue to reach the patient's kidney. (b) *Adiposity* can be reduced by going on a strict diet. (c) The librarian took down an *adipose* leather-bound volume from the shelf.

2. (a) She plays the harp well, but her favorite instrument is the *arpeggio*. (b) He sat at the piano and practiced *arpeggios* for a while. (c) The rippling *arpeggios* of the piece are a severe test of the pianist's skill.

3. (a) He takes care to obey the law as *behooves* the son of a police chief. (b) It ill *behooves* those who kept silent at that time to raise their voices now. (c) It would *behoove* us to examine our motives in wanting to help. (d) The dress *behooved* her as though it had been made for her.

4. (a) The *canon* at St. Matthew's Cathedral graciously offered to receive us. (b) The books of the Apocrypha are not accepted by Protestants as part of the Biblical *canon*. (c) Her outrageous behavior flouts all the *canons* of good taste. (d) The *canons* mounted in the aircraft's wings fire two thousand rounds a minute.

5. (a) Pressure causes the two halves to *cohere*, and great force is needed to separate them. (b) She was a firm *coherent* of the views of Charles Darwin. (c) The book forms a *coherent* whole, with each chapter falling neatly into place. (d) The *cohesion* of the tribe is accounted for by the fact that marriage to persons outside the tribe is banned.

6. (a) After years of *desuetude* the helium-filled airship may be making a comeback. (b) A note of *desuetude* crept into her voice when she realized her request was not going to be met. (c) The old customs are neglected and fall into a state of *desuetude*.

7. (a) Her *factitious* gaiety did not deceive me, and I asked her what was troubling her. (b) The *factitiousness* of the applause was evidenced by the suddenness with which it stopped when the chairperson motioned for silence. (c) To keep the story as *factitious* as possible, the author has eliminated all events that are of doubtful authenticity.

8. (a) The man who had *impugned* his honor was promptly challenged to a duel. (b) She seems to

think that she can break the law with *impugnity*, but she is mistaken. (c) In going over these figures you submitted, I am not *impugning* your honesty.

9. (a) The first word of each paragraph should be *indented* slightly. (b) Columns of figures are *indented* one inch from the margin. (c) There should be an *indentation* here to indicate the new paragraph. (d) You will be *indented* for any expenses incurred by you.

10. (a) Holding it by the handle, she polished the lenses of her *lorgnette* vigorously. (b) The duchess peered at the young man through her *lorgnette,* then lowered it and turned to me. (c) She finished the dance with a graceful *lorgnette* and bowed low to the audience.

11. (a) Members of the legislature grew so *obstreperous* that the sitting was suspended. (b) She stubbornly refuses to cooperate, and I could see no reason for her *obstreperousness.* (c) The penicillin shots quickly cured the *obstreperous* infection in his throat.

12. (a) She was always uttering *plenitudes* like "Haste makes waste." (d) Death came to him in the *plenitude* of health, vigor, and fortune. (c) Grain was in short supply, but there was a *plenitude* of wildlife in the region.

13. (a) He was quite at home in the *rarefied* realm of country houses and grand balls. (b) The *rarefied* air at the mountain top makes breathing difficult. (c) These coins are extremely *rarefied*; this one, for example, costs two thousand dollars.

14. (a) He believes that flying saucers manned by *sentient* and intelligent beings have landed. (b) *Sentience,* though most marked in human beings, is not exclusive to them. (c) In his madness he addressed the stones as though they were *sentient* and could sympathize with his plight. (d) She wants nothing to do with you, and these are my *sentients* also.

15. (a) The two ends of the blood vessel were carefully *sutured* together. (b) His arm was immobilized to prevent his moving it and breaking open the *sutures.* (c) The surgeons use fine silk to *suture* wounds because it is non-absorbent. (d) She *sutured* three ribs and bruised her spine in the fall.

16. (a) The year 1920 marked the *tercentenary* of the landing of the *Mayflower.* (b) *Tercentenaries* have passed since Caesar's legions occupied Gaul. (c) People came from miles around to attend the *tercentenary* celebration of the founding of the town back in 1666.

17. (a) The errors in this book are *venial* and in no way detract from its importance. (b) The book distinguishes between *venial* sins, which are forgivable, and mortal sins, which are not. (c) The bottles of wine and *venials* they had brought with them were quickly consumed.

EXERCISE 17C

Complete the analogies below by underlining the numbered pair of words that stand in the same relationship to each other as do the first pair of words.

1. sentient:feel:: (1) audible:hear (2) olfactory:smell (3) visible:see (4) tactile:touch (5) mobile:move

2. pig:porcine:: (1) bacon:oleaginous (2) ape:simian (3) pork:meat (4) human:simian (5) giraffe:tall

3. vernal:spring::(1) rococo:art (2) carnal:spirit (3) venial:sin (4) freshet:stream (5) nocturnal:night

4. genocide:race:: (1) migration:nation (2) robbery:theft (3) crime:punishment (4) suicide:oneself (5) homicide:murder

5. zenith:nadir:: (1) furthest:nearest (2) earliest:latest (3) highest:lowest (4) innermost:outermost (5) widest:narrowest

6. millenium:tercentenary:: (1) 1,000:3,000 (2) 100:300 (3) 1,000:300 (4) 100:50 (5) 1,000:100

7. seamstress:stitch:: (1) surgeon:suture (2) stitch:needle (3) needle:thread (4) suture:thread (5) dress shop:surgery

8. tier:tear:: (1) cry:weep (2) new:flow (3) row:balcony (4) night:day (5) canon:cannon

9. ring:annular:: (1) square:circle (2) cancel:annul (3) year:annual (4) season:vernal (5) ball:spherical

10. descry:see:: (1) decry:hear (2) observe:denounce (3) hear:observe (4) decry:denounce (5) ear:eye

WORDLY WISE 17

FACTITIOUS means "not genuine; artificial" (factitious applause); *fictitious* means "represented as real but not actually existing" (fictitious characters in a novel); *factious* (Word List 15) means "causing or produced by strife or quarrelling." A factitious report is one that is not genuine and is perhaps got up for some ulterior purpose; a fictitious report is one that is wholly imaginary; a factious report is one calculated to stir up strife and quarrelling.

VENIAL means "capable of being forgiven" (a venial sin); *venal* (Word List 1) means "characterized by bribery or corruption" (venal officials); *vernal* (Word List 15) means "of or relating to spring" (vernal flowers).

LORGNETTE is pronounced *lor-NYET*.

Etymology

Study the roots and prefix given below together with the English words derived from them. Capitalized words are those given in the Word List. You should look up in a dictionary any words that are unfamiliar to you.

Prefix: *co-* (together) Latin — Examples: *CO-HERE*, *co*habit

Roots: *here, hes* (cling) Latin — Examples: *CO-HERE*, ad*here*, ad*hes*ive

sens, sent (feel) Latin — Examples: *SENT*IENT, in*sens*ate, *sens*e

plenus (full) Latin — Examples: *PLENI-TUDE*, *plen*ty, *plen*ary

---

Word List 18

AFFIDAVIT	FRESHET	RECALCITRANT
AVUNCULAR	INCHOATE	SIMULATE
BENEDICTION	LACUNA	TEMPERA
CEREMENTS	NEXUS	TRADUCE
COLLOQUY	ORTHODOX	VERDIGRIS
ENERVATE	PROLIX	

Look up the words above in your dictionary. Note that many of them have more than one meaning. When you feel that you know *all* the meanings of *all* the words, go on to the exercises below.

EXERCISE 18A

From the four choices following each phrase or sentence, you are to circle the letter preceding the one that is closest in meaning to the italicized word. Where the same word appears more than once, you should note that it is being used in different senses.

1. to sign the *affidavit*
(a) order requisitioning military supplies (b) statement bequeathing property to one's heirs (c) bill passed by both houses of Congress (d) written statement made under oath

2. an *avuncular* manner
(a) like that of a king (b) like that of a stranger (c) like that of a brother (d) like that of an uncle

3. to utter a *benediction*
(a) trite saying (b) curse (c) blessing (d) sign of relief

4. *cerements* of rich satin
(a) coronation robes (b) christening clothes (c) burial wrappings (d) heavy drapes

5. to hold a *colloquy*
(a) inquiry as to the cause of death (b) mass

meeting (c) informal discussion (d) view that is intensely unpopular

6. to *enervate*
   (a) restore energy to (b) refer indirectly to (c) deprive of vitality (d) indicate forcefully

7. a spring *freshet*
   (a) shower of brief duration (b) flooding of a stream (c) cleaning of a house or room (d) growth of a plant

8. an *inchoate* plot
   (a) large-scale (b) minutely detailed (c) rebellious (d) incompletely formed

9. a large *lacuna*
   (a) error (b) gap (c) inheritance (c) reserve

10. to see the *nexus*
    (a) connection (b) result (c) parallel (d) purpose

11. *orthodox* views
    (a) conforming to what is generally accepted (b) opposed to what is generally accepted (c) lacking precise form or substance (d) outdated

12. *prolix* arguments
    (a) tricky (b) false (c) unavoidable (d) wordy

13. a *recalcitrant* child
    (a) emotionally disturbed (b) stubbornly disobedient (c) physically handicapped (d) intellectually gifted

14. to *simulate* fear
    (a) increase (b) show (c) feign (d) hide

15. to use *tempera*
    (a) pigments suspended in oils (b) pigments suspended in wax (c) dry pigments (d) pigments suspended in gelatinous substances

16. to *traduce* someone
    (a) greet (b) encounter (c) trick (d) slander

17. to *traduce* a principle
    (a) betray (b) establish (c) defend (d) preserve

18. to prevent *verdigris*
    (a) a disease of the skin caused by vitamin deficiency (b) a greenish film formed on copper, brass, and bronze (c) a slimy film formed on underwater structures (d) a dizzy feeling caused by looking down from a height

Check your answers against the correct ones given below. The answers are not in order; this is to prevent your eye from catching sight of the correct answers before you have had a chance to do the exercise on your own.

12d. 2d. 14c. 8d. 5c. 16d. 4c. 18b. 10a. 11a. 7b. 17a. 1d. 15d. 3c. 13b. 9b. 6c.

Look up in your dictionary all the words for which you gave incorrect answers. Only when you have done this should you go on to the next exercise.

EXERCISE 18B

Each word in Word List 18 is used several times in the sentences below to illustrate different meanings or usage. One of the sentences for each word uses the italicized word incorrectly. You are to circle the letter preceding that sentence.

1. (a) The senator signed an *affidavit* disclaiming any financial interest in the proposed deal. (b) The governor's name will be entered in the primary unless she signs an *affidavit* stating that she is not a candidate. (c) He raised his right hand and swore an *affidavit* to tell the truth, the whole truth, and nothing but the truth.

2. (a) He regarded his daily walk with his nephew as one of his *avuncular* duties. (b) His *avuncular* manner won over the children, who addressed him as "Uncle Fred." (c) He was the children's *avuncular*, the man to whom they took all their troubles.

3. (a) She drank the *benediction* I had prepared and was soon fast asleep. (b) She departed for

74

the city with her parents' *benediction* but with little else. (c) The old man knelt to receive the *benediction* of the rabbi.

4. (a) The body, clothed in rich linen *cerements,* was laid to rest in the burial vault. (b) Makeup was used to smooth the harsh *cerements* of the performer's face before she appeared on television. (c) The jewels and richly embroidered *cerements* of the dead kings and queens were stolen by thieves who broke into the royal tombs.

5. (a) The two senators held a brief *colloquy* before entering the chamber to cast their votes. (b) Informal *colloquies* are held before the meeting so that delegates can sound out each other's views. (c) Hamlet's most famous *colloquy* begins, "To be, or not to be."

6. (a) The government had been *enervated* by corruption and was ripe for overthrow. (b) The heat and humidity are extremely *enervating*; no one wants to do anything. (c) These malarial attacks leave me quite *enervated*, and only rest can restore my vitality. (d) She *enervated* indirectly to her own part in the affair but did not elaborate on it.

7. (a) *Freshets,* gathered from the river bank, are strewn on the dirt floors of the huts. (b) Repairs to roads and bridges must wait until the spring *freshets* have subsided. (c) *Freshets* caused by thawing snow have washed out parts of the road ahead. (d) Interest in the forthcoming election is apparent from the *freshet* of campaign biographies.

8. (a) Plans so far are *inchoate* and need the arrival of a leader who can pull them together. (b) Out of this *inchoate* mass of stellar dust and gases was formed our solar system. (c) Her strength lies in her ability to express the *inchoate* needs of the people. (d) Those refusing to go along with his plans were ruthlessly *inchoated.*

9. (a) Research is filling the *lacuna* of these early years of Columbus' life. (b) Our knowledge of these sources of radiation is increasing, but many *lacunae* remain. (c) A full-length *lacuna* coat can cost over one thousand dollars.

10. (a) Cash payment is the only universal *nexus* linking person to person. (b) The *nexus* between the needs of the individual and the aspirations of the society should be a close one. (c) Light rays are brought to a *nexus* after passing through the lens.

11. (a) Her *orthodox* views and standing in the community make her ideal for the position of community relations director. (b) *Orthodoxes* grew in profusion around the edge of the lake. (c) She was a profound thinker who successfully challenged the *orthodoxies* of her time. (d) The revisionist theories of Yugoslavia's Tito were at odds with the *orthodox* Marxism of Moscow.

12. (a) Her style is *prolix*, bursting with subordinate clauses and parenthetical asides. (b) To a generation brought up on Hemingway, the Victorian novelists must seem unduly *prolix*. (c) The *prolixity* of her speeches discourages audiences from giving them the attention they perhaps deserve. (d) The firefighters are required to live in close *prolixity* to the firehouse.

13. (a) *Recalcitrant* elements were packed off to labor camps for reeducation by the regime. (b) This is a particularly *recalcitrant* form of the disease for which no cure has been discovered. (c) The mule, though a useful beast of burden, is the most *recalcitrant* of animals. (d) The walls and ceilings had been painted a *recalcitrant* shade of brown.

14. (a) The prospective buyer *simulated* indifference in the hope of bringing the price down. (b) This purse costs fifty dollars, but a similar one of *simulated* alligator sells for only ten dollars. (c) Soldiers train for weeks under *simulated* battle conditions. (d) The appearance of the astronaut at the school did much to *simulate* interest in .space exploration among the students.

15. (a) The dog has *tempera* and should be taken to a veterinarian immediately. (b) The artist prepared her own *tempera* by mixing the pigments with egg white. (c) He works mostly in *tempera* but does an occasional oil painting on commission.

16. (a) He is known for *traducing* anyone he doesn't like. (b) The correct answer can easily be *traduced* once the value of "x" is known. (c) I shall sue those who have slandered me, and I dare my *traducers* to face me in court. (d) Those who would *traduce* this great and good person should examine their motives carefully.

17. (a) The brasses can be treated to prevent *verdigris* from forming if this is desired. (b) A *verdigrised* bronze statue graced the village square. (c) The patina of old copper is actually a greenish-blue copper carbonate known as *verdigris*. (d) An acute attack of *verdigris* assailed me when I looked down from the top of the tower.

EXERCISE 18C

This exercise combines synonyms and antonyms. You are to underline the word which is *either* most similar in meaning *or* most nearly opposite in meaning to the capitalized word. Underline only one word for each question after deciding that it is either an antonym or a synonym and write A (for antonym) or S (for synonym) after the capitalized word. Allow only fifteen minutes for this test. If you cannot answer a question, go on to the next one without delay. If you have time left over at the end, go back and try to fill in unanswered questions.

26 or over correct:	excellent
22 to 25 correct:	good
21 or under correct:	thorough review of A exercises indicated

1. GENUINE . . . .
venial sentient adipose factitious contumacious

2. FORGIVABLE . . . .
unctuous obstreperous retrograde venial nihilistic

3. ATTACHMENT . . . .
provender appendage mountebank periphery affidavit

4. FEIGN . . . .
simulate traduce behoove impugn indent

5. DENSE . . . .
factious recalcitrant avuncular inchoate rarefied

6. ENERGIZE . . . .
philander cohere beget incubate enervate

7. SHORTENED . . . .
kinetic orotund rarefied adipose truncated

8. BLESSING . . . .
affidavit mountebank prelate benediction levy

9. SCARCITY . . . .
plenitude provender nexus suture concatenation

10. FATHER (verb) . . . .
behoove enervate traduce beget calcify

11. DISCUSSION . . . .
obloquy nexus lorgnette liaison colloquy

12. SEPARATE . . . .
resuscitate impugn simulate descry cohere

13. SATIATED . . . .
rarefied jaded obstreperous orotund porcine

14. FATTY . . . .
avuncular inchoate adipose truncated redundant

15. SLANDER . . . .
enervate beget calcify traduce adjure

16. COMPLETE . . . .
factitious sentient kinetic fulsome inchoate

17. REVIVE . . . .
resuscitate indent impute anneal permeate

18. TOUGHEN . . . .
abrade cohere incubate anneal resuscitate

19. FEELING . . . .
savant factitious sentient contumacious ubiquitous

20. COOPERATIVE . . . .
prolix obstreperous tenable redundant sanguine

21. COMMAND . . . .
descry abrade adjure philander permeate

22. PRINCIPLE . . . .
arpeggio periphery tempera canon colloquy

23. DISUSE . . . .
desuetude tautology verdigris recalcitrance colloquy

24. OBEDIENT . . . .
jaded recalcitrant retrograde unctuous nihilistic

25. HONOR . . . .
tempera verdigris obloquy colloquy quarantine

26. GAP . . . .
lorgnette suture dialectic nexus lacuna

27. DEFENSIBLE . . . .
tenable carnal porcine kinetic ubiquitous

28. CONNECTION . . . .
periphery garrote junto nadir nexus

29. ENCOMIUM . . . .
natation stricture liaison quarantine freshet

30. TERSE . . . .
contumacious truncated prolix unmitigated ubiquitous

WORDLY WISE 18

INCHOATE is pronounced *in-KO-et* or *IN-kə-wate.*

The plural of LACUNA is *lacunae* or *lacunas.*

ORTHODOX means "conforming to generally accepted beliefs." Its antonym is *heterodox*, which means "contrary or opposed to some acknowledged standard or belief." A more common antonym is *unorthodox.*

SIMULATE means "to feign" (to simulate death). *Dissimulate* means "to conceal one's true feelings under a false appearance" (he dissimulates, hoping not to betray his true feelings).

Etymology

Study the roots given below together with the English words derived from them. Capitalized words are those given in the Word List. You should look up in a dictionary any words that are unfamiliar to you.

Roots:　*bene* (good) Latin – Examples: *BENE-*DICTION, *bene*volent, *bene*fit
(Review) *dic, dict* (say) Latin – Examples: BENE*DICT*ION, pre*dict*, *dict*ion
loqui (speak) Latin – Examples: COL-*LOQUY*, *loqu*acious, e*loqu*ent
ortho (straight) Greek – Examples: *ORTHO*DOX, *ortho*graphy, *ortho*dontist

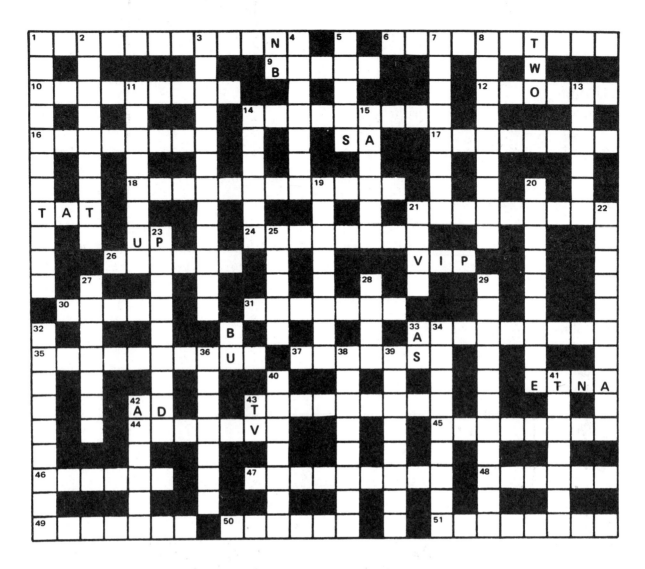

ACROSS

1. stubbornly disobedient
6. an imposed isolation
9. to become the father of
10. adverse criticism; a critical remark
12. excessively wordy
14. to become semi-solid; to clot
16. to imitate or feign
17. the systematic killing of a whole race
18. stubbornly or noisily defiant
21. a pair of eyeglasses with a handle
24. to deprive of vitality; to enfeeble
26. of or relating to woodland (8)
30. an important principle
31. intercommunication between units
33. kindly and indulgent as befits an uncle
35. not genuine; artificial or forced
37. of animal fat; fatty
43. having a part cut off; shortened
44. to be fitting or necessary
45. to protect until ready for hatching
46. that can be forgiven; pardonable
47. to love lightly and insincerely
48. to call into question
49. a painting medium of pigment and egg white
50. surgical stitch used to close a wound
51. capable of feeling; conscious

DOWN

1. to revive from near death
2. burial clothes
3. a three hundredth anniversary
4. that can be held or maintained
5. a link or connection
7. the notes of a chord played in quick succession
8. a (usually inessential) attachment
11. a speaking together; an informal discussion
13. to space a word or line in from the margin
14. to stick together
15. a gap or blank space
19. lacking density
20. a state of disuse
21. to wage or conduct, as a war (14)
22. one who chooses to live in exile
23. fullness; abundance
25. the low point, as of a career (14)
27. to become hard and stony
28. a highly successful suddenly executed stratagem
29. a blessing spoken by a person
32. a written statement made on oath
34. a greenish coating formed on copper, brass, and bronze
36. utter disgrace
38. recently begun; rudimentary
39. conforming to what is generally accepted
40. a flooding or overflowing, as of a stream
41. to attack or lower the reputation of
42. to rub the surface of; to scrape

Chapter Seven

Word List 19

ALLUVIAL	INFIDEL	PEON
ATELIER	LAMPOON	RECIPIENT
COLLATION	LEONINE	RUSTIC
EFFUSIVE	MALLEABLE	SINGULAR
FETID	NUMISMATIST	SUBORN
IGNEOUS	OUSTER	UNCTION

Look up the words above in your dictionary. Note that many of them have more than one meaning. When you feel that you know *all* the meanings of *all* the words, go on to the exercises below.

EXERCISE 19A

From the four choices following each phrase or sentence, you are to circle the letter preceding the one that is closest in meaning to the italicized word. Where the same word appears more than once, you should note that it is being used in different senses.

1. *alluvial* clays
   (a) deposited by glacial action (b) deposited by flowing water (c) deposited by erupting volcanoes (d) deposited on the sea bed

2. a crowded *atelier*
   (a) artist's studio (b) hotel for transients (c) horse drawn bus (d) motor-driven pleasure craft

3. an enjoyable *collation*
   (a) round of cards (b) brief rest (c) short trip (d) light meal

4. *effusive* thanks
   (a) unwillingly expressed (b) overly demonstrative (c) haltingly expressed (d) suitably phrased

5. *fetid* slums
   (a) broken-down (b) crime-ridden (c) widespread (d) foul-smelling

6. *igneous* rocks
   (a) laid down by water (b) produced by volcanic action (c) of very great age (d) of a diamondlike hardness

7. an *infidel* sect
   (a) without a recognized leader (b) pro-Christian (c) nonviolent (d) nonbelievers in the prevailing religion

8. to *lampoon* someone
   (a) emulate (b) envy (c) satirize (d) desert

9. a *leonine* head
   (a) ferretlike (b) foxlike (c) horselike (d) lionlike

10. *malleable* metals
    (a) capable of withstanding enormous strain without bending (b) incapable of conducting electricity (c) incapable of being magnetized (d) capable of being hammered into shape

11. a *malleable* personality
    (a) sunny (b) gloomy (c) cast in a rigid mold (d) easily influenced

12. an ardent *numismatist*
    (a) collector of stamps (b) collector of coins (c) collector of butterflies (d) collector of birds' eggs

13. to call for one's *ouster*
    (a) ticket of admission (b) personal servant (c) forcible expulsion (d) weatherproof outer garment

14. a Latin-American *peon*
    (a) unskilled laborer (b) small farm (c) wealthy landowner (d) large estate

15. the *recipient* of money
    (a) donor (b) offer (c) receiver (d) amount

16. *rustic* homes
    (a) of the wealthy (b) of the country (c) of the city (d) of the poor

17. a *singular* noun
    (a) denoting maleness (b) denoting femaleness
    (c) denoting only one (d) denoting many

18. a *singular* affair
    (a) secret (b) forbidden (c) lengthy (d) strange

19. a person of *singular* charm
    (a) unctuous (b) carefully cultivated (c) rare
    (d) disturbing

20. the *singularity* of the individual
    (a) separateness (b) totality (c) moodiness (d)
    incomprehensibility

21. The guards were *suborned.*
    (a) bludgeoned from behind (b) dismissed (c)
    punished for insolence (d) secretly induced to
    do something unlawful

22. to *suborn* a witness
    (a) call before a court (b) utter slander against
    (c) inflict pain upon (d) induce to commit
    perjury

23. the act of *unction*
    (a) creating a masterpiece (b) anointing with
    oil (c) crowning a monarch (d) renouncing
    one's sins

24. to prepare an *unction*
    (a) paper giving one's views (b) sacrifice to the
    gods (c) substance or thing that soothes (d)
    dinner celebrating a religious holiday

Check your answers against the correct ones given below. The answers are not in order; this is to prevent your eye from catching sight of the correct answers before you have had a chance to do the exercise on your own.

16b. 5d. 15c. 22d. 10d. 21d. 7d. 13c. 17c. 2a. 12b. 1b. 20a. 4b. 8c. 11d. 18d. 19c. 6b. 23b. 14a. 3d. 9d. 24c.

Look up in your dictionary all the words for which you gave incorrect answers. Only when you have done this should you go on to the next exercise.

EXERCISE 19B

Each word in Word List 19 is used several times in the sentences below to illustrate different meanings or usage. One of the sentences for each word uses the italicized word incorrectly. You are to circle the letter preceding that sentence.

1. (a) The *alluvial* soil of the valley is extremely fertile. (b) An *alluvial* plain is one formed from materials deposited by rivers and streams. (c) The *alluvium* of the area consists of silty clay deposited over the past million years. (d) They constructed an *alluvium* from which they could observe the birds without being seen.

2. (a) Most of the artists had their *ateliers* on the famed Left Bank of Paris. (b) The *atelier* took our suitcases and led us to our room. (c) The young painter appeared at Rembrandt's *atelier* and begged to be taken on as an apprentice.

3. (a) A *collation* was taken up among the members which raised the sum of sixty dollars. (b) After a *collation* of cheese and pickled beets we continued our journey. (c) She was too busy to go out to lunch and contented herself with a *collation* at her desk.

4. (a) She thanked him *effusively* for what had been, after all, a very small favor. (b) So *effusive* was he in his greeting to us that I was actually a little embarrassed. (c) Their goal proved a lot more *effusive* than they had at first thought it would be. (d) They are highly demonstrative people, so don't be surprised by their *effusiveness.*

5. (a) The German army made a *fetid* of discipline. (b) The *fetid* air assailed our nostrils, and we made haste to open the windows. (c) The streets were *fetid* with rotting vegetables and strewn garbage.

6. (a) *Igneous* rocks are formed by the solidifying of molten material called magma. (b) Lava and

other *igneous* rocks are found in areas of volcanic activity. (c) He was a person of such *igneous* crudity that I was ashamed of him.

7. (a) The book questioning the government's ethics was dismissed as the work of an *infidel*. (b) His wife recounted numerous *infidels* of her husband when she sued for divorce. (c) The Moslems fought to repel the *infidel* Crusaders from the Holy Land.

8. (a) The book *lampoons* some of the more prominent figures in the nation. (b) Goya's official portraits of Spanish royalty were actually thinly veiled *lampoons*. (c) An anonymously-written *lampoon* of a presidential press conference has been circulating in Washington. (d) He stood in the prow of the boat and fired the *lampoon* at the whale.

9. (a) His proud bearing and shaggy golden locks gave him a *leonine* appearance. (b) The lioness was captured with her two *leonines* and shipped off to a European zoo. (c) With a *leonine* roar he flung himself at his tormentor. (d) The book contains just about every fact known about lions and should appeal to all lovers of things *leonine*.

10. (a) When iron is mixed with carbon, it becomes very *malleable*. (b) Gold is so *malleable* that it can be beaten into leaf four-millionths of an inch thick. (c) I am quite *malleable* to your suggestion that we delay discussions. (d) The *malleability* of young minds places a great responsibility on those who teach.

11. (a) This particular coin is so common that it has no *numismatic* value. (b) The coin auction was attended by *numismatists* from all over the country. (c) She has written extensively on *numismatics* and has catalogued many coin collections for museums. (d) The coins are kept in *numismatically* sealed cases to control temperature and humidity.

12. (a) When the team lost five straight games, fans called for the *ouster* of the coach. (b) The children at the orphanage are taken for an *ouster* every Saturday afternoon. (c) His inability to bring together the various factions in the party led to his *ouster* from the position of leadership. (d) She was *ousted* from her position as treasurer when the shortage of funds was discovered.

13. (a) The system of *peonage*, under which convicts are leased out to contractors, should be brought to an end. (b) The people object to working such long hours for a *peon's* wages. (c) The *peons* who work on the large estates have been forced into servitude by debt. (d) The people who work on the farm earn less than ten *peons* a day.

14. (a) I took two aspirin tablets in the hope of breaking a *recipient* cold. (b) She was the *recipient* of over twenty honorary degrees from universities here and abroad. (c) The *recipient* of the package must sign for it.

15. (a) I addressed my questions to one of the *rustics* who sat outside the village inn. (b) The *rustic* charm of the village brings visitors from all over the state. (c) *Rustic* work is the name given to furniture made of roughly-finished tree limbs. (d) At ninety, his joints were *rustic* with age, and he walked with considerable difficulty.

16. (a) If the subject is plural, then the verb must agree and cannot be *singular*. (b) Sherlock Holmes believed it to be the most *singular* case he had ever been called upon to solve. (c) Why did she *singular* me out for punishment and ignore the others? (d) The *singularity* of the individual is expressed in an infinite variety of ways.

17. (a) She was accused of *subornation* after her attempt to induce the witness to give false evidence was revealed. (b) If the lawyer did *suborn* the witness, then the witness's evi-

dence is worthless. (c) The kidnap plot depended on whether the child's nurse could be *suborned*. (d) She was *suborned* to appear in court to answer charges of perjury.

18. (a) The doctor applied an *unction* to the patient's burns. (b) The *unction* in her voice annoyed me as I don't believe she was sincere in her sympathy. (c) The accident occurred at the *unction* of the highway and the railroad. (d) The act of *unction*, in which the monarch is anointed with holy oil, is the most sacred part of the coronation.

EXERCISE 19C

LEONINE means "of or like a lion," and *simian* (Word List 13) means "of or like an ape." Some other similar adjectival forms are given below. Match these adjectives with the names of the animals in the right hand column.

1. murine	(	)	bear
2. cervine	(	)	cat
3. porcine	(	)	cow
4. caprine	(	)	deer
5. vulpine	(	)	dog
6. ovine	(	)	fox
7. equine	(	)	goat
8. bovine	(	)	horse
9. canine	(	)	mouse
10. feline	(	)	pig
11. lupine	(	)	sheep
12. ursine	(	)	wolf

WORDLY WISE 19

A COLLATION was originally a light meal served in monasteries during the reading of "Collations," the lives of the Church fathers. It refers now to any meal served at an irregular hour.

Etymology

Study the following root together with the English words derived from it. Capitalized words are those given in the Word List. You should look up in a dictionary any words that are unfamiliar to you.

Root: *ignis* (fire) Latin — Examples: *IGNE*OUS, *igni*te, *igni*tion

---

Word List 20

ABEYANCE	INDEMNITY	RATIFY
AFFLATUS	JOCULAR	ROSEATE
ARCHIPELAGO	LEGATE	SCINTILLA
CASUISTRY	MACHINATIONS	SPATIAL
DULCET	MUNDANE	TYRO
EXTIRPATE	OSTRACIZE	
FULMINATE	PENDANT	

Look up the words above in your dictionary. Note that many of them have more than one meaning. When you feel that you know *all* the meanings of *all* the words, go on to the exercises below.

EXERCISE 20A

From the four choices following each phrase or sentence, you are to circle the letter preceding the one that is closest in meaning to the italicized word. Where the same word appears more than once, you should note that it is being used in different senses.

1. held in *abeyance*
(a) temporary suspension (b) secret session (c) contempt of court (d) high esteem

2. a powerful *afflatus*
(a) being (b) purpose (c) inspiration (d) event

3. They explore the *archipelago*.
(a) upper reaches of the atmosphere (b) coastal strip bordering dense jungle (c) elevated area of level land (d) sea containing many scattered islands

4. familar with the *archipelago*
(a) lower reaches of the atmosphere (b) cluster of islands (c) area of land below sea level (d) dense jungle

5. to employ *casuistry*
(a) delaying tactics (b) subtle but false reasoning (c) overwhelming physical force (d) supernatural powers

6. *dulcet* tones
   (a) pleading (b) harsh (c) threatening (d) soothing

7. to *extirpate* something
   (a) root out (b) favor (c) cultivate (d) shape

8. to cause it to *fulminate*
   (a) end (b) explode (c) subside (d) expand

9. to ignore the *fulminations*
   (a) inevitable repercussions (b) cries for help (c) warning signs (d) vigorous denunciations

10. to demand an *indemnity*
    (a) apology for insulting behavior (b) repayment for loss or damage (c) guarantee of good behavior (d) detailed profit and loss statement

11. a *jocular* remark
    (a) offensive (b) joking (c) ambiguous (d) concise

12. the Roman *legate*
    (a) council (b) palace (c) reign (d) envoy

13. an opponent's *machinations*
    (a) crafty schemes (b) rough calculations (c) gross tactical errors (d) protestations of innocence

14. *mundane* affairs
    (a) foreign (b) worldly (c) protracted (d) spiritual

15. to *ostracize* someone
    (a) flatter insincerely (b) inoculate against disease (c) heap praise upon (d) banish from favor

16. a large *pendant*
    (a) curved arch (b) jewelled casket (c) hanging ornament (d) roll of money

17. to *ratify* an agreement
    (a) angrily denounce (b) read carefully (c) work for (d) formally approve

18. *roseate* views
    (a) strongly expressed (b) secretly felt (c) overly optimistic (d) overly pessimistic

19. *roseate* petals
    (a) blue (b) white (c) yellow (d) pink

20. a *scintilla* of evidence
    (a) abundance (b) irrefutable chain (c) tiny particle (d) brilliant presentation

21. *spatial* concerns
    (a) relating to space (b) large (c) short-lived (d) interconnected

22. a *tyro*
    (a) expert (b) brute (c) dictator (d) beginner

Check your answers against the correct ones given below. The answers are not in order; this is to prevent your eye from catching sight of the correct answers before you have had a chance to do the exercise on your own.

4b. 20c. 1a. 12d. 2c. 10b. 21a. 7a. 13a. 17d. 16c. 5b. 15d. 22d. 6d. 19d. 18c. 11b. 8b. 14b. 3d. 9d.

Look up in your dictionary all the words for which you gave incorrect answers. Only when you have done this should you go on to the next exercise.

EXERCISE 20B

Each word in Word List 20 is used several times in the sentences below to illustrate different meanings or usage. One of the sentences for each word uses the italicized word incorrectly. You are to circle the letter preceding that sentence.

1. (a) The deal was held in *abeyance* until all the parties to it had expressed agreement. (b) The practice has fallen into *abeyance*, and there is no immediate prospect of reviving it. (c) The *abeyance*, drawn by a pair of spirited horses, pulled up outside the house.

2. (a) A poem is not created by some mysterious *afflatus* descending into the poet from on

high. (b) Apparently in the grip of a sudden *afflatus*, the artist had never before been so inspired. (c) The *afflatus* of the balloon was caused by a leak near the opening.

3. (a) As one crosses the *archipelago*, one is never more than ten miles from the nearest island. (b) The *archipelago* comprises a total of eighty islands, half of them uninhabited. (c) After a visit to Athens, we leave for a tour of the Aegean *archipelago*. (d) Philip of Macedonia was the *archipelago* of the entire Greek mainland.

4. (a) No amount of *casuistry* can conceal the fact that we suffered a great defeat. (b) Numerous *casuistries* were inflicted on both sides in the bloody battle. (c) Those *casuistical* arguments may have convinced you, but I was not deceived by them.

5. (a) The dessert was a rich cherry concoction, a little too *dulcet* for my taste. (b) Her *dulcet* voice was like music to our ears. (c) The *dulcet* tones of the violin played by a virtuoso is one of the most heavenly of sounds.

6. (a) The government will make every effort to *extirpate* discrimination based on racism. (b) The growth on the patient's lung can be *extirpated* by radiation without resorting to surgery. (c) The lights at the camp must be *extirpated* promptly at ten o'clock. (d) The *extirpation* of evil is an endeavor that should not be left solely to religion.

7. (a) Ammonia and silver oxide *fulminate* when combined under the right conditions. (b) "I'll have the law on you for this," he *fulminated* when he saw how he had been tricked. (c) Mercury *fulminate* is an explosive compound used in detonators and blasting caps. (d) Her scientific career *fulminated* in her appointment to the National Academy of Sciences.

8. (a) The plan offers an *indemnity* to workers who are unable to find new jobs. (b) All those who suffered loss were *indemnified* by the company. (c) The army paid a large *indemnity* to those whose land it had taken over. (d) The people sought *indemnity* from the floods by moving to higher ground.

9. (a) The war was a topic too tragic to be dealt with seriously, so they spoke of it *jocularly*. (b) I thought his *jocular* remarks were out of place at his brother's funeral. (c) The *jocular* veins are the two large veins of the neck that carry blood from the head. (d) Her speech was enlivened with numerous *jocularities* and witticisms.

10. (a) Marc Antony's *legate* requested Caesar's permission for Antony to remain in Egypt. (b) Members of the Swiss *legation* were housed at the capital's best hotel for the duration of the conference. (c) The papal *legates* are meeting with representatives of the Protestant and Greek Orthodox churches. (d) The case was *legated* right up to the Supreme Court.

11. (a) The *machinations* of the mass media manipulators are so obvious that we are scarcely aware of them. (b) The looms are run by small one-horsepower *machinations* that require little maintenance. (c) I was too clever for her and easily thwarted her *machinations*.

12. (a) The reviewer is not expected to refer to such *mundane* matters as the price of the book. (b) The *mundaneness* of their lives was enlivened by an occasional visit to the movies. (c) Some people think the clergy should concern itself with people's spiritual needs and leave more *mundane* matters to the social agencies. (d) It was *mundaned* by the government that all adult males were eligible for military service.

13. (a) Animals brought into the country are *ostracized* for six months to prevent the spread of disease. (b) The players who had been accused of taking bribes were *ostracized* by their teammates. (c) In the past in some places, marrying beneath one's station in life led to one's social *ostracism*.

14. (a) The *pendants* that swung from her ears were tiny pieces of carved jade. (b) The chandeliers were enormous; some had over five hundred crystal *pendants*. (c) The administration of justice is very slow with some cases having been *pendant* in the courts for four years.

15. (a) All senior presidential appointments must be *ratified* by the Senate. (b) All members must be *ratified* of the meeting at least three days before. (c) Heads of state of the countries involved have agreed to *ratify* the mutual aid treaty.

16. (a) The *roseates* I planted in the spring are now in full bloom. (b) The *roseate* tips of the petals merge with the deep crimson of the centers. (c) I'm afraid I don't take such a *roseate* view of the situation as my colleagues do.

17. (a) There is not a *scintilla* of evidence linking her with the crime. (b) A *scintilla* of doubt in the witness's voice encouraged the lawyer to press her cross-examination. (c) A magnificent *scintilla* of ships appeared on the horizon on their way to the Indies.

18. (a) To meet the exacting demands of the client, the architect had had to overcome a number of *spatial* problems. (b) *Spatial* balance consists of the judicial arrangement of building masses with open spaces. (c) In addition to its *spatial* dimensions, an object has a dimension in time. (d) She was delighted with her new office, which was much more *spatial* than her old one.

19. (a) Ski classes are conducted for everyone from the veriest *tyro* to the expert. (b) His attempts to *tyro* over his employees led to much dissatisfaction. (c) For a *tyro*, you show a lot of ability.

EXERCISE 20C

In each of the following sentences a word is omitted. From the four words provided, select the one that best completes the sentence. Allow ten minutes for this test. If you cannot answer a question, go on to the next one without delay. If you have time left over at the end, go back and try to fill in unanswered questions.

18 or over correct:	excellent
14 to 17 correct:	good
13 or under correct:	thorough review of A exercises indicated

1. The .... consists of over fifty islands, half of them uninhabited.
   maelstrom isthmus scintilla archipelago

2. .... deposits are brought down by the river and enrich the soil of the plain.
   forensic orotund alluvial inchoate

3. The .... seized power last month and established a military regime.
   lacuna argot schism junto

4. The nobleman felt that the accusation of cowardice had .... his honor.
   imputed imbibed inveighed impugned

5. Copper, when exposed to the atmosphere, becomes coated with ....
   chimera penumbra verdigris detritus

6. The witnesses were charged with perjury after admitting they had been .... by the defendant.
   suborned jaded annealed elided

7. She is skillful at employing ....
   to conceal the truth from her listeners.
   desuetude ostracism apotheosis casuistry

8. A(n) .... from Albania arrived this morning to attend the meeting.
   curia sobriquet atelier legate

9. You should .... the first line of each paragraph one inch.
   traduce impute suborn indent

10. His . . . . manner led to his being called "Uncle Ned" by the children.
unmitigated avuncular leonine obstreperous

11. His refusal to pay his dues led to his . . . . from the club.
espousal ouster liaison atonement

12. The plan . . . . in her mind over the next few weeks.
behooved enervated estranged incubated

13. These . . . . were caused by glaciers moving over the rocks.
sutures exegeses abrasions gaffs

14. Politicians make every effort to . . . . themselves with the voters.
resuscitate traduce ingratiate impute

15. The Senate yesterday . . . . the president's ambassadorial appointments.
benighted ratified despoiled fulminated

16. . . . . rocks are formed through fiery volcanic action.
oleaginous adipose igneous sidereal

17. Her taste in music is . . . . and covers all fields.
fulsome endemic eclectic redundant

18. His opponent was a . . . . of a man, twice as big as he was.
behemoth dialectic behoove diapason

19. One's bones . . . . and become brittle as one reaches old age.
egress anneal ratify calcify

20. Think of the cost of . . . . before proceeding with your lawsuit.
litigation patrimony mensuration supplication

WORDLY WISE 20

SPATIAL means "of or pertaining to space" (spatial considerations in the design of a building); *spacious* means "having plenty of space" (spacious closets).

The *ch* in MACHINATIONS is pronounced *k*.

OSTRACIZE derives from the Athenian practice of voting into exile a public figure deemed dangerous to the state. Ballots were shards of pottery (*ostrakoi*) on which the name of the person to be banished was written. There was no specific accusation or trial, and if 6,000 citizens cast ballots against him, a person was exiled for five to ten years.

Etymology

Study the roots given below together with the English words derived from them. Capitalized words are those given in the Word List. You should look up in a dictionary any words that are unfamiliar to you.

Roots: *dulcis* (sweet) Latin – Examples: DULCET, *dulc*imer
pendere (hang) Latin – Examples: PENDANT, *pend*ulum, *pend*ulous
jocus (joke) Latin – Examples: JOCULAR, *joc*und, *joc*ose

Word List 21

ADO	IMMUNIZE	PASSE
ANIMADVERSION	INIMICAL	PREAMBLE
BATTEN	LASCIVIOUS	RECREANT
CUMULATIVE	LIMN	SADISTIC
ELIXIR	MIKADO	SOPORIFIC
FIAT	OSSIFY	TRAVAIL

Look up the words above in your dictionary. Note that many of them have more than one meaning. When you feel that you know *all* the meanings of *all* the words, go on to the exercises below.

EXERCISE 21A

From the four choices following each phrase or sentence, you are to circle the letter preceding the one that is closest in meaning to the italicized word. Where the same word appears more than once, you should note that it is being used in different senses.

1. much *ado*
   (a) excitement (b) labor (c) provocation (d) delay

2. to ignore the *animadversion*
   (a) malfunctioning of a part (b) critical remark (c) inherent contradiction (d) alternative route

3. to *batten*
   (a) give away all that one has (b) become weak from hunger (c) engage in warlike acts (d) thrive at another's expense

4. to *batten* down the hatch
   (a) break (b) glance (c) fasten (d) lower oneself

5. a long *batten*
   (a) gun barrel (b) seige of a walled town (c) stretch of highway (d) strip of wood

6. a *cumulative* effect
   (a) that was not anticipated (b) calculated to attain the desired end (c) that cannot be predicted with accuracy (d) increasing by successive additions

7. a strong *elixir*
   (a) medicinal preparation (b) condemnatory utterance (c) line of argument (d) defense barrier

8. the *elixir* of life
   (a) ultimate secret (b) magical prolonger (c) humdrum sameness (d) enormous variety

9. government by *fiat*
   (a) a ruling council (b) the traditions of the past (c) consent of the governed (d) command of the ruler

10. to *immunize* someone
    (a) severely restrict the movements of (b) spread false and malicious stories about (c) make resistant to a disease (d) shut off from all social intercourse

11. *inimical* to us
    (a) indifferent (b) friendly (c) useful (d) hostile

12. *lascivious* talk
    (a) inspirational (b) treasonable (c) lustful (d) boastful

13. to *limn* their plight
    (a) ignore (b) describe (c) sympathize with (d) gloat over

14. to *limn* the tree
    (a) trim the branches of (b) chop down (c) draw (d) climb

15. a visit to the *mikado*
    (a) Japanese capital (b) Japanese emperor (c) Japanese parliament (d) Japanese mainland

16. to *ossify*
    (a) turn into stone (b) act indecisively (c) act the fool (d) develop into bone

17. *ossified* views
    (a) childishly immature (b) rigidly fixed (c) sweepingly comprehensive (d) easily changed

18. That is *passé*.
    (a) acceptable (b) first class (c) out of date (d) up to date

19. a long *preamble*
    (a) unhurried stroll (b) round of discussions (c) physical warmup (d) introductory statement

20. *recreant* vassals
    (a) disloyal (b) in name only (c) low-ranking (d) newly created

21. a *recreant* person
    (a) cowardly (b) audacious (c) immature (d) dishonest

22. a *sadistic* person
    (a) who delights in inflicting pain (b) who is in constant pain (c) who constantly seeks sympathy (d) who refuses to accept sympathy

23. a *soporific* drug

    (a) antibiotic (b) sleep-inducing (c) pain-killing (d) mind-expanding

24. three years' *travail*

    (a) imprisonment (b) seclusion (c) on the move (d) hard work

25. to end the *travail*

    (a) enforced idleness (b) uncertainty (c) agony (d) fun

Check your answers against the correct ones given below. The answers are not in order; this is to prevent your eye from catching sight of the correct answers before you have had a chance to do the exercise on your own.

8b. 4c. 17b. 24d. 16d. 13b. 20a. 11d. 9d. 1a. 18c. 3d. 25c. 7a. 5d. 15b. 21a. 12c. 19d. 14c. 23b. 6d. 2b. 10c. 22a.

Look up in your dictionary all the words for which you gave incorrect answers. Only when you have done this should you go on to the next exercise.

EXERCISE 21B

Each word in Word List 21 is used several times in the sentences below to illustrate different meanings or usage. One of the sentences for each word uses the italicized word incorrectly. You are to circle the letter preceding that sentence.

1. (a) She answered the questions without much *ado* and then excused herself. (b) The war scare resulted in considerable *ado* on the New York Stock Exchange yesterday. (c) What made him *ado* like that over such a trivial matter?

2. (a) As an activist, the first lady, Eleanor Roosevelt, was used to the *animadversions* of the press. (b) He was flying a roughly put together *animadversion* of a World War I biplane. (c) I shall ignore her *animadversions* because she is motivated solely by malice.

3. (a) A heavy *batten* was placed against the door to prevent persons from breaking in. (b) When the storm broke, the sailors hastened to *batten* down the hatches. (c) These unscrupulous officials have been *battening* on the very people they were supposed to help. (d) The man was *battened* over the head as he stooped to tie his shoelace.

4. (a) The drug has been tested for such a short time that its *cumulative* effects are not known. (b) A *cumulative* index is one that can be easily added to. (c) Amounts are added each day to form a *cumulative* total for the month. (d) The two students exchanged *cumulative* looks when I asked which of them had done it.

5. (a) The search for the *elixir* of life, a substance with the power of bestowing eternal youth, was vigorously pursued in the Middle Ages. (b) The bottled *elixirs* sold by itinerant peddlers were aromatic preparations containing alcohol. (c) The sound of drums and fifes acted like an *elixir* upon the tired soldiers and they fought back determinedly. (d) The *elixir*, summoned by a rubbing of the lamp, sped away to do his master's bidding.

6. (a) The general made himself governor of the area under the *fiat* of the queen. (b) Senators who tried to *fiat* the bill through Congress soon gave up their attempts. (c) Rule by *fiat* is resented by the people, who feel they should have a say in the government.

7. (a) Since everyone has been *immunized* against smallpox, the disease has almost been wiped out. (b) Scientists are trying to find out why some people have a natural *immunity* to the disease. (c) *Immunization* is carried out by teams of doctors who go from village to village. (d) The whole nation *immunized* for the expected attack along its eastern border.

8. (a) The two groups, though mutually *inimical*, nevertheless contrive to get along with each other. (b) The measures suggested are *inimical* to our interests and should be opposed.

(c) The *inimical* way the child's leg was twisted indicated that it had been badly broken.

9. (a) *Lascivious* amounts of money were spent by the two candidates in their campaigns. (b) Various enterprises around the docks cater to the *lascivious* tastes of sailors on shore leave. (c) The *lasciviousness* of the court of Charles II shocked his more puritanical subjects.

10. (a) The artists presented her with a beautiful *limn* of herself executed in charcoal. (b) Portraits of their ancestors, not all of them *limned* by masters, graced the walls. (c) So vividly are the characters *limned* in this novel that they seem to step out of the pages.

11. (a) The Japanese people regarded the *mikado* as a divine being. (b) The *mikados* formerly resided in the ancient Japanese capital of Kyoto. (c) Al Capone was the uncrowned *mikado* of the Chicago underworld.

12. (a) The poet's worst enemy is the emotional *ossification* that creeps up on him or her unawares. (b) The cartileges of the joints *ossify* with age and make movement difficult. (c) Institutions which begin with revolutionary fervor soon *ossify* into rigidly maintained preserves of privilege. (d) Trees that grew a million years ago are now *ossified* into coal.

13. (a) He was once a good writer, but most of his ideas are now *passé*. (b) She is an excellent swimmer but is barely *passé* at field sports. (c) The Riviera is becoming *passé* as a tourist area as more visitors are discovering Spain.

14. (a) The *preamble* to the Constitution of the United States states the purpose of the document. (b) Without any *preamble*, the union's leader delivered the list of grievances that needed redress. (c) She *preambled* back and forth like a caged tiger as she awaited further news.

15. (a) The *recreant* was only slightly wounded, but he dropped his sword and begged for mercy. (b) The disease proved *recreant* to every remedy that was tried. (c) The *recreant* way his soldiers dropped their weapons and fled filled the general with shame. (d) The prime minister asked for the resignations of her *recreant* cabinet members and planned to replace them with more loyal followers.

16. (a) She derived a *sadistic* pleasure from seeing her victims squirm. (b) He must be a *sadist* to have treated those children so cruelly. (c) When her acts of *sadism* came to the notice of the authorities, she was committed to an institution for psychiatric observation. (d) So *sadistic* was the pain in his leg that he passed out several times.

17. (a) She spoke only in the most general way and promised to get down to *soporifics* later. (b) A warm bath before retiring makes an excellent *soporific* for those unable to sleep. (c) The professor's lectures are so *soporific* that I have to pinch myself to stay awake.

18. (a) Her drawn face and clenched fists were evidence of the *travail* she was undergoing. (b) Sometimes drugs are administered to ease the *travail* of intense physical pain. (c) The projectile is *travailing* at a thousand feet per second when it leaves the gun barrel. (d) After much *travail*, the trees were cleared and a cabin built.

EXERCISE 21C

This exercise combines synonyms and antonyms. You are to underline the word which is *either* most similar in meaning *or* most nearly opposite in meaning to the capitalized word. Underline only one word for each question after deciding that it is either an antonym or a synonym and write A (for antonym) or S (for synonym) after the capitalized word. Allow only fifteen minutes for this test. If you cannot answer a question, go on to the next one without delay. If you have time left over at the end, go back and try to fill in unanswered questions.

26 or over correct: excellent
22 to 25 correct: good

1. SPIRITUAL . . . .
dulcet inimical soporific mundane comatose

2. JOKING . . . .
sanguine perspicuous sentient adipose jocular

3. SNACK . . . .
collation atelier benediction arpeggio obloquy

4. OUTDATED . . . .
turbid fecund soporific passé obdurate

5. SCHEMES . . . .
sutures cerements machinations animadversions elixirs

6. GIVER . . . .
provender recipient atelier apotheosis egress

7. FRIENDLY . . . .
endemic malleable mundane dulcet inimical

8. STINKING . . . .
splenetic jaded adipose fetid simian

9. EXPLODE . . . .
lampoon behoove enervate simulate fulminate

10. INSPIRATION . . . .
coup liaison tautology lacuna afflatus

11. COMMAND . . . .
scintilla fiat affidavit codicil elixir

12. BRITTLE . . . .
covert arrant malleable singular germane

13. FAITHFUL . . . .
expeditious egregious jocular recreant roseate

14. ERADICATE . . . .
extirpate suborn limn supplicate enervate

15. SUSPENSION . . . .
appendage inhibition acumen abeyance collation

16. BEGINNER . . . .
atelier scintilla infidel recreant tyro

17. EXCITEMENT . . . .
desuetude extrusion ado scintilla plenitude

18. RIDICULE . . . .
behoove ratify gainsay mulct lampoon

19. CHASTE . . . .
unguent inimical lascivious stentorian palpable

20. ABUNDANCE . . . .
plenitude emolument moiety abeyance desuetude

21. CACOPHONOUS . . . .
jocular dulcet roseate malleable factitious

22. BACKWARD . . . .
eclectic moot frenetic retrograde perfunctory

23. OPTIMISTIC . . . .
mundane palpable soporific recreant roseate

24. STRANGE . . . .
inchoate singular recalcitrant avuncular rarefied

25. TORMENT . . . .
travail aberration declivity exegesis paradigm

26. CONVENTIONAL . . . .
obstreperous prolix inimical orthodox sentient

27. COMMUNICATION . . . .
lampoon soporific collation abeyance liaison

28. LIONLIKE . . . .
lucent infidel leonine oleaginous lambent

29. WEAKEN . . . .
limn fulminate suborn simulate enervate

30. SLEEP-INDUCING . . . .

emetic adipose orthodox soporific malleable

WORDLY WISE 21

To IMMUNIZE a person is to give him or her *immunity* to a particular disease. *Immunity* has a broader application and can mean "exemption from a duty or liability" (diplomatic immunity protects diplomats from arrest).

PASSÉ (pronounced *pa-SAY*) comes from the French and must be written with an acute accent (´).

SADISTIC means "deriving pleasure from inflicting pain on others." The word derives from the Marquis de Sade, an eighteenth-century French nobleman, who showed marked symptoms of this condition in his life and writings. The reverse of sadism is *masochism*, "the deriving of pleasure from having pain inflicted on oneself." The word is derived from Leopold von Sacher-Masoch, a nineteenth-century German novelist.

Etymology

Study the roots given below together with the English words derived from them. Capitalized words are those given in the Word List. You should look up in a dictionary any words that are unfamiliar to you.

Roots: *cumulus* (heap) Latin — Examples: *CUMULATIVE,* ac*cumul*ate, *cumulus*
ambulare (walk) Latin — Examples: PRE*AMBLE,* per*ambula*tor, *ambula*tory

ACROSS

1. crafty maneuvers; evil schemes
7. an artist's studio or workshop
10. of or relating to space
11. an unskilled laborer of South America
12. exciting lustful thoughts
14. a light meal
16. a medicinal preparation
17. overly demonstrative
18. a person who collects coins
20. very hard work
21. a sea containing many scattered islands
24. an emperor of Japan
26. a forcible ejection from a place or position
30. a protruding stud or ornament (4)
31. the act of anointing with oil
32. to explode
34. a critical or hostile remark
35. given to joking
37. a repayment for loss or damage
38. of the country; rural
40. not believing in a particular religion
42. detestable (4)
45. the smallest trace; a tiny particle
48. reverting to a worse state (13)
50. to exclude or banish from favor
51. relating to deposits laid down by water
52. a divine imparting of knowledge or inspiration
53. sweet to the ear
54. to root out; to eradicate

DOWN

1. capable of being hammered into shape
2. the use of subtle but false reasoning
3. hostile; unfavorable to
4. to develop into bone
5. deriving pleasure from inflicting pain
6. to thrive at another's expense; to fatten oneself
8. a beginner; a novice
9. one that receives
13. a tall, four-sided monument tapering to a pyramidal top (10)
14. increasing by successive addition
15. to hold up; to satirize
19. intensely hot; scorching (1)
21. great bustle and excitement
22. overly optimistic
23. a hanging object, as an ornament
24. worldly as opposed to spiritual; ordinary
25. temporary suspension, as of an activity
27. sleep-inducing
28. to induce (a person) to commit an unlawful act
29. to make resistant to a disease
33. to portray in words or picture
36. an introduction to a formal document
38. yielding in a cowardly way
39. denoting one rather than many
40. produced by heat or volcanic action
41. relating to or suggestive of a lion
43. to give formal approval to
44. an envoy
46. foul-smelling; stinking
47. out of date
49. a decree or command

Chapter Eight

Word List 22

APOSTATE	INGENUOUS	POMMEL
BULLION	INVIDIOUS	PROROGUE
DEBILITATED	MISCARRY	RHAPSODIZE
FLAGELLATE	ORISON	TANTAMOUNT
HIATUS	PERIPATETIC	TITULAR

Look up the words above in your dictionary. Note that many of them have more than one meaning. When you feel that you know *all* the meanings of *all* the words, go on to the exercises below.

EXERCISE 22A

From the four choices following each phrase or sentence, you are to circle the letter preceding the one that is closest in meaning to the italicized word. Where the same word appears more than once, you should note that it is being used in different senses.

1. to be an *apostate*
   (a) person who abandons his or her faith (b) person who takes religious vows (c) person who spreads the faith (d) person who dies for his or her faith

2. a cargo of *bullion*
   (a) metals in their unrefined state (b) goods illegally brought into a country (c) precious metals in bulk form (d) sand used as ballast

3. to be *debilitated*
   (a) deceived (b) in debt (c) encircled (d) enfeebled

4. to *flagellate* someone
   (a) whip (b) signal to (c) overtake (d) tickle

5. a long *hiatus*
   (a) introductory passage (b) open wound (c) lapse of time (d) summing up

6. an *ingenuous* person
   (a) unscrupulous (b) naive (c) resourceful (d) dull

7. *invidious* remarks
   (a) designed to placate (b) barely audible (c) self-deprecating (d) designed to create ill will

8. She may *miscarry*.
   (a) become physically ill (b) become mentally deranged (c) give birth to two or more babies (d) fail to carry a baby to its full term

9. The plan *miscarried*.
   (a) went ahead (b) was dropped (c) became known (d) went awry

10. to hear the *orison*
    (a) bird (b) bell (c) prayer (d) oath

11. *peripatetic* teaching
    (a) done part time (b) done while traveling (c) done without payment (d) done by setting an example

12. to grasp the *pommel*
    (a) essential point of an argument (b) rail around a ship's deck (c) free end of a swinging rope (d) protuberance on the front of a saddle

13. to *pommel* them
    (a) herd together (b) house (c) overload (d) beat

14. to *prorogue* parliament
    (a) extend the sitting of (b) be a member of (c) end a session of (d) formally address

15. to *rhapsodize*
    (a) sing in a soft and soothing voice (b) speak in an ecstatic manner (c) speak sadly of the past (d) rap out commands crisply

16. *tantamount* to an attack
    (a) resistant (b) prior (c) equivalent (d) leading

17. a *titular* chief of state
    (a) hereditary (b) democratically elected (c) with absolute powers (d) in name only

Check your answers against the correct ones given below. The answers are not in order; this is to prevent your eye from catching sight of the correct answers before you have had a chance to do the exercise on your own.

2c. 12d. 8d. 17d. 1a. 5c. 9d. 6b. 11b. 7d. 14c. 16c. 15b. 13d. 3d. 10c. 4a.

Look up in your dictionary all the words for which you gave incorrect answers. Only when you have done this should you go on to the next exercise.

EXERCISE 22B

Each word in Word List 22 is used several times in the sentences below to illustrate different meanings or usage. One of the sentences for each word uses the italicized word incorrectly. You are to circle the letter preceding that sentence.

1. (a) Long ago persons who questioned the divinity of Christ were denounced as *apostates* by the Catholic Church. (b) Martin Luther *apostated* his beliefs in a ringing denunciation of the Church. (c) Charges of *apostasy* were levelled against them for joining the opposition party.

2. (a) The gold ornaments had been melted into *bullion* for easier handling. (b) The missing aircraft was carrying gold *bullion* worth half a million dollars. (c) She admits to being one of the wealthiest women in the country but denies being a *bullionaire*.

3. (a) The disease has *debilitated* him so much that he can scarcely stand up. (b) The greater the *debilitation*, the greater the need for restorative measures. (c) She *debilitated* whether or not to join the rebels but finally decided against it. (d) The country, *debilitated* by four years of war, began the slow process of recovery.

4. (a) He picked up the heavy leather *flagellate* and scourged the prisoner. (b) In a fit of penance he *flagellated* himself until the blood ran down his back. (c) The prisoners were strapped to frames and *flagellated* with knotted whips. (d) The *flagellants* are a sect who practice whipping as a religious rite.

5. (a) There is a *hiatus* in the record of her early life that has puzzled her *biographers*. (b) After a *hiatus* of ten years one cannot pick up exactly where one left off. (c) The *hiatus* between the end of the Paleolithic and the beginning of the Neolithic period is filled largely by conjecture. (d) The members of the *hiatus* met in secret to plot the overthrow of the government.

6. (a) Her *ingenuousness* was made more hilarious by the air of experience she affected. (b) "The reason I didn't invite you to the party is that I don't like you," she said *ingenuously*. (c) His *ingenuous* pronouncements were a source of amusement to his more wordly colleagues. (d) She showed me an *ingenuous* device for recording sounds that was no bigger than a matchbox.

7. (a) Her *invidious* comparison of the two rival candidates only increased the bitterness between them. (b) The disease, unnoticed by the patient, works *invidiously* to destroy the blood cells. (c) At the risk of being accused of *invidiousness*, I have selected the following prize winners. (d) I do not envy the president his *invidious* task of choosing a cabinet.

8. (a) The plan *miscarried* through no fault of ours. (b) By a grave *miscarriage* of justice, he was acquitted of the crime he had freely confessed to. (c) She *miscarried* several times before giving birth to a seven-pound baby. (d) Don't *miscarry* the bag of groceries or you'll drop it.

9. (a) The *orison* is rung at daybreak to call the faithful to prayer. (b) Hamlet tells Ophelia, "Nymph, in thy *orisons* be all my sins remembered." (c) Her *orisons* completed, the woman rose to her feet and left the chapel.

10. (a) Her greatest poems were composed *peripatetically* as she strolled in her rose garden. (b) The machine has no *peripatetic* parts, so there

is nothing to wear out. (c) The *Peripatetic* school of philosophy was founded by Aristotle, who discussed philosophy with his students while walking about.

11. (a) When the horse started to gallop, the rider let the reins go and grabbed the *pommel*. (b) The other children *pommelled* him when they found he had betrayed their secret. (c) We bought a *pommel* of apples at a roadside stand outside of town.

12. (a) The king or queen no longer has the right to *prorogue* parliament. (b) Party leaders expect to *prorogue* the legislature this week-end at the latest. (c) The pay raise the workers receive will be *prorogued* to January 1st.

13. (a) The book ends with a *rhapsody* to America's vanished frontier. (b) The guests spoke in the most *rhapsodical* terms of the dinner you gave. (c) All the New York critics *rhapsodized* over the work of this brilliant young pianist. (d) The nurse *rhapsodized* the wound with antiseptic before bandaging it.

14. (a) He was the *tantamount* chief of all the tribes in the region. (b) Such unpatriotic remarks are *tantamount* to treason. (c) A refusal to lift the blockade would be *tantamount* to an act of war.

15. (a) The president is *titular* chief of state, but executive power is wielded by the prime minister. (b) Since the time of William and Mary, English monarchs have exercised only *titular* sovereignty. (c) As the nation's *titular*, she had only ceremonial duties to perform.

EXERCISE 22C

Few people know the meanings of such words as *chondrification, hidrosis,* or *kamelaukion* (for those who are interested, they can be found in any good unabridged dictionary), but we all know what *world* means. Or do we? The word has many meanings, among them the following.

(a) an infinite or vast amount

(b) a planet or other heavenly body

(c) a class of living things

(d) the sum of affairs affecting an individual

(e) an area of human activity having specific characteristics

(f) the total population of the earth

(g) a period of human history having specific characteristics

(h) a state of existence

(i) the planet earth

(j) the section of the population experienced in sophisticated aspects of modern life

(k) distances between places on earth

In the sentences below, the word is used in each of these meanings. In the spaces provided write out the letter corresponding to the particular meaning of the word *world* in the sentence.

1. He died in the belief that he was going to a better *world*. (   )

2. He has travelled around the *world* (   ) many times.

3. How's the *world* (   ) treating you these days?

4. There's a *world* (   ) of difference between the two types.

5. She is a woman of the *world* (   ).

6. The academic *world* (   ) is not for everyone.

7. The *world* (   ) faces a terrible famine by the end of this century.

8. She has made a number of films dealing with the animal *world*. ( )

9. This book tells us a great deal about the ancient *world*. ( )

10. Jet planes have made the *world* ( ) much smaller than it was a century ago.

11. Are flying saucers visiting us from other *worlds?* ( )

WORDLY WISE 22

INGENUOUS means "lacking in guile or sophistication"; this word is easily confused with *ingenious*, which means "clever; resourceful."

INVIDIOUS means "causing ill will or resentment" (an invidious comparison); *insidious* means "more dangerous than seems evident; treacherous" (the insidious course of a disease).

POMMEL as a verb meaning "to beat; to strike" is also spelled *pummel*.

Etymology

Study the root and prefixes given below together with the English words derived from them. Capitalized words are those given in the Word List. You should look up in a dictionary any words that are unfamiliar to you.

Prefixes: (review) *apo-* (away from) Greek — Examples: *APO*STATE, *apo*theosis, *apo*cryphal

(review) *peri-* (around) Greek — Examples: *PERI*PATETIC, *peri*pheral, *peri*meter

Root: *stasis* (standing) Greek — Examples: APO*STA*TE, *stat*ic, *stat*ionary

Word List 23

ANEMIA	INSULAR	PUERILE
APOTHEGM	KLEPTOMANIAC	SENTENTIOUS
CILIATED	NEOLOGISM	TIMPANI
DIURNAL	PARRICIDE	TOUPEE
GESTATION	PERMEABLE	
INDIGENT	PRECEPT	

Look up the words in Word List 23 in your dictionary. Note that many of them have more than one meaning. When you feel that you know *all* the meanings of *all* the words, go on to the exercises below.

EXERCISE 23A

From the four choices following each phrase or sentence, you are to circle the letter preceding the one that is closest in meaning to the italicized word. Where the same word appears more than once, you should note that it is being used in different senses.

1. suffering from *anemia*
(a) a habitual dependence on alcohol (b) insufficient red corpuscles in the blood (c) insufficient calcium in the bones (d) temporary loss of memory

2. to utter an *apothegm*
(a) prayer (b) plea (c) oath (d) maxim

3. a *ciliated* leaf
(a) dried out (b) having minute hairs (c) having a spear shape (d) having a tough, waxy surface

4. *diurnal* creatures
(a) microscopic (b) active at night (c) that hibernate in winter (d) active in the daytime

5. a *diurnal* cycle
(a) eccentric (b) tedious (c) historical (d) daily

6. the final days of *gestation*
(a) the serving of a prison sentence (b) an enforced isolation to prevent spread of disease (c) the carrying of young in the womb (d) the occupation of one's country by a foreign power

7. the *gestation* of a novel
(a) offering for publication (b) review in scathing terms (c) review in laudatory terms (d) development in the mind of the author

8. an *indigent* person
(a) poor (b) sick (c) outraged (d) wealthy

9. an *insular* people

    (a) wealthy (b) island (c) continental (d) impoverished

10. *insular* persons

    (a) sturdy (b) delicate (c) broad-minded (d) narrow-minded

11. to be a *kleptomaniac*

    (a) person with an obsession to steal (b) person with an obsession to start fires (c) person with an abnormal fear of heights (d) person with an abnormal fear of enclosed spaces

12. to explain the *neologism*

    (a) logical proposition (b) word puzzle (c) newly-coined word (d) poorly-phrased thought

13. guilty of *parricide*

    (a) murdering one's brother (b) murdering one's sister (c) murdering one's child (d) murdering one's parents

14. a *permeable* substance

    (a) brittle (b) heat resistant (c) porous (d) shatterproof

15. a useful *precept*

    (a) mechanical aid (b) rule of conduct (c) aid to memory (d) rule of thumb

16. a *puerile* plan

    (a) thoroughly tested (b) highly imaginative (c) childishly immature (d) long drawn out

17. *sententious* utterances

    (a) argumentative (b) prolix (c) soothing (d) pithy

18. a *sententious* person

    (a) given to quarreling (b) given to impractical dreaming (c) slow and dull-witted (d) given to trite moralizing

19. the *timpani* of the band

    (a) woodwinds (b) strings (c) kettledrums (d) leader

20. to wear a *toupee*

    (a) partial wig (b) floppy hat (c) steel helmet (d) conical hat

Check your answers against the correct ones given below. The answers are not in order; this is to prevent your eye from catching sight of the correct answers before you have had a chance to do the exercise on your own.

5d. 9b. 6c. 11a. 7d. 1b. 17d. 8a. 12c. 2d. 14c. 18d. 16c. 15b. 19c. 13d. 3b. 10d. 4d. 20a.

Look up in your dictionary all the words for which you gave incorrect answers. Only when you have done this should you go on to the next exercise.

EXERCISE 23B

Each word in Word List 23 is used several times in the sentences below to illustrate different meanings or usage. One of the sentences for each word uses the italicized word incorrectly. You are to circle the letter preceding that sentence.

1. (a) The lyrical tradition in poetry has grown *anemic* in recent years and is now almost extinct. (b) Persons suffering from *anemia* are usually advised to take an iron-rich tonic. (c) Persons undergoing surgery are given an *anemia* prior to the operation. (d) Until a blood count has been taken, we cannot be sure how *anemic* she is.

2. (a) "Haste makes waste" was one of her favorite *apothegms*. (b) The characters of the play prefer *apothegmatic* utterances to the normal remarks of everyday speech. (c) An *apothegm* of blood blocked the artery and led to the patient's collapse.

3. (a) After five days without shaving, he had a distinctly *ciliated* look about the face. (b) The minute hairs of the *ciliated* leaf show up clearly under the microscope. (c) The paramecium is a one-celled *ciliate* animal.

4. (a) Hunting dogs are mainly *diurnal* animals and sleep during the night. (b) *Diurnal* flowers open during the day and close their petals at night. (c) The *diurnal* rotation of the earth is responsible for the apparent motion of the fixed stars. (d) The last entry in the ship's *diurnal* was dated January 14th.

5. (a) *Gestation* periods for mammals vary from under thirteen days for an opossum to over 624 days for an elephant. (b) This extraordinary book, ten years in *gestation*, has now been published. (c) She *gestated* for us to go on without her. (d) While the author spent a month in apparent idleness, a novel was *gestating* in her mind.

6. (a) Welfare funds are available to help the *indigents* of the state. (b) *Indigence* is a kind of gray area between being in abject poverty and having just enough money to live on. (c) You are required to prove that you are *indigent* before you can draw welfare. (d) The kangaroo is *indigent* to Australia.

7. (a) The *insularity* of Great Britain has been the ultimate defense against invasion threats from the continent of Europe. (b) The *insular* is fourteen miles long, but is nowhere more than half a mile wide. (c) The people have little contact with outsiders and so grow *insular* and illiberal.

8. (a) Where a person steals with no economic motive, doctors usually suspect *kleptomania*. (b) The woman accused of shoplifting confessed to being a *kleptomaniac*. (c) He had a *kleptomaniac* seizure and fell writhing to the floor.

9. (a) "Madam, I'm Adam" is a *neologism*, or sentence that reads the same backward or forward. (b) Modern technology has introduced large numbers of *neologisms* into the language. (c) "Hydrofoil" is a *neologism*; it refers to a watercraft that moves by raising its hull out of the water.

10. (a) The *parricide* expressed no remorse at having murdered his parents. (b) When the daughter disappeared immediately following her parents' murder, *parricide* was suspected. (c) She murdered her husband by putting *parricide* in his tea. (d) The boy's *parricidal* tendencies terrified the parents and led to their having the boy committed.

11. (a) Limestone is extremely *permeable* to water. (b) With education available to all, one expects class barriers to become more *permeable*. (c) The *permeability* of the filter is an important factor in cigarette manufacture. (d) Is it *permeable* to ask why we have been brought here?

12. (a) A reverence for life was the dominant *precept* of Albert Schweitzer. (b) She taught a respect for the law by example and not just by *precept*. (c) She *precepted* a place for herself in the hearts of all who knew her. (d) "Honor thy father and thy mother" is a *precept* we should all take to heart.

13. (a) After reading some of his *puerile* verses, I advised him to stop trying to write poetry. (b) It *pueriled* her that I had won the first prize that she had coveted so much. (c) The *puerility* of most television shows did not deter him from spending all his free time in front of the set.

14. (a) Her prose style is clipped, epigrammatic, *sententious*. (b) "Contentment breeds idleness," she said *sententiously*. (c) Laertes squirmed silently as he was forced to listen to his father's *sententious* speech of farewell. (d) She was *sententious* of our needs and did everything she could to make us comfortable.

15. (a) He was for many years the *timpanist* with the Boston Symphony Orchestra. (b) She was made *timpani* of the string section while still a young woman. (c) A toy drum given to her when she was a child stirred within her the ambition to play the *timpani* in a famous orchestra.

16. (a) He wore a *toupee* to hide the fact that he was bald. (b) Since getting a *toupee*, he looks years younger. (c) He was able to *toupee* the $1,000 into $10,000 within a year.

EXERCISE 23C

Complete the analogies below by underlining the numbered pair of words that stand in the same relationship to each other as do the first pair of words.

1. simian:ape:: (a) tiger:lion (2) insect: beetle (3) Africa:lion (4) leonine:lion (5) ape:human

2. soporific:sleep:: (1) sleepy:tired (2) headache:aspirin (3) illness:cure (4) emetic:vomit (5) flagellate:whip

3. indigent:wealth:: (1) doctor:health (2) sickness:medicine (3) debilitated:strength (4) kleptomania:steal (5) rich:money

4. acclivity:declivity:: (1) near:far (2) agree: disagree (3) in:out (4) forward:backward (5) up:down

5. coins:numismatist:: (1) health:physician (2) votes:election (3) mail:postmaster (4) butterflies:net (5) stamps:philatelist

6. petrify:stone:: (1) limn:picture (2) porcine: pig (3) ossify:bone (4) suture:wound (5) impugn:honor

7. igneous:fire:: (1) archipelago:island (2) immunize:disease (3) elixir:health (4) rarefied:air (5) alluvial:water

8. paternal:father:: (1) father:son (2) malleable: gold (3) parricide:parents (4) avuncular:uncle (5) anemic:blood

9. flagellate:whip:: (1) gallows:noose (2) strangle: garrote (3) wound:scar (4) suffocate:die (5) wooden:club

10. collation:eat:: (1) beverage:imbibe (2) pommel:saddle (3) diurnal:day (4) infidel:faith (5) wisdom:savant

WORDLY WISE 23

ANEMIA is also written *anaemia*; both spellings are correct.

DIURNAL means "daily" or "of or relating to day"; its antonym is *nocturnal*, "of or relating to night."

PARRICIDE is the murder of a parent or parents; *patricide* and *matricide* are more specific terms and refer to the murder of one's father and mother respectively. Some related forms are: *regicide*, the murder of one's king; *genocide* (see Word List 16), the deliberate destruction of a race of people; *deicide*, the murder of a god or divine being; *fratricide*, the murder of a brother or sister; *filicide*, the murder of a son or daughter; *infanticide*, the murder of a newborn child; and *suicide*, the deliberate taking of one's own life.

Etymology

Study the roots given below together with the English words derived from them. Capitalized words are those given in the Word List. You should look up in a dictionary any words that are unfamiliar to you.

Roots: *caed*, *cid* (kill) Latin — Examples: see above
logos (word) Greek — Examples: NEO-*LOG*ISM, *log*ic, philo*logy*

Word List 24

BELLICOSE	INTESTATE	PROPITIATE
CONTENTIOUS	LIBRETTO	RANT
EBULLIENT	OPALESCENT	SEQUESTER
GRAPNEL	PENDENT	TINCTURE
INFINITESIMAL	PLENARY	VOTARY

Look up the words above in your dictionary. Note that many of them have more than one meaning. When you feel that you know *all* the meanings of *all* the words, go on to the exercises below.

From the four choices following each phrase or sentence, you are to circle the letter preceding the one that is closest in meaning to the italicized word. Where the same word appears more than once, you should note that it is being used in different senses.

1. a *bellicose* manner
   (a) foolish (b) friendly (c) warlike (d) docile

2. a *contentious* crew
   (a) satisfied (b) quarrelsome (c) satisfactory (d) cowardly

3. to be *ebullient*
   (a) quaking with fear (b) shaking with laughter (c) seething with rage (d) bubbling with enthusiasm

4. a large *grapnel*
   (a) wine barrel (b) bomb fragment (c) grappling hook (d) awning

5. an *infinitesimal* amount
   (a) immeasurably large (b) immeasurably small (c) incapable of being divided (d) imperceptibly increasing

6. to die *intestate*
   (a) without any assets (b) by foul play (c) in a foreign land (d) having left no will

7. a fine *libretto*
   (a) comic opera (b) music conductor (c) composer of musical works (d) text of a musical work

8. an *opalescent* surface
   (a) of deepest black (b) that reflects light back (c) of changing colors (d) that glows in the dark

9. *pendent* blossóms
   (a) unopened (b) flowering (c) cut (d) hanging

10. a *plenary* session
    (a) hastily summoned (b) attended by all members (c) regularly scheduled (d) with all nonmembers excluded

11. *plenary* power
    (a) loosely defined (b) carefully defined (c) complete (d) limited

12. to *propitiate* someone
    (a) antagonize (b) appease (c) like (d) abhor

13. to *rant*
    (a) become putrid (b) break down (c) talk wildly (d) become panicky

14. to *sequester* oneself
    (a) seclude (b) defend (c) adorn (d) praise

15. to *sequester* property
    (a) surreptitiously steal (b) buy at auction (c) put up for sale (d) lawfully seize

16. a *tincture* of pride
    (a) affirmation (b) gesture (c) trace (d) look

17. a *tincture* of iodine
    (a) small bottle (b) alcohol solution (c) small application (d) pure form

18. to *tincture* something
    (a) break down into its parts (b) give a metallic sheen to (c) taint with impurities (d) tinge with color

19. a *votary* of the church
    (a) outstanding architectural feature (b) object venerated by the faithful (c) person bound by religious vows (d) chosen leader

20. a *votary* of gambling
    (a) defense (b) den (c) opponent (d) addict

Check your answers against the correct ones given below. The answers are not in order; this is to prevent your eye from catching sight of the correct answers before you have had a chance to do the exercise on your own.

2b. 5b. 14a. 19c. 13c. 18d. 9d. 12b. 8c. 6d. 16c. 3d. 10b. 15d. 11c. 17b. 1c. 7d. 20d. 4c.

Look up in your dictionary all the words for which you gave incorrect answers. Only when you have done this should you go on to the next exercise.

EXERCISE 24B

Each word in Word List 24 is used several times in the sentences below to illustrate different meanings or usage. One of the sentences for each word uses the italicized word incorrectly. You are to circle the letter preceding that sentence.

1. (a) This treaty demonstrates to *bellicose* nations that they cannot start wars with impunity. (b) They call themselves courageous, but I fear they confuse courage with *bellicosity*. (c) The two nations *bellicosed* insults at each other, but neither was prepared to go to war.

2. (a) One person spreads *contention* among the crew, and in no time we have a mutiny on our hands. (b) Discussions were broken off when they became *contentious* and will be resumed when tempers have cooled. (c) He expressed his objections so *contentiously* that I refused even to consider them. (d) They are perfectly *contentious* to remain behind provided they have enough food.

3. (a) Those taking part will receive an *ebullient* of ten dollars a day. (b) Her *ebullient* manner coupled with a cool head makes her an ideal leader. (c) The *ebullience* of the cruise director proved infectious, and soon everyone was joining in the fun.

4. (a) They used *grapnels* to drag the river bottom but failed to recover the swimmer's body. (b) They secured the boat by throwing out a *grapnel* that caught in the rocks. (c) The student showed a willingness to *grapnel* with the problem but lacked the ability to solve it.

5. (a) Space technology demands unprecedented accuracy, and the leeway for error is *infinitesimal*. (b) An *infinitesimal* number is one capable of being arbitrarily close to zero. (c) The universe contains an almost *infinitesimal* number of stars. (d) Nuclear scientists probe the *infinitesimally* small particles that comprise the atom.

6. (a) *Intestate* highways are primarily the responsibility of the federal government. (b) The father died *intestate*, and the heirs have been squabbling over the estate ever since. (c) The disposition of *intestate* property is left to the court.

7. (a) Frederick Loewe wrote the music of *My Fair Lady*, and Alan Jay Lerner wrote the *libretto*. (b) The next passage should be played *libretto*. (c) She was both the composer and the *librettist* of the opera.

8. (a) The milky *opalescence* of the stone is what gives it its rare beauty. (b) The myriad changing colors of the *opalescent* seashell fascinated us. (c) The glass had an *opalescent* sheen resembling mother-of-pearl. (d) The jeweler made the *opalescent* into a pendant.

9. (a) The vines were laden with *pendent* bunches of grapes. (b) I admired the perfect symmetry of the icicles *pendent* from the eaves. (c) His *pendent* for modern European paintings leads him to overlook many fine American works.

10. (a) Parties to the negotiations must have *plenary* powers if a settlement is to be reached. (b) The *plenary* of wildlife in the area is due to the strictness of the game laws. (c) The minister's recommendations will be voted on in *plenary* session of the legislature.

11. (a) Try to *propitiate* them by doing as they ask. (b) He realized that he had angered his boss and so worked long hours overtime as an act of *propitiation*. (c) Young maidens from the tribe were sacrificed to *propitiate* the wrathful gods. (d) You could hardly have chosen a more *propitiate* time to ask me.

12. (a) The huge *rant* in the side of the tent will have to be repaired. (b) He *ranted* and raved, but the guards refused to let him pass. (c) The actress thought she was portraying rage when she was merely *ranting*.

13. (a) She *sequestered* herself in her room while considering her next move. (b) Following his lonely *sequestration* on the island, he was never quite the same. (c) The property was *sequestered* by order of the court and held until the rightful ownership could be established. (d) We *sequestered* far and wide in our search for the missing child.

14. (a) The president's gloomy speech contained not a *tincture* of hope. (b) *Tincture* of iodine was applied to the cut before it was bandaged. (c) The petals were roseate, *tinctured* with a deep crimson at the center. (d) He *tinctured* the scene in pencil and added a color wash later.

15. (a) She became a *votary* of the church and henceforth was bound by the vow she had taken. (b) All political viewpoints have their *votaries*, but all will rally in a common cause. (c) A *votary* was taken, and the motion passed seventy votes to six. (d) She spoke scornfully of those who are *votaries* of the daily horoscopes published in the newspapers.

EXERCISE 24C

This exercise combines synonyms and antonyms. You are to underline the word which is *either* most similar in meaning *or* most nearly opposite in meaning to the capitalized word. Underline only one word for each question after deciding that it is either an antonym or a synonym and write A (for antonym) or S (for synonym) after the capitalized word. Allow only fifteen minutes for this test. If you cannot answer a question, go on to the next one without delay. If you have time left over at the end, go back and try to fill in unanswered questions.

26 or over correct: excellent
22 to 25 correct: good
21 or under correct: thorough review of A exercises indicated

1. COMPLETE . . . .
titular ebullient plenary sententious intestate

2. STRENGTHENED . . . .
orotund abraded traduced fetid debilitated

3. TRACE . . . .
encomium tier freshet hiatus tincture

4. PACIFIC . . . .
alluvial bellicose malleable salubrious sedulous

5. SUCCEED . . . .
ratify lampoon miscarry suborn sequester

6. PRAYER . . . .
unction prelate natation orison plenitude

7. BANISH . . . .
rhapsodize garrote flagellate ostracize abrade

8. HANGING . . . .
igneous contentious pristine kinetic pendent

9. MAXIM . . . .
stricture savant apothegm collation nepotism

10. PORTRAY . . . .
limn suborn batten rhapsodize propitiate

11. NOCTURNAL . . . .
venial carnal sylvan vernal diurnal

12. QUARRELSOME . . . .
puerile sentient adipose contentious inchoate

13. WHIP . . . .
ostracize flagellate ratify limn suture

14. STUDIO . . . .
mountebank dory isthmus atelier tempera

15. RURAL . . . .
singular alluvial igneous spatial rustic

16. BROAD-MINDED . . . .
    indigent permeable inimical insular intestate

17. CONCISE . . . .
    passé inimical prolix puerile pendent

18. NAIVE . . . .
    ingenuous effusive fetid ebullient diurnal

19. DISGRACE . . . .
    colloquy collation natation quarantine obloquy

20. PESSIMISTIC . . . .
    effusive leonine recreant sanguine sadistic

21. POROUS . . . .
    diurnal sententious permeable titular peripatetic

22. APPEASE . . . .
    resuscitate ostracize sequester enervate propitiate

23. WEALTHY . . . .
    titular opalescent ebullient indigent bellicose

24. ASTRONOMICAL . . . .
    spatial alluvial apostate infinitesimal insular

25. NOMINAL . . . .
    peripatetic passé roseate plenary titular

26. SECLUDED . . . .
    mundane debilitated ciliated sequestered opalescent

27. CHILDISH . . . .
    puerile rustic permeable apostate truncated

28. WIG . . . .
    timpani votary toupee tyro tempera

29. BEAT . . . .
    fulminate pommel prorogue limn indent

30. APATHETIC . . . .
    ciliated indigent ebullient peripatetic mundane

WORDLY WISE 24

INFINITESIMAL means "extremely small"; it conveys the meaning of an amount so small as to be approaching zero. *Infinite* conveys the meaning of an amount capable of being made arbitrarily close to infinity, i.e., extremely large.

PENDENT is an adjective and means "hanging" (pendent branches); *pendant* (Word List 20) is a noun and means "a hanging object, as an ornament."

Etymology

Study the roots given below together with the English words derived from them. Capitalized words are those given in the Word List. You should look up in a dictionary any words that are unfamiliar to you.

Roots: *bellum, bellus* (war) Latin – Examples: *BELLICOSE, belligerent, antebellum*

votum (vow) Latin – Examples: *VOTARY, votive, vote*

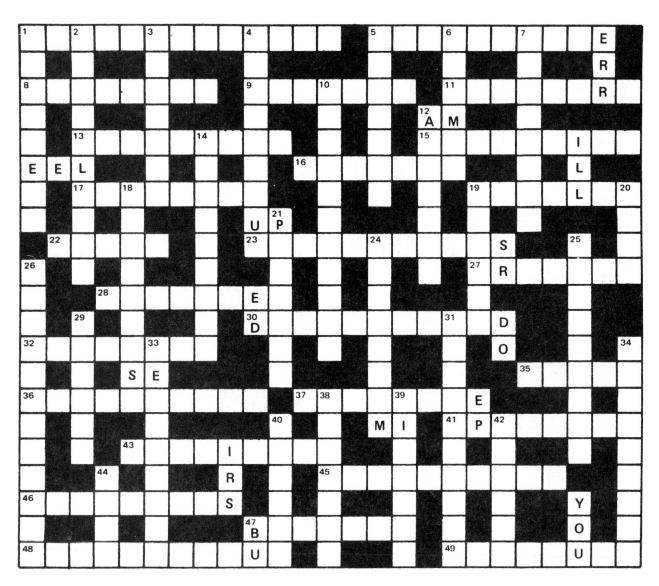

ACROSS

1. immeasurably small
5. to try to please; to appease
8. the entire range, as of the voice (1)
9. a grappling hook
11. to go awry
13. bubbling with enthusiasm
15. a newly coined word
16. of the daytime; daily
17. the text of a musical work
19. in name only
22. a ring-shaped coral island (2)
23. given to trite moralizing
27. a rule of conduct
28. having minute hairs
30. weakened; enfeebled
32. to adjourn, as a legislative session
35. out of date; old-fashioned (21)
36. having a milky surface with changing colors
37. one who abandons his faith
41. a short, pointed saying; a maxim
43. the act of murdering one's parents
45. to speak in an ecstatic manner
46. creating envy or animosity
47. precious metals in bulk form
48. quarrelsomely argumentative
49. to tinge with color

DOWN

1. lacking money; poor
2. to whip
3. of an island or islanders
4. lacking guile or sophistication
5. attended by all members
6. to beat
7. recently begun; rudimentary (18)
10. moving from place to place
12. an insufficiency of red blood corpuscles (variant spelling)
14. having made no will
18. warlike; aggressive
19. a small wig
20. to talk wildly; to rave
21. supported from above; hanging
24. the rejection of all beliefs (14)
25. to set or draw apart; to seclude
26. one with an obsession to steal
29. one bound by vows or by devotion to a cause
31. equal in effect; equivalent
33. the carrying of young in the womb
34. allowing the passage of liquids through
38. childishly immature
39. the kettledrums of a band or orchestra
40. a blank space; a lapse of time
42. a prayer
44. a decree or command (21)

Chapter Nine

Word List 25

ADDUCE	DOTAGE	OCCULT
APPELLATION	EMEND	PECULATE
BELABOR	EQUIVOCATE	RESONANT
CABAL	FEALTY	STRIATED
CORPOREAL	HEINOUS	VETO
DEPRECATE	MERCURIAL	

Look up the words above in your dictionary. Note that many of them have more than one meaning. When you feel that you know *all* the meanings of *all* the words, go on to the exercises below.

EXERCISE 25A

From the four choices following each phrase or sentence, you are to circle the letter preceding the one that is closest in meaning to the italicized word. Where the same word appears more than once, you should note that it is being used in different senses.

1. to *adduce* evidence
   (a) collect (b) refute (c) present (d) question

2. a curious *appellation*
   (a) figure (b) description (c) result (d) name

3. to *belabor* the obvious
   (a) tersely point out (b) fail to see (c) pretend not to see (d) expound lengthily on

4. to *belabor* someone
   (a) work alongside (b) attack (c) hire (d) dismiss

5. to break up the *cabal*
   (a) statue of a person on horseback (b) gold-bearing ore (c) large crowd of rioters (d) small group of plotters

6. a vicious *cabal*
   (a) rumor (b) riot (c) conspiracy (d) attack

7. a *corporeal* being
   (a) physical (b) ghostly (c) invisible (d) disembodied

8. to *deprecate* something
   (a) lower the value of (b) express disapproval of (c) estimate the value of (d) express approval of

9. in one's *dotage*
   (a) weak state following an illness (b) early years of childhood (c) prime of life (d) feeble-minded state due to old age

10. to *emend* the passage
    (a) omit (b) underline (c) correct (d) memorize

11. to *equivocate*
    (a) speak evasively (b) render a decision (c) speak forcefully (d) grow weary

12. *fealty* to one's lord
    (a) disloyalty (b) loyalty (c) insolence (d) honor

13. a *heinous* act
    (a) benevolent (b) foolish (c) wicked (d) unplanned

14. a *mercurial* person
    (a) given to outbursts of rage (b) given to unreasonable pessimism (c) given to unreasonable optimism (d) given to changes of mood

15. *occult* powers
    (a) overwhelming (b) limited (c) harnessed (d) supernatural

16. *occult* properties
    (a) manifest (b) worthless (c) valuable (d) hidden

17. to *peculate*
    (a) embezzle (b) gamble (c) complain (d) beg

18. a *resonant* sound
    (a) diminishing (b) echoing (c) high-pitched (d) intermittent

19. *striated* rocks
    (a) formed by great heat (b) rising above the earth's surface (c) marked with thin parallel lines (d) composed of a mixture of elements

20. to *veto* the proposal
    (a) vote for (b) discuss at length (c) strengthen (d) put a stop to

Check your answers against the correct ones given below. The answers are not in order; this is to prevent your eye from catching sight of the correct answers before you have had a chance to do the exercise on your own.

10c. 2d. 6c. 15d. 1c. 12b. 19c. 14d. 5d. 7a. 18b. 3d. 16d. 13c. 20d. 11a. 9d. 17a. 4b. 8b.

Look up in your dictionary all the words for which you gave incorrect answers. Only when you have done this should you go on to the next exercise.

EXERCISE 25B

Each word in Word List 25 is used several times in the sentences below to illustrate different meanings or usage. One of the sentences for each word uses the italicized word incorrectly. You are to circle the letter preceding that sentence.

1. (a) Since you make this accusation without *adducing* a shred of evidence, you cannot expect us to believe you. (b) Facts may be *adduced* to support either side in the dispute. (c) The salesperson did everything possible to *adduce* us to buy the appliance.

2. (a) He had received the *appellation* "Lefty" because he wrote with his left hand. (b) There was an overgrown patch of weeds there, but nothing that I would dignify with the *appellation* of "garden." (c) The *appellation* appears at midnight and walks the battlements of the castle.

3. (a) I don't wish to *belabor* the point, but I would like to make one thing clear. (b) He habitually *belabored* the horse with a stick despite his neighbors' threats to report him to the police. (c) The crew worked until dusk when they *belabored* for the night. (d) He *belabored* the children for playing in the mud and getting their clothes filthy.

4. (a) Members opposed to the senator formed a *cabal* to deny her the nomination. (b) The members of the *cabal* fled when their plot was discovered. (c) The *cabal* to seize the throne was easily put down and the plotters imprisoned. (d) She's a generous person, but sometimes she'll *cabal* over a dime just to prove a point.

5. (a) She believes that only when the soul has escaped its *corporeal* prison can it be free. (b) Disobedient students were once soundly thrashed, but *corporeal* punishment is now forbidden. (c) A poet's work may be touched with divine inspiration, but it should be rooted in his or her *corporeal* baseness.

6. (a) While *deprecating* violence, she acknowledged that one sometimes has to resort to force. (b) Her self-*deprecating* manner is inoffensive, but we need a more aggressive person. (c) He *deprecates* the tendency of young people to espouse causes they do not understand. (d) Some of the paintings have increased in value, while others have *deprecated*.

7. (a) Grandfather showed his *dotage* by losing his way when he went to the mailbox. (b) She is now in her *dotage* and sits quietly, chuckling at the memories of her eighty years. (c) The old *dotage* really should be in a nursing home.

8. (a) She offered to look over the article and make any *emendations* she thought necessary. (b) He spotted the error in the report and offered to *emend* it before I had it typed. (c) She bases her theory on the views of Sartre, *emending* them to suit her purpose. (d) She

asked what she could do to make *emends* for her foolish remark.

9. (a) Not wishing to lie, and afraid to tell the truth, the candidate *equivocated*. (b) The proceeds will be *equivocated* among those taking part. (c) "Answer the question without *equivocation*," the judge told the witness. (d) That I cannot give you a direct answer does not prove me to be an *equivocator*.

10. (a) With her hand on the Bible, she swore *fealty* to the Constitution of the United States. (b) In feudal times a vassal had to kneel and swear *fealty* to his lord. (c) Though not bound to accept the ruling of the board, he does owe strong *fealty* to it. (d) Soldiers soon become *fealty* under the strain of battle and are sent back for a brief rest.

11. Blackmail is the most *heinous* of crimes and deserving of the harshest punishment. (b) Hitler's murder of six million Jews was a *heinous* crime. (c) Smallpox, typhoid, and other *heinous* diseases have been almost wiped out in this country. (d) To say that he committed acts of treason is a most *heinous* accusation.

12. (a) A shudder passed through him as he gazed into the *mercurial* waters of the moat. (b) The wide range of moods exhibited in his works is evidence of his *mercurial* temperament. (c) Her *mercurial* spirits were never depressed for long, and soon she was laughing again.

13. (a) The wizard consulted his books of *occult* lore to find an appropriate spell. (b) She is a student of the *occult* and believes in black magic. (c) Witches were believed to possess *occult* powers and to be in league with the devil. (d) A number of *occults* devoted to devil worship flourished in this area.

14. (a) The candidate refused to *peculate* on the outcome of the election until all the results were in. (b) A large sum was *peculated* from the club, and the treasurer is suspected.

(c) The *peculation* of state funds led to a scandal involving many public officials.

15. (a) The wood used in violins is chosen for its *resonant* qualities. (b) In a rich, *resonant* baritone, the speaker urged his listeners to give him their support. (c) The *resonance* of the concert hall enhances the beauty of the music. (d) The people stood *resonantly* against the enemy, confident that victory would be theirs.

16. (a) *Striated* muscles are formed of long, thin fibers packed tightly together. (b) This blue and white *striated* shirt will go well with your suit. (c) *Striated* rocks are formed by the scraping of glaciers over them.

17. (a) The governor may exercise the right of *veto* if the bill passes the legislature. (b) Each of the four major powers has the right to *veto* any proposal. (c) We had made plans to go away for the weekend, but our parents *vetoed* the idea. (d) No one has the *veto* to exercise his rights if they infringe on the rights of others.

EXERCISE 25C

It was once believed (and still is by some people) that the planets exercised control over human destiny, and persons born under a particular planet were believed to have certain characteristics. Those born under Mercury, for example, were thought to be particularly subject to sudden and unpredictable changes of mind; the word MERCURIAL came to be applied to such people. Other words describing mental or emotional states have come into the language through the influence of the planets; give the origins and meanings of the similarly derived words below.

SATURNINE . . . .

. . . .

. . . .

. . . .

JOVIAL . . . .

. . . .

. . . .

. . . .

MARTIAL . . . .

. . . .

. . . .

. . . .

WORDLY WISE 25

To ADDUCE means "to give as a reason or proof" (to adduce evidence); *deduce* means "to infer by reasoning" (to deduce the cause from the effects observed).

The adjectives CORPOREAL and *corporal*, meaning "physical; bodily" were once synonymous; *corporal*, in this meaning, is now restricted to the phrase "corporal punishment."

To DEPRECATE is to express disapproval of (to deprecate illegal practices); to *depreciate* is to belittle or lessen the value of (to depreciate in value; to depreciate one's own contribution to something).

EMEND means "to correct or improve, as a literary text"; *amend* also means "to improve" but is more general in its application and can suggest change merely rather than improvement. We emend a text by making a specific correction in it; we amend the Constitution by attaching amendments to it.

STRIATED means "marked with thin parallel lines" (Striated rocks give evidence of glacial action). A single such mark is called a *stria* (plural, *striae*) or a *striation*.

Etymology

Study the roots and prefix given below together with the English words derived from them. Capitalized words are those given in the Word List. You should look up in a dictionary any words that are unfamiliar to you.

Prefix: *ad-* (to, toward) Latin – Examples:
    ADDUCE, *adjure*, *advert*
Roots: *corpus* (body) Latin – Examples:
    CORPOREAL, *corpse*, *corporation*
    voc, vox (voice) Latin – Examples:
    EQUIVOCATE, *vocal*, *equivocal*

Word List 26

ACERBITY	DONOR	OBVERSE
APHORISM	EJACULATION	PECTORAL
ATROPHY	ENDOW	RECTITUDE
BURGEON	EXTRINSIC	SALACIOUS
COQUETTE	GYRATE	TRIPTYCH
DECOCTION	JOCUND	

Look up the words above in your dictionary. Note that many of them have more than one meaning. When you feel that you know *all* the meanings of *all* the words, go on to the exercises below.

EXERCISE 26A

From the four choices following each phrase or sentence, you are to circle the letter preceding the one that is closest in meaning to the italicized word. Where the same word appears more than once, you should note that it is being used in different senses.

1. to speak with *acerbity*
   (a) authority (b) an air of sadness (c) difficulty (d) sharpness of temper

2. to utter an *aphorism*
   (a) prayer of thanks (b) mildly blasphemous oath (c) concise statement of a principle (d) malicious or hurtful remark

3. the *atrophy* of freedom
   (a) vigorous defense (b) wasting away (c) ultimate triumph (d) triumphant hymn

4. to *burgeon*
   (a) fall into decay (b) refuse to budge (c) grow or flourish (d) fall back

5. a young *coquette*
   (a) overdressed man (b) gossipy person (c) boastful woman (d) flirtatious woman

6. to obtain by *decoction*
   (a) filtering through successive layers (b) underhanded or illegal methods (c) translating from code into ordinary language (d) boiling so as to extract the essence

7. a generous *donor*
   (a) share (b) offer (c) giver (d) gift

8. a sudden *ejaculation*
   (a) sword thrust (b) exclamation (c) withdrawal (d) understanding

9. to *endow* an institution
   (a) assure the leadership of (b) formally join (c) formally establish (d) provide funds for

10. *extrinsic* features
    (a) costly (b) outside (c) rare (d) essential

11. to *gyrate*
    (a) climb to a higher level (b) undergo a change of heart (c) move in a spiral path (d) change into a new form

12. to *gyrate* wildly
    (a) wave one's arms (b) cheer for one's team (c) move irregularly (d) utter nonsensical sounds

13. a *jocund* group
    (a) merry (b) somber (c) tightly-knit (d) traveling

14. the *obverse* of a coin
    (a) front (b) back (c) condition (d) inscription

15. *pectoral* muscles
    (a) chest (b) stomach (c) leg (d) facial

16. a person of *rectitude*
    (a) reckless bravery (b) doubtful character (c) spareness of frame (d) uprightness of character

17. *salacious* talk
    (a) wise (b) boring (c) witty (d) lewd

18. a large *triptych*
    (a) design formed of inlaid tiles (b) picture painted on a wall (c) picture formed of three panels (d) three-sided stone monument

Check your answers against the following correct ones. The answers are not in order; this is to prevent your eye from catching sight of the correct answers before you have had a chance to do the exercise on your own.

17d. 4c. 8b. 16d. 13a. 11c. 5d. 7c. 18c. 3b. 10b. 2c. 6d. 15a. 1d. 12c. 14a. 9d.

Look up in your dictionary all the words for which you gave incorrect answers. Only when you have done this should you go on to the next exercise.

EXERCISE 26B

Each word in Word List 26 is used several times in the sentences below to illustrate different meanings or usage. One of the sentences for each word uses the italicized word incorrectly. You are to circle the letter preceding that sentence.

1. (a) "Get out of here!" she said with some *acerbity* in her voice. (b) He is one of our more *acerbic* critics, so don't let his scathing review upset you. (c) The *acerbity* of her muscles is caused by her failure to exercise regularly.

2. (a) My boss is always quoting the *aphorism* "The early bird gets the worm." (b) She tends to be too self-consciously *aphoristic* in her speechmaking. (c) Francis Bacon wrote his essays in a beautifully *aphoristic* style. (d) When Columbus returned to the colony he had founded, he discovered that it was in a state of *aphorism*.

3. (a) The disease had *atrophied* the man's legs, making it impossible for him to walk. (b) Muscles *atrophy* if they are not used. (c) The *atrophy* of our major cities can be prevented only at a cost of tens of billions of dollars. (d) One team will *atrophy* over the others, and that team will be the champion.

4. (a) The arts festival, which was on the point of being abandoned, is *burgeoning* under its new director. (b) Hope *burgeoned* anew as we saw that we were to be given a second chance. (c) The *burgeoning* plants in the garden are a tribute to the gardener's skill. (d) A heavy oak

109

burgeon was placed against the door to prevent anyone from entering.

5. (a) Supporters of the team wore blue and white *coquettes* pinned to their coats. (b) She loves to *coquette* at parties. (c) Her *coquettish* airs seemed out of place on such a serious occasion. (d) She loved playing the *coquette* and thought nothing of promising her heart to three men at one time.

6. (a) The herbs are boiled for an hour, and the resulting *decoction* is used as a medicine. (b) I *decocted* a dessert for the children made of ice cream, cherries, and chocolate. (c) If the mixture is too weak, it can be *decocted* further until it is the desired strength.

7. (a) The Red Cross has put out an urgent appeal for blood *donors*. (b) The committee offered to *donor* the use of the hall for our meeting. (c) Here is a list of *donors* to the museum fund.

8. (a) "Oh, no!" he *ejaculated* when he heard that the money had been stolen. (b) A surprised *ejaculation* escaped his lips when he heard the news. (c) Any persons trying to disrupt the meeting will be *ejaculated* from the hall.

9. (a) The family was *endowed* with intelligence, good health, and an unusual talent in music. (b) The Greek writers of tragedies *endowed* many of the old myths with new meanings. (c) The university's *endowment* is one of the largest in the country. (d) The *endow* that she received on her marriage was used as a down payment on a house.

10. (a) The matters you bring up are *extrinsic* to the main issue and cannot be considered here. (b) The husband and wife grew more and more *extrinsic* and finally agreed to separate. (c) The pressures being applied to the organization are *extrinsic* and are not the doing of any of its members. (d) Style should not be something *extrinsic* to the subject matter but an intrinsic part of it.

11. (a) Prices on the stock exchange *gyrated* wildly yesterday in the wake of the President's announcement. (b) Clouds of dust raised by the storm *gyrated* about the housetops. (c) The wild *gyrations* of the plane indicated that the rudder was stuck. (d) She *gyrated* the wheel a few times to make sure that it was no longer sticking.

12. (a) Our teacher's *jocundities* usually took the form of bad puns. (b) The *jocund* host bade us eat, drink, and be merry. (c) A party of young *jocunds* was making merry in the room below.

13. (a) The *obverse* of the one cent piece shows the head of Lincoln, and the reverse shows the Lincoln Memorial. (b) The *obverse* side of an object is the side facing the observer. (c) The prolonged drought is bound to have an *obverse* effect on the crops.

14. (a) He complains of pains in the *pectoral* region, so he may have a pulled chest muscle. (b) A *pectoral* cross is one worn on the breast by certain members of the clergy. (c) The *pectoral* girdle is the bony arch that supports the forelimbs in vertebrates. (d) *Pectoral* creatures sleep during the day and are active at night.

15. (a) She stood up bravely to the *rectitude* that was hurled against her. (b) The *rectitude* of her behavior has never been questioned. (c) Despite our misgivings, he is convinced of the *rectitude* of what he is doing.

16. (a) The talk of the sailors embarking for shore leave was cheerfully *salacious*. (b) The *salaciousness* of this novel led to its being banned in Boston. (c) The *salaciousness* of the water is due to its high salt content.

17. (a) The artist was working on the two outside panels of the *triptych* when I called on her. (b) The three paintings had been *triptyched*

with a clear varnish to protect them. (c) The center panel of the *triptych* that stood above the altar portrayed religious figures.

EXERCISE 26C

In each of the sentences below a word is omitted. From the four words provided, select the one that best completes the sentence. Allow ten minutes for this test. If you cannot answer a question, go on to the next one without delay. If you have time left over at the end, go back and try to fill in unanswered questions.

18 or over correct: excellent
14 to 17 correct: good
13 or under correct: thorough review of A
                        exercises indicated

1. The president has the power to
   . . . . bills passed by the
   Congress.
   observe veto belabor endow

2. His father was a man of . . . .
   and incapable of acting immorally.
   dialectic casuistry benediction rectitude

3. The . . . . on South American
   plantations work long hours for low pay.
   temperas canons tyros peons

4. She was . . . . by her associates
   because of her unethical practices.
   rarefied ostracized simulated striated

5. A small . . . . was paid to anyone
   suffering loss.
   appellation collation precept indemnity

6. Political leaders are expected to
   . . . . the legislature by the
   weekend.
   prorogue moot ossify abrade

7. His low red blood-cell count indicates that he
   is suffering from . . . .
   animadversion apothegm anemia aphorism

8. We used a . . . . to drag the river
   bottom.
   pommel lampoon sobriquet grapnel

9. Grandfather is in his . . . . and
   sometimes says silly things.
   abeyance dotage apostate declivity

10. I never knew such a . . . . person,
    sad one minute and happy the next.
    malleable peripatetic bellicose mercurial

11. Prices on the stock market . . . .
    wildly in the wake of yesterday's news.
    burgeoned striated limned gyrated

12. As a . . . . of the church, he is
    bound forever by his vows.
    sequester precept codicil votary

13. *Telecast* is a . . . . formed
    from the words *television* and *broadcast*.
    neophyte nepotism neologism natation

14. Her . . . . teaching was done
    while she strolled the grounds of the academy.
    peripatetic annular apocryphal indigent

15. Even a small daily intake of the drug has a
    harmful . . . . effect.
    itinerant inimical cumulative extrinsic

16. The orator spoke like a man in the grip of a
    divine . . . .
    afflatus aphorism cognomen apotheosis

17. There is not a . . . . of truth in
    what that mountebank says.
    diva cabal scintilla codicil

18. The . . . . branches of the willow
    trailed in the water.
    germane endemic pendent dative

19. Apart from a minor . . . . in her
    youth, she has never been in any trouble.
    anathema peccadillo archipelago concatenation

20. This book helps fill the . . . . in Shakespeare's early life.

fiat desuetude argot hiatus

WORDLY WISE 26

A DECOCTION is an essence or extract obtained by boiling; a *concoction* is anything, an item of food, a scheme, that is put together.

A DONOR is one who gives; a *donee* is the recipient of such an act.

JOCUND, *jocular* (Word List 20), and *jocose* (Word List 6) all mean "given to joking; happy." *Jocund* suggests the feeling or showing of cheeriness of spirit; *jocular* and *jocose* suggest a playful humorousness with the latter term conveying a sense of facetiousness also.

A TRIPTYCH is a picture formed of three panels. A *triptyque* (pronounced the same as *triptych*) is a customs pass for the temporary importation of one's car into a country.

Etymology

Study the roots given below together with the English words derived from them. Capitalized words are those given in the Word List. You should look up in a dictionary any words that are unfamiliar to you.

Roots: *jac*, *joc* (throw) Latin — Examples: E*JAC*ULATION, e*jec*t, pro*jec*t
tri (three) Greek — Examples: *TRI*PTYCH, *tri*ad, *tri*logy

Word List 27

ANCHORITE	EFFULGENT	MACROSCOPIC
APPOSITE	ENAMORED	OLIGARCHY
BRACKISH	ESCUTCHEON	PROSODY
CAVIL	FOIBLE	REVELATION
DECIMATE	INORDINATE	STULTIFY
DEVOLVE		

Look up the words above in your dictionary. Note that many of them have more than one meaning. When you feel that you know *all* the meanings of *all* the words, go on to the exercises below.

EXERCISE 27A

From the four choices following each phrase or sentence, you are to circle the letter preceding the one that is closest in meaning to the italicized word. Where the same word appears more than once, you should note that it is being used in different senses.

1. to become an *anchorite*
   (a) source of concern to others (b) ship's cabin boy (c) senior naval officer (d) religious recluse

2. an *apposite* remark
   (a) contradictory (b) fitting (c) peculiar (d) embarrassing

3. The water is *brackish*.
   (a) poisonous (b) slightly dirty (c) somewhat salty (d) not moving

4. to *cavil*
   (a) raise trivial objections (b) move at a fast trot (c) offer a salute to one's foe (d) keep a sharp lookout

5. to *decimate* an army
   (a) withdraw under heavy fire (b) add reinforcements to (c) disband and send home (d) destroy a large part of

6. to *devolve* upon
   (a) turn around (b) transfer (c) seize (d) rest

7. an *effulgent* light
   (a) of changing colors (b) flashing (c) brilliant (d) dim

8. *enamored* of a person
   (a) filled with boredom (b) filled with love (c) filled with hatred (d) filled with disgust

9. a family *escutcheon*
   (a) gathering held on certain occasions (b) servant who is treated as a member of the family (c) quarrel, the cause of which has been forgotten (d) shield bearing a coat of arms

10. a petty *foible*
    (a) weakness (b) quarrel (c) grudge (d) remark

11. an *inordinate* desire
    (a) secret (b) strange (c) immoderate (d) repressed

12. *macroscopic* creatures
    (a) having an extremely short life (b) invisible to the naked eye (c) attracted to bright light (d) visible to the naked eye

13. to establish an *oligarchy*
    (a) government by a single person (b) government by a few persons (c) government by all the people (d) government by a foreign power

14. the *prosody* of Milton
    (a) complete works (b) richness of imagery (c) method of versification (d) prose writings

15. a *revelation* in the last chapter
    (a) striking disclosure (b) terrible warning (c) disappointing letdown (d) missing section

16. a *revelation* to me
    (a) major setback (b) unfriendly warning (c) show of affection (d) pleasant surprise

17. to *stultify* oneself
    (a) hold back the physical growth of (b) loudly proclaim the merits of (c) cause to appear inconspicuous (d) cause to appear foolish

18. to *stultify* the system
    (a) open up (b) overcome the limitations of (c) render worthless (d) openly oppose

Check your answers against the correct ones given below. The answers are not in order; this is to prevent your eye from catching sight of the correct answers before you have had a chance to do the exercise on your own.

2b. 8b. 17d. 1d. 5d. 9d. 6b. 11c. 7c. 14c. 18c. 16d. 15a. 12d. 13b. 3c. 10a. 4a.

Look up in your dictionary all the words for which you gave incorrect answers. Only when you have done this should you go on to the next exercise.

EXERCISE 27B

Each word in Word List 27 is used several times in the sentences below to illustrate different meanings or usage. One of the sentences for each word uses the italicized word incorrectly. You are to circle the letter preceding that sentence.

1. (a) A small bay provided a good *anchorite* for the vessel after the storm-tossed crossing. (b) He was the son of a wealthy merchant, but he renounced his riches and became an *anchorite*. (c) The *anchorite* said she had withdrawn from the bustle of life the better to contemplate God's will.

2. (a) The example he gave was particularly *apposite* to the subject under discussion. (b) Her lecture was replete with *apposite* quotations from Emily Dickinson. (c) The blue hat he wore was strikingly *apposite* to the rest of his outfit.

3. (a) The water had a slightly *brackish* taste, but we were thirsty and drank it. (b) We hacked our way through the *brackish* tangle of undergrowth. (c) The water that collects in the marshes is *brackish* and unfit for drinking.

4. (a) She accepted without *cavil* the conditions that we laid down. (b) These *cavilling* shoppers who have all day to haggle are the bane of the shopkeepers' lives. (c) He *cavilled* at the price asked and was pleased when the price was lowered a dollar. (d) A dish of *cavilled* beef was set before the child.

5. (a) Rampant inflation has *decimated* the buying power of the consumer. (b) Injuries and disease had *decimated* the army and it was in no condition to fight. (c) The cannons fired point blank into the advancing soldiers, *decimating* their ranks. (d) The general *decimated* whether to withdraw his army or to stay and fight.

6. (a) On the death of the president, the presidency *devolves* upon the vice-president. (b) She was *devolved* of any responsibility for the accident. (c) He spoke of the risks of *devolving* political authority upon those not yet prepared for it.

7. (a) The monarch, *effulgent* in scarlet robes, greeted the cheering subjects. (b) Poets have hymned and painters have limned Helen of Troy's *effulgent* beauty. (c) The sinking sun lit up the mountaintops with a fiery *effulgence*. (d) He was feeling *effulgent* toward his children and gave them all an extra dollar.

8. (a) The copper plates were *enamored* to the sides of the box with brass rivets. (b) They became *enamored* of the town and returned every year. (c) He was *enamored* with the girl and could not wait to declare his love.

9. (a) The family *escutcheon* consisted of a white cross on a blue and gold ground. (b) The son's scrapes with the law are a blot on the family *escutcheon*. (c) In a quavering voice the aged family *escutcheon* announced the guests as they arrived.

10. (a) Sarah Bernhardt's only *foible* was her refusal to accept the fact that she was getting old. (b) A husband and wife must learn to live with each other's *foibles*. (c) As a judge with forty years' experience, he is used to human *foibles* and frailties. (d) She was given her chance and *foibled* it, and she will not get another one.

11.
(a) She was *inordinately* fond of seafood and never ordered anything else when eating out. (b) The book's *inordinate* length could be overlooked if the author had tried to make it interesting. (c) Her *inordinate* ambition led her to take many chances in her bid for the leadership. (d) The place where the two *inordinates* cross on the map marks the position.

12. (a) *Macroscopic* creatures are large enough to be seen with the unaided eye. (b) The scientists examined the specimens under a powerful *macroscope*. (c) *Macroscopic* equations deal with unusually large numbers.

13. (a) Many of these countries are *oligarchies* with a handful of powerful landowners controlling the government. (b) If the people do not involve themselves in government, democracy quickly degenerates into *oligarchy*. (c) Those who distrusted the common people were in favor of an *oligarchic* society. (d) After destroying all opposition to his rule, he proclaimed himself *oligarch* with dictatorial powers.

14. (a) This article on the *prosody* of English deals chiefly with the rhythmic aspects of the language. (b) The *prosody* of Shakespeare's early plays is marked by a reliance on rhymed couplets. (c) He was a musical *prosody* and could play six instruments before he was five. (d) Her book on *prosody* will deal with all aspects of versification, particularly metrical structure.

15. (a) The family experienced a *revelation* when the new will was read. (b) They believe that divine truth is obtained by *revelation* and not by studying. (c) This *revelationary* device cuts in half the time needed to do the job. (d) The ease with which she won the race was a *revelation* to me.

16. (a) Is it true that cigarette smoking can *stultify* your growth? (b) The system of automatic promotion for time served *stultifies* initiative. (c) You *stultify* your research papers by failing to provide adequate references. (d) She found that running her own business was less *stultifying* than working for a large corporation.

EXERCISE 27C

This exercise combines synonyms and antonyms. You are to underline the word which is *either* most similar in meaning *or* most nearly opposite in meaning to the capitalized word. Underline only one word for each question after deciding that it is either an antonym or a synonym and write A (for antonym) or S (for synonym) after the capitalized word. Allow only fifteen minutes for this test. If you cannot answer a question, go on to the next one without delay. If you have time left over at the end, go back and try to fill in unanswered questions.

26 or over correct: excellent
22 to 25 correct: good
21 or under correct: thorough review of A
                       exercises indicated

1. FLOURISH . . . .
   adduce atrophy equivocate prorogue pommel

2. NAME . . . .
   cabal prosody escutcheon appellation casuistry

3. DULL . . . .
   inordinate apposite occult corporeal effulgent

4. ORDINARY . . . .
   bellicose peripatetic striated extrinsic mundane

5. CORRECT . . . .
   deprecate belabor peculate encroach emend

6. LEWD . . . .
   salacious salubrious sanguine sedulous obstreperous

7. RECIPIENT . . . .
   obelisk legate votary donor tyro

8. ATTACK . . . .
   descry beget behoove imbibe belabor

9. SOLEMN . . . .
   immanent igneous inimical jocund itinerant

10. SALTY . . . .
    brackish sylvan germane chimerical lachrymose

11. DEFALCATE . . . .
    abrogate anneal genuflect peculate lucubrate

12. OUTSIDE . . . .
    extrinsic prolix indigenous corporeal ubiquitous

13. EXCESSIVE . . . .
    lachrymose macroscopic fulsome mercurial unguent

14. EXTOL . . . .
    adduce deprecate permeate lucubrate emend

15. SHARPNESS . . . .
    abeyance incubus acerbity detritus mensuration

16. ASTUTE . . . .
    perspicuous perspicacious invidious igneous factious

17. WEAKNESS . . . .
    tautology moiety fealty desuetude foible

18. WITHER . . . .
    deprecate equivocate emend divine burgeon

19. CLEAR . . . .
    sidereal perspicuous perspicacious inordinate forensic

20. EXCLAMATION . . . .
    aberration affidavit animadversion ejaculation trumpery

21. REVERSE . . . .
    triptych retrograde diurnal adipose obverse

22. HIDDEN . . . .
    unmitigated lambent covert rarefied moot

23. LOYALTY . . . .
    equanimity equity fetish fealty acumen

24. SUPERNATURAL . . . .
    lambent opalescent passé occult orotund

25. DAILY . . . .
    fecund germane diurnal eclectic annular

115

26. PRESENT . . . .

emend adduce deprecate peculate simulate

27. WARLIKE . . . .

inchoate peripatetic singular bellicose itinerant

28. INAPPROPRIATE . . . .

apposite indigent indeterminate unequivocal apocryphal

29. EXCESSIVE . . . .

inimical immanent inordinate ingenuous insensate

30. WICKED . . . .

forensic frenetic fetid comatose heinous

WORDLY WISE 27

DEVOLVE is usually followed by the preposition *on* or *upon* (It devolved upon me to break the news).

ENAMORED takes the preposition *of* (enamored of someone) or *with* (enamored with someone).

MACROSCOPIC means "large enough to be seen with the unaided eye" (macroscopic insects); *microscopic* means "so small as to be visible only under a microscope."

Etymology

Study the roots given below together with the English words derived from them. Capitalized words are those given in the Word List. You should look up in a dictionary any words that are unfamiliar to you.

Roots: *decem* (ten) Latin – Examples: *DECI-MATE, December, decade*

macro (large) Greek – Examples: *MACRO-SCOPIC, macrocosm, macroeconomics*

ACROSS

1. sharpness of temper
6. to express disapproval of
11. to provide or be provided with
12. to embezzle
13. government by a few
14. to grow or flourish
16. fitting; apt
20. a concise statement of a principle
21. to speak evasively
22. marked with thin, parallel lines
23. excessive; immoderate
25. given to sudden changes of mood
28. of or occurring in the spring (15)
30. one who gives or contributes
32. marked by lewdness; lustful
35. loyalty, especially to a feudal lord
36. to quote from (3)
38. the power to prohibit action
40. a flirtatious woman
41. weakminded because of old age
44. a picture made up of three panels
45. the method or study of versification
47. an extract obtained by boiling
50. somewhat salty
51. a slight fault or weakness
52. to pass to another; to transfer
53. radiant; brilliant
54. to raise trivial objections

DOWN

1. a name or title
2. a shield bearing a coat of arms
3. to expound on at great length
4. a religious recluse; a hermit
5. open to question; debatable (11)
7. filled with love
8. uprightness of character; moral correctness
9. a sudden exclamation
10. of the body; physical
15. echoing; resounding
17. of or located in the chest
18. atrociously wicked
19. cheerful; merry
22. to cause to appear foolish
24. a striking disclosure
26. able to be seen by the naked eye
27. to correct or improve
29. a soft mass of chewed food (7)
31. the front side, as of a coin or medal
33. to waste away
34. to close, as a wound, with surgical stitches (17)
37. operating from outside; external
39. to destroy a large part of
42. to move or spin in a spiral path
43. to present as proof or evidence
46. secret; mysterious; supernatural
48. a small group of plotters
49. a female opera star (3)

Chapter Ten

Word List 28

ABJURE	EXTEMPORIZE	PLEONASM
BADINAGE	INEFFABLE	RECONDITE
BRIO	ITERATE	SANGUINARY
CONCURRENT	MANIAC	TERPSICHOREAN
DEPRAVED	OBEISANCE	UNEQUIVOCAL

Look up the words above in your dictionary. Note that many of them have more than one meaning. When you feel that you know *all* the meanings of *all* the words, go on to the exercises below.

EXERCISE 28A

From the four choices following each phrase or sentence, you are to circle the letter preceding the one that is closest in meaning to the italicized word. Where the same word appears more than once, you should note that it is being used in different senses.

1. to *abjure* allegiance
   (a) demand (b) swear (c) renounce (d) pretend

2. to exchange *badinage*
   (a) letters of introduction (b) small gifts (c) dire threats (d) teasing remarks

3. with *brio*
   (a) fear and trembling (b) spirited zest (c) grim determination (d) great uncertainty

4. *concurrent* events
   (a) occurring one after the other (b) of the present time (c) occurring together (d) of the past

5. a *depraved* person
   (a) mentally alert (b) terribly unhappy (c) without money or a job (d) thoroughly corrupt

6. to *extemporize* a speech
   (a) make additions or deletions to (b) deliver from memory (c) tone down the inflammatory parts of (d) make up as one goes along

7. *ineffable* joy
   (a) unending (b) unutterable (c) unrelieved (d) unjustified

8. to *iterate* the complaint
   (a) repeat (b) reject (c) answer (d) act on

9. the work of a *maniac*
   (a) person of enormous strength (b) person with great strength of will (c) violently insane person (d) brilliantly imaginative person

10. to make one's *obeisances*
    (a) gestures of respect (b) formal apologies (c) final farewells (d) final preparations

11. to question the *pleonasm*
    (a) outdated form of a word (b) omission of a word or phrase (c) newly coined word (d) superfluous word or phrase

12. *recondite* books
    (a) freely available (b) reprinted in cheap editions (c) in very short supply (d) beyond ordinary understanding

13. a *sanguinary* threat
    (a) veiled (b) empty (c) murderous (d) humorously intended

14. a *sanguinary* battle
    (a) brief (b) simulated (c) bloodless (d) bloody

15. *terpsichorean* skills
    (a) oratorical (b) singing (c) dancing (d) dramatic

16. an *unequivocal* reply
    (a) deliberately ambiguous (b) clear and explicit (c) hesitant and tentative (d) unintentionally ambiguous

Check your answers against the following correct ones. The answers are not in order; this is to prevent your eye from catching sight of the correct answers before you have had a chance to do the exercise on your own.

2d. 8a. 1c. 5d. 9c. 6d. 11d. 7b. 14d. 16b. 15c. 12d. 13c. 3b. 10a. 4c.

Look up in your dictionary all the words for which you gave incorrect answers. Only when you have done this should you go on to the next exercise.

EXERCISE 28B

Each word in Word List 28 is used several times in the sentences below to illustrate different meanings or usage. One of the sentences for each word uses the italicized word incorrectly. You are to circle the letter preceding that sentence.

1. (a) Galileo was called before the Inquisition and made to *abjure* his heretical theories. (b) She continues to hold these absurd views despite the *abjurations* she made. (c) He *abjurately* refuses to do as he is told. (d) Before receiving her citizenship, she was made to *abjure* allegiance to her former country.

2. (a) Just before going on the air, the announcer exchanged *badinage* with the two guest speakers. (b) The candidate's lighthearted *badinage* was taken seriously by the reporters. (c) Grandfather is in his *badinage*, so you must excuse the foolish things he says.

3. (a) The next passage suggests the exuberance of spring and must be played with *brio*. (b) The old man sang with enormous *brio*, if a little off key. (c) She flew the plane with all the *brio* of a fighter pilot. (d) Thorns tore our clothes as we made our way through the *brio* thicket.

4. (a) Our speaker is a professor of Spanish, and *concurrent* to that taught my adult education class. (b) She was given five years on each charge, the sentences to run *concurrently*. (c) *Concurrent* with Germany's plans to invade Russia were her vows of nonaggression with that country.

5. (a) This man is a monster who *depraves* everyone he comes in contact with. (b) Is human nature so *depraved* that people need war, even relish it? (c) Only a *depraved* mind could have conceived and executed such a ghastly crime. (d) He was *depraved* of a normal childhood and so grew up with a warped mind.

6. (a) She had had no time to prepare a speech, so she spoke *extemporaneously* when called upon. (b) The director made the film without a script, preferring to *extemporize* as she went along. (c) Defensive barriers were quickly *extemporized* to give warning of any enemy attack. (d) He has *extemporized* both groups of supporters by his refusal to take a stand on this issue.

7. (a) His manner was always subdued, as though he bore the burden of some *ineffable* secret. (b) The door proved *ineffable* to our attempts to break it down. (c) Her radiant face spoke of her *ineffable* joy as mere words never could. (d) Jehovah's name was *ineffable*; to utter it was a sin.

8. (a) A bird perched on a branch, *iterating* a single note. (b) She *iterated* her request that she be allowed to remain behind. (c) The *iterate* salesperson never stayed more than a week in any one place.

9. (a) The *maniacal* laugh of the murderer sent chills down my spine. (b) He had been raving like a *maniac*, but a few minutes after taking the drug he was sleeping like a child. (c) Hitler's *maniac* desire to impose his will on Europe met with astonishingly little resistance. (d) A *maniac*-depressive person alternates between moods of euphoria and melancholy.

10. (a) She was terrified of being accused of disloyalty and was forever making *obeisances* to her superiors. (b) The *obeisance* shown the king by his courtiers took the form of an elaborate ritual. (c) After making her *obeisance* before the queen, she turned and left the room. (d) The matter will be held in *obeisance* until the committee has its next meeting.

11. (a) She suffered a *pleonasm* of the heart recently, but she has made a good recovery. (b) In the phrase "a true fact," the word "true" is a *pleonasm*. (c) Try to avoid such *pleonastic* phrases as "with my own eyes" in the sentence "I saw it with my own eyes."

12. (a) He was not a specialist in the field and so found the subject matter too *recondite* for him. (b) He *reconditied* himself to the fact that he would never see her again. (c) She was an expert in Sanskrit and other *recondite* languages.

13. (a) Blackbeard was one of the most *sanguinary* pirates of the Caribbean. (b) This *sanguinary* war will not stop until both sides have been bled white. (c) He gazed stunned at the *sanguinary* stream flowing from his slashed artery. (d) She was rushed to the first-aid post where a waiting *sanguinary* bound her wounds.

14. (a) Her weekly column on the *terpsichorean* scene in New York is read by all students of the dance. (b) He plays the harpsichord beautifully, although his favorite instrument is the *terpsichore*. (c) Her *terpsichorean* abilities were recognized when she began taking ballet lessons.

15. (a) The plain and *unequivocal* language of the contract leaves no room for misunderstanding. (b) Edna St. Vincent Millay speaks *unequivocally* in the language of a new age. (c) She *unequivocaled*, uncertain whether to agree or disagree. (d) She answered his proposal of marriage with an *unequivocal* no.

EXERCISE 28C

There are two distinct levels of vocabulary in English — the first consists of familiar, everyday words, often Anglo-Saxon in origin; the second is made up of rarer, more bookish words that are generally of Latin origin. Shakespeare uses both styles in the last two lines of this speech from *Macbeth* (Act II, scene ii, lines 60–64).

Will all great Neptune's Ocean wash this blood
Clean from my hand? No; this my hand will rather
The multitudinous seas incarnadine,
Making the green one red.

The advantage of the Latinate style is that it is dignified and possesses a stately grandeur; its disadvantage is that it may be obscure or absurdly pompous. The advantage of the Anglo-Saxon style is that it is simple, plain, direct; its disadvantage is that it can sound childish and may result in oversimplification.

Rewrite each of the sentences below, substituting the more common word for each Latinate word italicized. Which version do you prefer?

1. These *colloquies* require *minimal cerebration*.

. . . .

2. Although *impecunious*, he was *immaculate* in his *habiliments*.

. . . .

3. The *pulchritude* of her *physiognomy* was temporarily marred by her *sanguinary proboscis*.

. . . .

4. The *collation* that the *somnambulist consumed* while *ambulatory* will not be *deleterious*.

. . . .

5. The *altercation* was so *ephemeral* it scarcely deserves such an *appellation*.

. . . .

WORDLY WISE 28

To EXTEMPORIZE is to speak, play, or act in an impromptu manner; to *temporize* is to act evasively in order to gain time.

SANGUINARY means "bloodthirsty" or "covered with blood" (the sanguinary hands of Lady Macbeth); *sanguine* (Word List 14) means "cheerful; optimistic" (to take a sanguine view of events).

The adjectives MANIAC and *maniacal* mean "violently insane" (maniac desires); *manic* means "mentally or physically hyperactive" (a manic-depressive person alternates between frenzied excitement and deep melancholy).

The nine Muses were goddesses born of Zeus and Mnemosyne (Memory) who presided over song, poetry, and the arts and sciences. Besides TERPSICHORE, the Muse of dance, they were: *Calliope* (chief of the Muses), *Clio* (history and heroic exploits), *Euterpe* (music), *Thalia* (gaiety and comedy), *Melpomene* (tragedy), *Erato* (the lyre and love poetry), *Polyhymnia* (inspired and stately hymns), and *Urania* (astronomy).

Etymology

Study the roots given below together with the English words derived from them. Capitalized words are those given in the Word List. You should look up in a dictionary any words that are unfamiliar to you.

Roots: *sang* (blood) Latin – Examples: *SANGUI-NARY*, *sang*uine, con*sang*uinity

jura (swear) Latin – Examples: AB*JURE*, per*jury*

Word List 29

ASCRIBE	HEGEMONY	QUIESCENT
BICAMERAL	INTERDICT	REDEEM
CAULK	JINGOISM	SHIBBOLETH
DAIS	MAWKISH	TOPOGRAPHY
ELUCIDATE	OVERRULE	UXORIOUS

Look up the words above in your dictionary. Note that many of them have more than one meaning. When you feel that you know *all* the meanings of *all* the words, go on to the exercises below.

EXERCISE 29A

From the four choices following each phrase or sentence, you are to circle the letter preceding the one that is closest in meaning to the italicized word. Where the same word appears more than once, you should note that it is being used in different senses.

1. to *ascribe* blame
   (a) accept (b) avoid (c) deny (d) attribute

2. a *bicameral* legislature
   (a) having two chambers (b) elected for two years (c) holding sessions twice yearly (d) meeting in secret

3. to *caulk* the cracks
   (a) point out (b) stop up (c) clean out (d) paste over

4. to approach the *dais*
   (a) mountain peak (b) appointed time (c) church dignitary (d) raised platform

5. to *elucidate* something
   (a) think one is seeing (b) make more confusing (c) explain (d) come to understand

6. to establish *hegemony*
   (a) peace (b) dominance (c) partnership (d) trade

7. to *interdict* trade
   (a) engage in (b) establish (c) encourage (d) prohibit

8. an increase in *jingoism*
   (a) lip service paid to religion (b) the movement for a world government (c) optimism unjustified by events (d) stridently aggressive patriotism

9. a *mawkish* pride
   (a) motherly (b) patriotic (c) sentimental (d) deep

10. to *overrule* someone
    (a) promote over the head of (b) give precedence to (c) decide against (d) estimate the worth of

11. to be *quiescent*

(a) seething (b) inactive (c) in agreement (d) jubilant

12. to *redeem* a sinner

(a) condemn (b) lead into temptation (c) detect (d) deliver from evil

13. to *redeem* his amateur status

(a) win back (b) give up (c) question (d) assert

14. to *redeem* a promise

(a) renege on (b) put in writing (c) give verbally (d) make good on

15. to *redeem* the slaves

(a) buy (b) sell (c) release (d) capture

16. to ignore the *shibboleth*

(a) thing that serves to separate one group from another (b) sign that is a warning of impending danger (c) religious teacher who instructs the young (d) ultimatum that threatens a nation with war

17. to utter a *shibboleth*

(a) warning (b) piece of gibberish (c) oath (d) catchword

18. the *topography* of the region

(a) plants and animals (b) climatic variations (c) surface features (d) latitude and longitude

19. to be *uxorious*

(a) excessively loyal to one's country (b) excessively fond of sensual pleasures (c) given to expressing views not sincerely held (d) excessively devoted to one's wife

Check your answers against the correct ones given below. The answers are not in order; this is to prevent your eye from catching sight of the correct answers before you have had a chance to do the exercise on your own.

4d. 10c. 3b. 13a. 14d. 18c. 16a. 15c. 12d. 7d. 11b. 6b. 19d. 5c. 2a. 8d. 17d. 1d. 9c.

Look up in your dictionary all the words for which you gave incorrect answers. Only when you have done this should you go on to the next exercise.

EXERCISE 29B

Each word in Word List 29 is used several times in the sentences below to illustrate different meanings or usage. One of the sentences for each word uses the italicized word incorrectly. You are to circle the letter preceding that sentence.

1. (a) The authorship of this poem has been variously *ascribed* but it is probably by Milton. (b) The plane *ascribed* a perfect arc in the sky before levelling out. (c) She *ascribed* her victory to careful training and a strict diet. (d) The peculiar religiosity *ascribed* to the Middle Ages is challenged in this book.

2. (a) Congress is a *bicameral* institution, consisting of a Senate and House of Representatives. (b) The upper house of a *bicameral* legislature usually reviews laws passed by the lower house. (c) A *bicameral* attack was launched on the enemy positions, the left flank being a decoy.

3. (a) A huge hole was *caulked* in the side of the boat where it struck the rock. (b) The seams of the boat are *caulked* with a special sealing compound. (c) The *caulking* has come loose from the seams, and they should be stopped up again.

4. (a) The chairperson ascended the *dais* and brought the meeting to order. (b) The members were seated facing the *dais*, which was draped with flags for the occasion. (c) He was a *dais* in the union before accepting his present position.

5. (a) She must have been having *elucidations* if she thought her dead father spoke to her. (b) His *elucidation* of the problem was a triumph of scientific methodology. (c) She *elucidated* the problem so clearly that I had no trouble understanding it. (d) Can you *elucidate* the

nature of the government's policy toward Southeast Asia?

6. (a) It is claimed that Egypt is trying to establish its *hegemony* in the Middle East. (b) A *hegemony* of ten thousand dollars was offered for the rebel leader's capture. (c) The *hegemonic* policies of this nation are bound to mean trouble for its neighbors. (d) Hitler's plan for world *hegemony* was frustrated by the allied powers.

7. (a) The *interdiction* of the marriage was ordered by the courts at the request of the bride's parents. (b) Enemy supply routes have been bombed in an attempt to *interdict* the flow of guns to the front. (c) The government has taken action to *interdict* all trade with the offending countries. (d) She was *interdicted* on charges of burglary and resisting arrest.

8. (a) Unbridled *jingoism* can very easily lead to war. (b) The *jingoists* are out in force declaring that their country isn't going to be pushed around by other nations. (c) *Jingoistic* slogans appeared on walls accusing the nation's leaders of being chicken-hearted. (d) The marchers wore red, white, and blue *jingoes* pinned to their coats.

9. (a) His *mawkish* tears and hand-wringing made him a pitiable, even despicable figure. (b) Her speech was simple and sincere, without a trace of *mawkishness*. (c) The scene in the movie where the child's dog is killed is a piece of pure *mawkish*. (d) The poems were so *mawkishly* written that it was embarrassing to have to listen to them.

10. (a) The defense attorney's objection was *overruled* by the judge. (c) The Supreme Court *overruled* the decision of the lower court. (c) I raised a point of order at the meeting, but the chairperson *overruled* me. (d) We cannot *overrule* the possibility that something has happened to them.

11. (a) The melancholy *quiescence* of the deserted town affected us strangely. (b) His *quiescence* with our plan enabled us to move ahead quickly. (c) The volcano has been *quiescent* for years, but it could erupt at any time. (d) When the progress of a disease has been arrested, the disease is said to be *quiescent*.

12. (a) You can *redeem* the goods you pawned by paying the amount of the loan plus interest. (b) The coupons that come with each package are *redeemable* for gifts. (c) I *redeemed* it necessary to speak to you privately on this matter. (d) You can *redeem* yourself by making a public apology for your thoughtless remark.

13. (a) Our listeners type us by the words we use, language itself being the great *shibboleth*. (b) Dressing for dinner was the *shibboleth* that separated the elite from the common people. (c) Words like "freedom" and "peace" have degenerated into *shibboleths*, devoid of meaning. (d) Much of what she said was unintelligible *shibboleth*, but I understood a word here and there.

14. (a) Hills, streams, and other *topographical* features are clearly marked on the map. (b) The general studied the *topography* of the region where he expected the battle to take place. (c) Mapmakers work from data supplied by *topographers* who have surveyed the area. (d) Indiscriminate hunting and fishing have greatly reduced the *topography* of the area.

15. (a) His bachelor apartment had been furnished so *uxoriously* that he was the envy of all his friends. (b) His wife shamelessly took advantage of her husband's *uxorious* nature. (c) His *uxoriousness* was carried to such extremes that he was almost a slave to his wife.

EXERCISE 29C

Complete the following analogies by underlining the numbered pair of words that stand in the same relationship to each other as the first pair of words.

1. uxorious:wife:: (1) luxurious:pleasure (2) patriotic:flag (3) terpsichorean:dance (4) parricidal:parents (5) chauvinistic:country

2. ebullient:enthusiasm:: (1) intestate:will (2) boil:pot (3) bellicose:warlike (4) concurrent:events (5) jocose:humor

3. donor:recipient:: (1) gift:giver (2) take:leave (3) give:take (4) arrive:leave (5) please:thank you

4. libretto:opera:: (1) terpsichorean:dance (2) performer:audience (3) ballet:music (4) lyrics:song (5) rhyme:poetry

5. macroscopic:microscopic:: (1) deadly:harmless (2) dead:alive (3) sky:earth (4) visible:invisible (5) hear:see

6. monarchy:oligarchy:: (1) king:country (2) rule:preside (3) part:whole (4) one:few (5) top:bottom

7. emotional:mawkish:: (1) pleonasm:word (2) love:country (3) fealty:lord (4) lachrymose:tears (5) patriotic:jingoistic

8. diurnal:day:: (1) century:year (2) ten:decade (3) annual:year (4) annular:anneal (5) centennial:decade

9. limn:limb:: (1) branch:twig (2) paint:picture (3) arm:leg (4) rant:rave (5) plum:plumb

10. pectoral:chest:: (1) helmet:head (2) pelvic:hips (3) skull:spine (4) limbs:legs (5) muscle:bone

WORDLY WISE 29

The *l* in CAULK is silent; this word rhymes with *talk*.

In England in 1878, popular feeling ran high against Czarist Russia, and war seemed likely. A popular music-hall song of the time had as its chorus:

We don't want to fight, but, by Jingo! if we do,
We've got the ships, we've got the men, we've got the money too.

This song, with its appeal to primitive patriotism, has added the word JINGOISM to the language.

There is a fascinating story behind the word SHIBBOLETH. It is told in Judges, chapter 12, verses 5 and 6, of the Bible. The Gileadites were at war with the Ephraimites, and the following test was devised to determine whether a captured person was an Ephraimite. The word *shibboleth* (Hebrew for "an ear of grain") was pronounced *sibboleth* by the Ephraimites. A prisoner was simply made to say this word; if he mispronounced it, he was not a Gileadite and was promptly slain.

Etymology

Study the roots and prefix given below together with the English words derived from them. Capitalized words are those given in the Word List. You should look up in a dictionary any words that are unfamiliar to you.

Prefix: *inter-* (between) Latin – Examples: *INTER*DICT, *inter*cept, *inter*rupt

Roots: *scrip, scriba* (write) Latin – Examples: A*SCRIBE, scrip*ture, *scribe*

Word List 30

AVAIL	INDETERMINATE	RECIPROCAL
BILINGUAL	INVIOLABLE	SACERDOTAL
CHOREOGRAPHY	LICENTIOUS	SUBALTERN
DEMURE	MODE	UNDERWRITE
ENSCONCED	PISCATORIAL	VERACIOUS

Look up the words above in your dictionary. Note that many of them have more than one meaning. When you feel that you know *all* the meanings of *all* the words, go on to the exercises below.

EXERCISE 30A

From the four choices following each phrase or sentence, you are to circle the letter preceding the one that is closest in meaning to the italicized word. Where the same word appears more than once, you should note that it is being used in different senses.

1. to *avail* against something
   (a) cry out (b) put up a resistance (c) make a declaration (d) be of use

2. a *bilingual* person
   (a) able to see both sides of a question (b) having citizenship in two countries (c) able to speak two languages (d) able to write with either hand

3. to change the *choreography*
   (a) design of stage costumes (b) dance movements on stage (c) style of singing on stage (d) overall design of a stage production

4. a *demure* manner
   (a) modestly shy (b) aggressively bold (c) offensively sly (d) coldly polite

5. to *ensconce* oneself
   (a) excuse (b) praise (c) reveal (d) conceal

6. to be *ensconced*
   (a) settled in place (b) on the move (c) accused (d) damaged

7. of *indeterminate* size
   (a) greatly enlarged (b) not clearly established (c) greatly reduced (d) rigidly defined

8. an *inviolable* oath
   (a) that cannot be uttered (b) that cannot be enforced (c) that cannot be revealed (d) that cannot be broken

9. *licentious* behavior
   (a) circumspect (b) eccentric (c) wanton (d) normal

10. a new *mode*
    (a) discovery (b) development (c) manner (d) purpose

11. to be *modish*
    (a) awkward (b) unassuming (c) sentimental (d) fashionable

12. the *piscatorial* art
    (a) of fishing (b) of hunting (c) of dancing (d) of conversation

13. *reciprocal* parts
    (a) easily replaced (b) corresponding but reversed (c) identical in form and function (d) alternately stopping and starting

14. *reciprocal* love
    (a) with certain conditions attached (b) given without thought of return (c) mutually experienced (d) that has no end

15. *sacerdotal* garments
    (a) costly (b) pure white (c) royal (d) priestly

16. a *subaltern* in the British army
    (a) senior officer (b) junior officer (c) non-commissioned officer (d) private soldier

17. a *subaltern* position
    (a) substantial (b) superior (c) subjective (d) subordinate

18. to *underwrite* the project
    (a) call off (b) take charge of (c) agree to finance (d) casually dismiss

19. to *underwrite* an insurance policy
    (a) take out (b) make a financial claim under (c) cancel (d) assume any liability under

20. a *veracious* person
    (a) habitually truthful (b) extremely attractive (c) ravenously hungry (d) very eager

Check your answers against the following correct ones. The answers are not in order; this is to prevent your eye from catching sight of the correct answers before you have had a chance to do the exercise on your own.

15d. 5d. 16b. 17d. 13b. 7b. 1d. 10c. 20a. 12a. 4a. 8d. 11d. 18c. 19d. 6a. 14c. 3b. 9c. 2c.

Look up in your dictionary all the words for which you gave incorrect answers. Only when you have done this should you go on to the next exercise.

EXERCISE 30B

Each word in Word List 30 is used several times in the sentences below to illustrate different meanings or usage. One of the sentences for each word uses the italicized word incorrectly. You are to circle the letter preceding that sentence.

1. (a) I was delighted to *avail* myself of the opportunity of speaking to you. (b) J.P. Morgan poured millions into the stock market to prevent a crash, but to no *avail*. (c) He was a big, hearty man who *availed* from somewhere in eastern Texas. (d) You think your scheme will make you rich, but it will *avail* you nothing.

2. (a) I speak some German but not enough to describe myself as *bilingual*. (b) She speaks English, French, German, and Spanish and is *bilingual* in all of them. (c) Canada is a *bilingual* country, the two official languages being French and English.

3. (a) The *choreography* of the show needs a lift, so we have inserted some new dance routines. (b) Agnes de Mille has *choreographed* a number of much acclaimed shows. (c) The dances in the show are a tribute to the *choreographer*. (d) The dancer *choreographed* her way across the stage with almost feline grace.

4. (a) Those children are extremely *demure* and would never raise their voices in anger. (b) She smiled *demurely* when I complimented her on her charming manners. (c) I didn't think he would accept the money, but he took it without *demure*.

5. (a) The treasurer *ensconced* with the money and fled to South America. (b) I *ensconced*

myself behind the curtain so that I could hear without being seen. (c) The statue was *ensconced* in a niche in the main hallway of the building. (d) He was comfortably *ensconced* in his favorite armchair when I arrived.

6. (a) Prisoners given *indeterminate* sentences have no idea when they will be released. (b) A kitten of *indeterminate* sex was left on our doorstep last night. (c) I *indeterminated* them from going ahead with their plan. (d) He was a grizzled fellow of *indeterminate* years.

7. (a) The frontier is regarded as *inviolable* and has never been crossed by an invader. (b) The king's person was *inviolable*, and anyone laying a hand on him would be killed instantly. (c) The vows she had taken were *inviolable*; only death would release her. (d) She *inviolably* stopped by on her way home, and today was no exception.

8. (a) He deplored the *licentiousness* of the stage and urged theatrical producers to show more restraint. (b) The table was filled with cakes, pastries, and other *licentious* things to eat. (c) Their *licentious* behavior scandalized even the more broad-minded members of society.

9. (a) They are conservative people and depart only with reluctance from the established *modes* of behavior. (b) Poets who set out to establish new *modes* in literature are frequently misunderstood. (c) I found that the people in the capital dressed very *modishly*. (d) She was in a somber *mode* when she returned from her visit to the condemned man.

10. (a) She was the best *piscatorial* in the county and usually won the annual fishing competition. (b) For those who enjoy *piscatorial* pursuits, there are excellent trout streams in the area. (c) The best-known *piscatorial* work is Izaak Walton's *The Compleat Angler.*

11. (a) The agreement must be truly *reciprocal*, with both parties sharing the benefits equally. (b) Although the two books are quite

dissimilar, certain themes are *reciprocal* to them both. (c) In the sentence "Bill and Mary like each other," "each other" is a *reciprocal* pronoun. (d) Each contracting flexor muscle has its *reciprocal* extensor muscles which operate in the reverse direction.

12. (a) The priest regarded his visits to the poor as the greatest of his *sacerdotal* duties. (b) Roman Catholicism, with its emphasis on priestly offices, is a supremely *sacerdotal* religion. (c) The doctrine of *sacerdotalism* assumes the necessity for a priestly mediator between people and God. (d) The priest, followed by the *sacerdotals* of the church, walked up the aisle.

13. (a) The captain spoke to the newly-commissioned *subalterns* shortly after their arrival. (b) She occupied a *subaltern* position in the hierarchy and had little hope of rising in it. (c) He did everything he could to *subaltern* my position with the people I commanded.

14. (a) A group of local citizens have agreed to *underwrite* the symphony orchestra's deficit for the year. (b) An insurance *underwriter* sometimes becomes responsible for claims under the contract. (c) Any stocks left would be bought by those who had offered to *underwrite* the issue. (d) Don't *underwrite* her off until you have seen what she can do.

15. (a) Her *veracious* manner of answering the questions impressed all of us. (b) He is so *veracious* that he could not tell a lie to save his life. (c) The members of the jury had complete confidence in the *veracity* of the witness. (d) She reads *veraciously*, everything from westerns to the most recondite works of philosophy.

EXERCISE 30C

This exercise combines synonyms and antonyms. You are to underline the word which is *either* most similar in meaning *or* most nearly opposite in meaning to the capitalized word.

Underline only one word for each question after deciding that it is either an antonym or a synonym and write A (for antonym) or S (for synonym) after the capitalized word. Allow only fifteen minutes for this test. If you cannot answer a question, go on to the next one without delay. If you have time left over at the end, go back and try to fill in unanswered questions.

26 or over correct:	excellent
22 to 25 correct:	good
21 or under correct:	thorough review of A exercises indicated

1. EXPLICIT . . . .
deleterious heinous incipient unequivocal inordinate

2. ATTRIBUTE . . . .
sequester abjure adjure incubate ascribe

3. SETTLED . . . .
unmitigated truncated retrograde ensconced obdurate

4. SIMPLE . . . .
mawkish sanguinary quiescent recondite mundane

5. FITTING . . . .
puerile soporific splenetic apposite vernal

6. UNUTTERABLE . . . .
licentious jocund nuptial incipient ineffable

7. PLATFORM . . . .
cabal schism dais mountebank batten

8. MANNER . . . .
hegemony incubus orison mode moot

9. BANTER . . . .
shibboleth badinage verdigris cacophony canard

10. SENTIMENTAL . . . .
forensic factious factitious mawkish reactionary

11. CONFUSE . . . .
    inhibit simulate elucidate divine apprise

12. BLOODY . . . .
    sanguine sentient sententious sedulous sanguinary

13. FIXED . . . .
    indeterminate pristine reciprocal subaltern tantamount

14. CHEERFUL . . . .
    factious sanguine factitious extrinsic chimerical

15. ZEST . . . .
    luminary lorgnette largo eclogue brio

16. ENFEEBLED . . . .
    recalcitrant recondite striated debilitated subversive

17. PRIESTLY . . . .
    corporeal germane sacerdotal unctuous avuncular

18. SUBORDINATE . . . .
    reactionary peripatetic obverse subaltern sedulous

19. REPEAT . . . .
    cavil iterate cohere imbibe impugn

20. EQUIVALENT . . . .
    inimical palpable mandible lachrymose tantamount

21. WANTON . . . .
    lambent pectoral licentious ensconced sentient

22. TRUTHFUL . . . .
    veracious sententious pendent intransigent apostate

23. DOMINANCE . . . .
    tenure patina tenet dictum hegemony

24. ACTIVE . . . .
    retrograde quiescent resonant obdurate venial

25. PLEDGE . . . .
    iterate inveigh abjure immolate emend

26. FRONT . . . .
    pendent sobriquet encomium pendant obverse

27. RECTITUDE . . . .
    patrimony natation tautology depravity vagary

28. CHEST . . . .
    lacuna mandible sacerdotal piscatorial pectoral

29. BOLD . . . .
    ubiquitous fulsome demure adipose uxorious

30. ALLOW . . . .
    mulct cavil cite beget interdict

WORDLY WISE 30

DEMURE is an adjective and means "modest in demeanor." *Demur* is a verb and means "to take exception to" (He wanted to accompany me, but I demurred).

RECIPROCAL has a mathematical meaning in addition to those given in the exercises. A reciprocal is a number that when multiplied by a given number gives 1 (1/4 is the reciprocal of 4).

Don't confuse VERACIOUS, which means "truthful," with *voracious*, which means "excessively eager; having a huge appetite."

Etymology

Study the roots and prefix given below together with the English words derived from them. Capitalized words are those given in the Word List. You should look up in a dictionary any words that are unfamiliar to you.

Prefix: *sub* (under) Latin — Examples: *SUB*ALTERN, *sub*marine, *sub*terranean

Roots: *verac* (truthful) Latin — Examples: *VERAC*IOUS, *verac*ity

pisc (fish) Latin — Examples: *PISCA*TORIAL, *pisces*

ACROSS

1. that cannot be corrupted or destroyed
4. relating to fishing or fishermen
9. of the dance or dancers
11. playful talk; teasing banter
14. beyond ordinary understanding
16. done or felt in return
18. expressed clearly and explicitly
20. having or using two languages
22. of or relating to sound (8)
24. not precisely fixed or known
26. of priests or the priesthood
28. weakly or sickeningly sentimental
31. leadership or dominance, especially over other nations
32. lacking all moral restraint
34. a group plotting to seize political power (14)
35. not to be spoken; unutterable
36. occurring together
38. self possession; poise (7)
39. to stop up cracks or seams
40. the surface features of a region
43. to do something impromptu
44. modest and shy
45. a superfluous word or phrase
46. inactive; at rest

DOWN

1. to prohibit or restrain
2. habitually truthful
3. to attribute or assign
5. to renounce upon oath
6. to decide against
7. thoroughly corrupt
8. a raised platform for a speaker
10. covered with blood; bloody
12. to be of use; to make use of
13. having two legislative chambers
15. to make clear; to explain
17. to agree to finance
19. a gesture of respect, as a bow
20. spirited zest or enthusiasm
21. excessively devoted to one's wife
23. the composition and arranging of stage dancing
25. to sing the praises of (13)
27. anything that serves to separate one group from another
29. to free, as from bondage or sin
30. settled in place
33. subordinate
34. stridently aggressive patriotism
35. to say again; to repeat
37. a violently insane person
40. one of a series of levels or rows (11)
41. an unskilled laborer of South America (19)
42. a manner of doing something